MW01174505

Canadian Daily

Grade 1

About this book:

These 32 weekly lessons will provide a strong phonetic background for Grade One students. The lessons cover a wide range of skills needed to develop strong reading skills. The skills taught are initial and final consonants, long and short vowels, vowel combinations, consonant blends and digraphs in the initial and final position, and singular and plural words. I strongly believe in the old saying 'practise makes perfect.'

Written by Ruth Solski
Illustrated by On The Mark Press

About the author:

Ruth Solski has been an educator for over 30 years and is the founder of S&S Learning Materials. As a writer, she strives to provide teachers with a useful tool to bring the joy of learning to many children.

Printed in Canada.

Published in Canada by:
On The Mark Press
15 Dairy Avenue, Napanee, Ontario, K7R 1M4
www.onthemarkpress.com

Canadian Daily Phonics

Grade One

Table of Contents

Week 1 6
Week 2 12
Week 3 18
Week 4 24
Week 5 30
Week 6 36
Week 7 42
Week 8 48
Week 9 54
Week 10 60
Week 11 66
Week 12 72
Week 13 78
Week 14 84
Week 15 90
Week 16 96
Week 17 102
Week 18.............................108
Week 19 114
Week 20 122
Week 21 126
Week 22 132
Week 23 138
Week 24 144
Week 25 150
Week 26 156
Week 27 162
Week 28 168
Week 29 174
Week 30 180
Week 31 186
Week 32 192
Student Assessment Sheet..198
Student Phonic Award........ 199 .
Student Phonic Award.........200

Canadian Daily Phonics

Sequential Development of Skills

Week 1: Initial Consonants: Ss, Mm, Tt

Week 2: Initial Consonants: Pp, Rr, Cc

Week 3: Initial Consonants: Gg, hh, Nn

Week 4: Initial Consonants: Bb, Kk, Ll

Week 5: Initial Consonants: Dd, Ff, Jj

Week 6: Initial Consonants: Qq, Vv, Ww

Week 7: Initial Consonants: Xx, Yy, Zz

Week 9: Final Consonants: g. l, d, f, p, n, l, m, t

Week 10: Final Consonants: d, m, t, l p, s

Week 11: Short Vowel 'Aa'

Week 12: Short Vowel 'Ee'

Week 13: Short Vowel ' Ii'

Week 14: Short Vowel 'Oo'

Week 15: Short Vowel 'Uu'

Week 16: Long Vowel 'Aa'

Week 17: Long Vowel ' Ee'

Week 18: Long Vowel 'Ii"

Week 19: Long Vowel 'Oo'

Week 20: Long Vowel ' Uu'

Week 21: S Blends: st, sk, sm, sn, sl, sw, sp, sc

Week 22: L Blends: bl, cl, fl, gl, pl, sl

Week 23: R Blends: br, cr, dr, fr, gr, pr

Week 24: Final Consonant Blends: st, lt, nk, nt, mp, sk

Week 25: Initial Consonant Digraphs: sh, ch, wh, wh

Week 26: Final Consonant Digraphs: sh, ch, th

Week 27: Vowel Pairs: ai, ay, ee, ea

Week 28: Vowel Pairs: oa, ou

Week 29: Double Vowel Combinations: oo, oa, ow

Week 30: Y as a consonant and as a vowel

Week 31: Final Consonant Blends: nt, nd, ng, nk

Week 32: Singular and Plural Words

How to Use This Book

The Canadian Phonics Book for Grade 1 contains thirty-two weekly lesson plans for the various phonetic skills required by Grade One students to help develop their reading, writing, anad spelling skills. Each week contains Weekly Lesson Plans, Daily Worksheets and a Weekly Test.

Weekly Planning Sheets

Week 1: **Initial Consonants 'Ss, Mm, Tt'**

Objective: To teach and review the initial consonants **Ss, Mm**,and **Tt**

Teacher Information: A. The initial consonant '**Ss**' is a voiceless continuant. The sound is issued from the front of the mouth instead of the throat. I call this sound the 'hissing' sound made by Sammy Snake. **B.** The initial consonant '**Mm**' is a nasal consonant. Nasal consonants are sounds made by the breath passing through the nostrils of the nose. When issuing this sound the lips are pressed together and a 'm-m-m' sound is issued. I call this the 'tastes good' sound. **C.** The initial consonant '**Tt**' is a voiceless stopped consonant. When issuing this sound the tongue touches the inside of the mouth above the front teeth to make a 'tih' sound. I call this the clock ticking sound 'tih, tih, tih'.

Day 1: Introduce the initial consonant 'Ss' using the following groups of words. 1. seal, snow, seven 2. sun, soap, sail 3. sap, seem, soup What sound do you hear at the beginning of each word? 'Ss' The tongue rests behind our teeth and blows out air. Can you think of something that makes the same sound. (snake, steam) I call this the Sammy Snake sound. Distribue the worksheet on page 7 and work with the students to complete it or instruct them to work independently.

Picture Key: Row 1: saddle, saw, cookie, hand Row 2: key, soap, soup, hammer Row 3: seal, pot, sandwich, mouse Row 4: mitten, six, pig, salad

Activity Sheet: Page 7: Students are to circle and name all the pictures that begin with the letter 'Ss.'

Day 2: Introduce the initial consonant '**Mm**' using the following names. Listen carefully to each animal's name: Mike Mouse, Marie Muskrat, Murray Monkey, Marty Mole. What sound do you hear at the beginning of each animal's name. (Mm) How do you make this sound. Our lips are pressed together and an 'm-m-m' sound is made. Have your students complete the worksheet on page 8.

Picture Key: Row 1: milk, match, ladder, pot Row 2: mitten, sun, tail, map Row 3: magnet, sun, mountain, rake, Row 4: monkey, mask, top, soap

Activity Worksheet: Page 8 Students are to circle and name all the pictures that begin with the letter '**Mm.**'

Day 3: Introduce the initial consonant '**Tt**' and its sound by using the following riddles. Record student answers on a white board, chalkboard, or chart paper. Riddles: 1. I live at the bottom of a pond and walk slowly. (turtle) 2. I can spin round and round. (top) 3. You eat me at special meals with your family. (turkey) 4. I am a large black and yellow striped jungle cat. (tiger) 5. I make bread warm and brown.(toaster) Have the students note how all the words are the same. (They all begin with the letter 'Tt.') Discuss the sound that it makes and where it is issued.

Picture Key: Row 1: tail, match, tent, goat Row 2: pig, top, duck, ten Row 3: net, toaster, kite, tape Row 4: television, raccoon, butterfly, toys

Activity Worksheet: Page 9 Students are to circle and name all of the pictures that begin with the letter '**Tt.**'

Day 4: Reiew the initial consonants and their sounds that were previously taught. **Auditory Game:** What letter makes the sound at the beginning of each of the following words: 1. tornado (Tt) 2. mother (Mm) 3. soon (Ss) 4. tulip (Tt) 5. moose (Mm) 6. soldier (Ss) 7. tar (Tt) 8. ten (Tt)

Picture Key: Row 1: tiger, sandwich, moon, man Row 2: tomato, saw, top, turtle Row 3: monkey, soap, mouse, towel Row 4: tire, mitten, seal, sink

Activity Worksheet: Page 10. Students will circle the letter heard at the beginning of each picture.

Day 5: Use the following instructions for an auditory and visual discrimination test for the consonants '**Ss, Mm**, and **Tt.**' The first section is an auditory test in which students follow the teacher's instructions. The second section is a visual discrimination test in which students record the initial sound.

Auditory Instructions: Use the following instructions to test the auditory recognition of '**Mm, Ss**, and **Tt.**' **Instructions:** Point to Box 1. Circle the letter that 1. monster (m) begins with. 2. sick (s) 3. tune (t) 4. munch (m) 5. tickle (t) 6. sap (s) 7. tank (t) 8. mess (m)

Visual Discrimination Instructions: Pictures: moon, sink, tape, meat, tap, snake, turnip, snowman The students will complete this part of the test independently. Letters to be circled: 1. m 2. s 3. t 4. m 5. t 6. s 7. t 8. m

SSR1140 ISBN: 9781771586863  6 © S&S Leaning Materials

Week 2: **Initial Consonants: 'Pp', 'Rr,' and 'Cc'**

Objective: To teach and review the initial consonants Pp, Rr, and Cc.

Teacher Information: A. The initial consonant '**Pp**' is a consonant that is completely obstructed or stopped for an instant. Stopped consonants at the end of a word end in an explosive sound. I call this sound the '*popcorn popping sound.*' **B.** The initial consonant '**Rr**' is a voiced consonant and the vocal cords vibrate in the throat when it is made. I call this sound '*the dog growling*' sound. **C.** The initial consonant '**Cc**' may be a voiced consonant with a hard sound or a soft voiceless sound that makes the same sound as the consonant'Ss.' As a hard sound I call the letter '**Cc**' '*the coughing sound.*'

Day 1: Introduce the initial consonant '**Pp**' using this sentence. '*Peter Piper picked a peck of pickled peppers and put the peppers in a purple bag.*' What sound do you hear at the beginning of most of the words in the sentence. (Pp) How do we make this sound? Our lips are pressed together at the beginning of the word. Think of other words that make the same sound at the beginning. List the words on a chart. Circle the beginning sounds. What letter makes this sound. (**Pp**) Tell your students that this is the '*popcorn popping*' sound. Distribute the worksheet on page 13 and work with the students to complete it or instruct them to work independently.

Picture Key: Row 1: parrot, bicycle, piano, door Row 2: girl, peanut, pencil, tent Row 3: soap, pot, goat, pear Row 4: puzzle, tie, puppet, leaf

Activity Worksheet: Page 13 Students are to circle and name all the pictures that begin with the letter '**Pp.**'

Day 2: Introduce the initial consonant '**Rr**' by using the following sentence. Listen carefully to this sentence: *Robbie Rabbit ran rapidly across Mr. Rogers' garden and nibbled on some radishes, raspberries, roses, rhubarb, and red peppers*. What is the name of the sound that you hear often at the beginning of the words in the sentence. (**Rr**) How do we make this sound? The mouth is slightly open, the tongue slides forward and the sound comes from the back of the throat. List other words on a chart that begin with the sound that 'Rr' makes. The sound that 'Rr' makes sounds like an *angry dog*. Duplicate the worksheet on page 14 and work with the students to complete it or instruct them to work independently.

Picture Key: Row 1: rope, pot, turtle, raccoon Row 2: button, ring, rooster, seal Row 3: rattle, desk, bus, rainbow Row 4: car, rug, star, roof

Activity Worksheet: Page 14 Students are to circle and name all the pictures that begin with the letter '**Rr.**'

Day 3: Introduce the initial consonant '**Cc**' by using the following sentence. Listen carefully to this sentence: *Carl Cowboy's favourite foods are corn, cake, carrots cookies, cauliflower, and candy.* What is the name of the sound that you hear often at the beginning of the words in the sentence? (*Cc*) How do we make this sound? The mouth is open at the beginning and air comes out from the back of the throat to make a '*cuh*' sound. I call this the coughing sound. Think of other words that begin with this sound. List the words on a chart. Circle the letter '*c*' at the beginning of each one.

Picture Key: Row 1: calendar, net, pencil, can Row 2: bear, camel, fish, cage Row 3: cow, fork, butterfly, candle Row 4: pumpkin, car, turtle, camera

Activity Sheet: Page 15 Distribute the worksheet and work with you students to complete it or instruct them to work independently. Students are to circle and name all of the pictures that begin with the initial consonant '**Cc.**'

Day Four: Review the consonants '**Pp, Rr**, and **Cc**' using the following riddles. 1. I am an animal with quills. (*porcupine*) What letter do I begin with? (*Pp*) 2. I am large, round and orange. (*pumpkin*) What letter do I begin with? (*Pp*) 3. I am a bird that lives on a farm and likes to wake people up in the morning.(*rooster*) What letter do I begin with ? (*Rr*)

Picture Key: Row 1: raccoon, pillow, ring, canoe Row 2. pot, rooster, cow, pencil Row 3: rose, cat, rake, camera Row 4: rope, candle, piano, camel

Activity Sheet: Page 16 Students will circle the initial consonant heard at the beginning of each picture.

Day 5: Use the following instructions for an auditory and visual discrimination test for the consonants '**Pp, Rr,** and **Cc.**'

A. Auditory Instructions: Use the following instructions to test the auditory recognition of **Pp, Rr**, and **Cc**. Circle the letter that you hear at the beginning of each word that I say. **Instructions:** Point to Box 1. Circle the letter that you hear at the beginning of 1. reindeer 2. pepper 3. moose 4. sand 5. robot 6. roof 7. bottle 8. maple
Answer Key: 1. r 2. p 3. m 4. s 5. r 6. r 7. b 8. m

B. Visual Discrimination: Review the names of the pictures. Instruct students to record the initial consonants on the lines in each box. **Answer Key:** Row 1: C, R, C Row 2: r, c, p Row 3: p, r, p Answer Key: Row 1: c, r, c Row 2: r, c, p Row 3 p, r, p

SSR1140 ISBN: 9781771586863  12 © S&S Leaning Materials

Student Worksheets

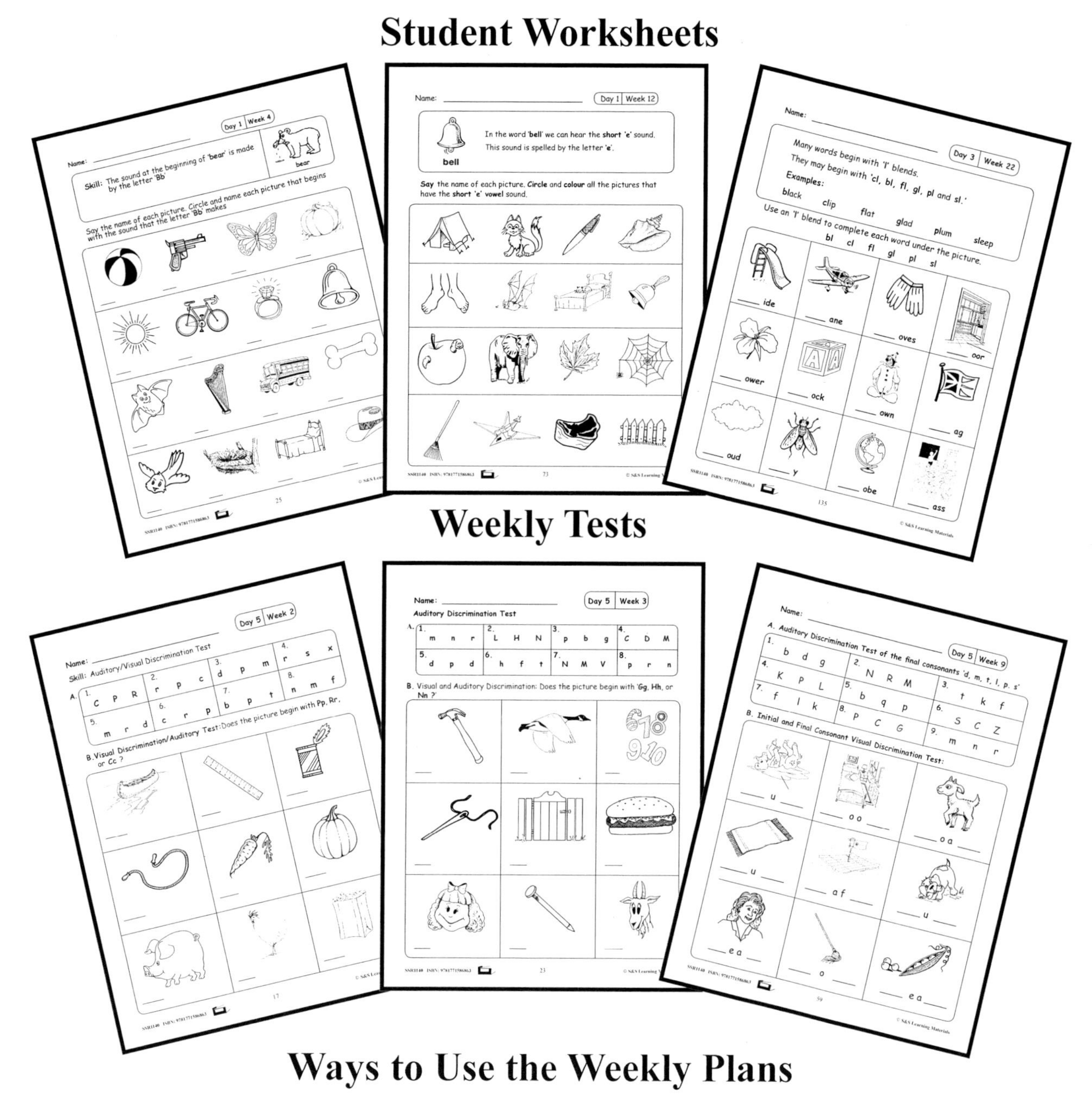

Weekly Tests

Ways to Use the Weekly Plans

The teaching plans and activity sheets can be used on a weekly basis or the ideas and worksheets can be used to suit students needs or they could be used for teaching ideas, reinforcing students' phonetic skills, and home study.

Each weekly plan contains an Objective, Teacher Information, Daily Planning Ideas containing games, listening activities, stories and riddles.

A Picture Key is provided for each worksheet so the pictures can be identified.

Four weekly activity worksheets focus on the concept(s) taught during the week.

Weekly tests are provided and could be held on the last day of the week or when it is necessary.

Week 1: Initial Consonants 'Ss, Mm, Tt'

Objective: To teach and review the initial consonants **Ss, Mm**,and **Tt**

Teacher Information: A. The initial consonant '**Ss**' is a voiceless continuant. The sound is issued from the front of the mouth instead of the throat. I call this sound the 'hissing' sound made by Sammy Snake. **B.** The initial consonant '**Mm**' is a nasal consonant. Nasal consonants are sounds made by the breath passing through the nostrils of the nose. When issuing this sound the lips are pressed together and a 'm-m-m' sound is issued. I call this the 'tastes good' sound. **C.** The initial consonant '**Tt**' is a voiceless stopped consonant. When issuing this sound the tongue touches the inside of the mouth above the front teeth to make a 'tih' sound. I call this the clock ticking sound 'tih, tih, tih'.

Day 1: Introduce the initial consonant 'Ss' using the following groups of words. 1. seal, snow, seven 2. sun, soap, sail 3. sap, seem, soup What sound do you hear at the beginning of each word? 'Ss' The tongue rests behind our teeth and blows out air. Can you think of something that makes the same sound. (snake, steam) I call this the Sammy Snake sound. Distribue the worksheet on page 7 and work with the students to complete it or instruct them to work independently.

Picture Key: Row 1: saddle, saw, cookie, hand Row 2: key, soap, soup, hammer Row 3: seal, pot, sandwich, mouse Row 4: mitten, six, pig, salad

Activity Sheet: Page 7: Students are to circle and name all the pictures that begin with the letter 'Ss.'

Day 2: Introduce the initial consonant '**Mm**' using the following names. Listen carefully to each animal's name: Mike Mouse, Marie Muskrat, Murray Monkey, Marty Mole. What sound do you hear at the beginning of each animal's name. (Mm) How do you make this sound. Our lips are pressed together and an 'm-m-m' sound is made. Have your students complete the worksheet on page 8.

Picture Key: Row 1: milk, match, ladder, pot Row 2: mitten, sun, tail, map Row 3: magnet, sun, mountain, rake, Row 4: monkey, mask, top, soap

Activity Worksheet: Page 8 Students are to circle and name all the pictures that begin with the letter '**Mm**.'

Day 3: Introduce the initial consonant '**Tt**' and its sound by using the following riddles. Record student answers on a white board, chalkboard, or chart paper. Riddles: 1. I live at the bottom of a pond and walk slowly. (turtle) 2. I can spin round and round. (top) 3. You eat me at special meals with your family. (turkey) 4. I am a large black and yellow striped jungle cat. (tiger) 5. I make bread warm and brown.(toaster) Have the students note how all the words are the same. (They all begin with the letter 'Tt.') Discuss the sound that it makes and where it is issued.

Picture Key: Row 1: tail, match, tent, goat Row 2: pig, top, duck, ten Row 3: net, toaster, kite, tape Row 4: television, raccoon, butterfly, toys

Activity Worksheet: Page 9 Students are to circle and name all of the pictures that begin with the letter '**Tt**.'

Day 4: Reiew the initial consonants and their sounds that were previously taught. **Auditory Game:** What letter makes the sound at the beginning of each of the following words: 1. tornado (Tt) 2. mother (Mm) 3. soon (Ss) 4. tulip (Tt) 5. moose (Mm) 6. soldier (Ss) 7. tar (Tt) 8. ten (Tt)

Picture Key: Row 1: tiger, sandwich, moon, man Row 2: tomato, saw, top, turtle Row 3: monkey, soap, mouse, towel Row 4: tire, mitten, seal, sink

Activity Worksheet: Page 10. Students will circle the letter heard at the beginning of each picture.

Day 5: Use the following instructions for an auditory and visual discrimination test for the consonants '**Ss, Mm**, and **Tt**.' The first section is an auditory test in which students follow the teacher's instructions. The second section is a visual discrimination test in which students record the initial sound.

Auditory Instructions: Use the following instructions to test the auditory recognition of '**Mm**, **Ss**, and **Tt**.' **Instructions:** Point to Box 1. Circle the letter that 1. monster (m) begins with. 2. sick (s) 3. tune (t) 4. munch (m) 5. tickle (t) 6. sap (s) 7. tank (t) 8. mess (m)

Visual Discrimination Instructions: Pictures: moon, sink, tape, meat, tap, snake, turnip, snowman The students will complete this part of the test independently. Letters to be circled: 1. m 2. s 3. t 4. m 5. t 6. s 7. t 8. m

Name: ______________________________ Day 1 | Week 1

Skill: The sound at the beginning of '**sun**' is made by the letter '**Ss**'.

Say the name of each picture. **Circle** and **name** each picture that begins with the sound that '**Ss**' makes in each row.

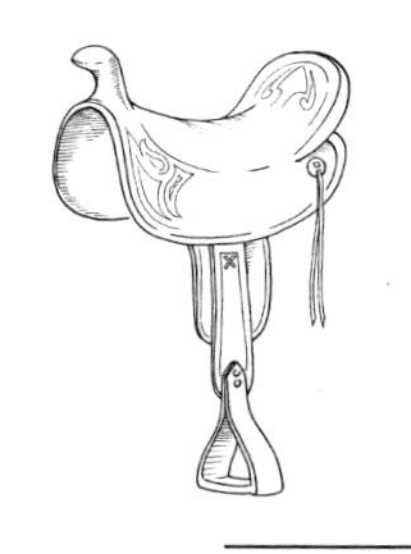

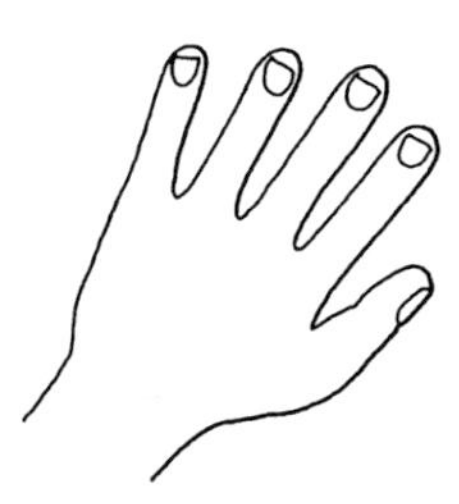

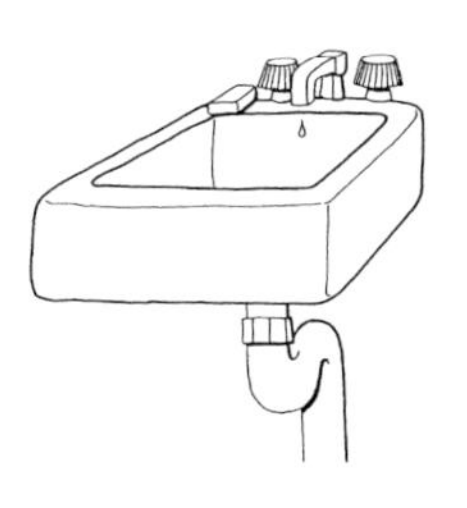

Name: ______________________________ Day 2 | Week 1

Skill: The sound at the beginning of mouse is made by the letter **Mm**

Say the name of each picture. **Circle** and name each picture that begins with the sound that **Mm** makes

____	____	____	____
____	____	____	____
____	____	____	____
____	____	____	____

Name: ______________________________

Day 3 | Week 1

Skill: The sound at the beginning of '**turtle**' is made by the letters '**Tt**'.

turtle

Say the name of each picture. **Circle** and **name** each picture that begins with the sound that '**Tt**' makes.

10

OFF

ON

 ISBN: 9781771586863

Name: ______________________________ | Day 4 | Week1 |

Skill: Auditory and visual recognition of the sounds made by the initial consonants '**s**, **m**, and **t**.'

Circle the letter that each sound is heard at the beginning of each picture.

 s m t	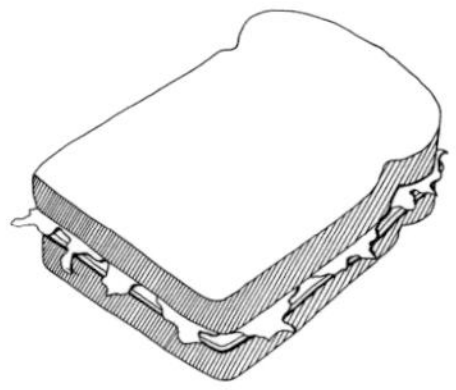 t s m	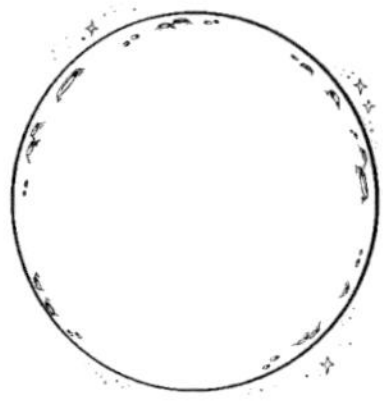 m s t	 t s m
 s t m	 t s m	 m s t	 t m s
 t m s	 m s t	 s m t	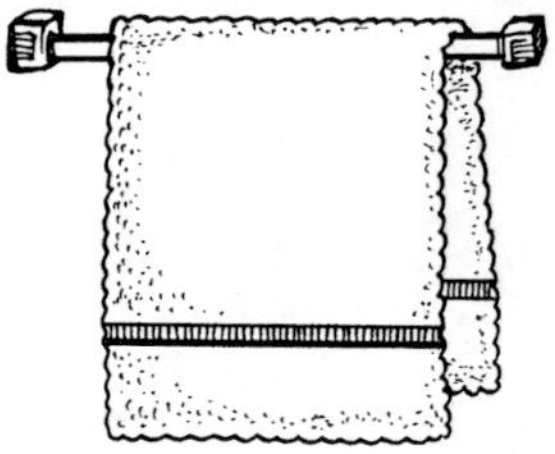 m s t
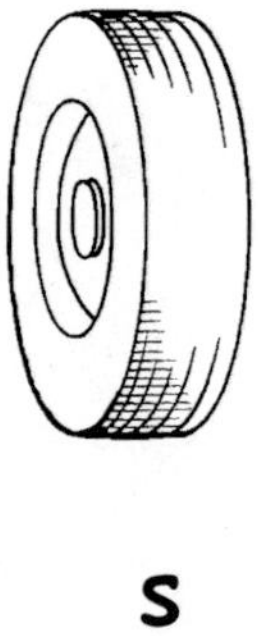 m s t	 s t m	 s t m	 t s m

Name: ______________________________

Day 5	Week 1

Skill: Auditory/Visual Discrimination Test

A.

1.	2.	3.	4.
M S T	m s t	s m t	T M S
5.	6.	7.	8.
m T s	S m t	M S T	S T M

B. Does the picture begin with '**Ss**', '**Mm**', or '**Tt**?'

____	____	____
____	____	____
____	____	____

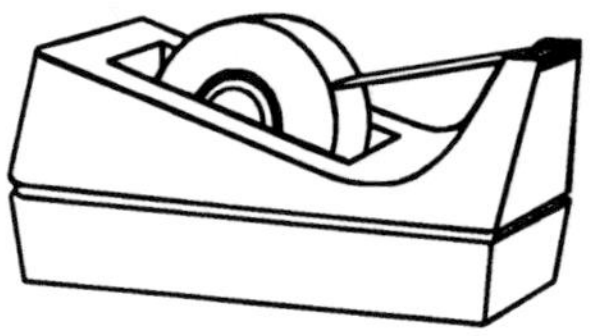

Week 2: Initial Consonants: 'Pp', 'Rr,' and 'Cc'

Objective: To teach and review the initial consonants Pp, Rr, and Cc.

Teacher Information: A. The initial consonant '**Pp**' is a consonant that is completely obstructed or stopped for an instant. Stopped consonants at the end of a word end in an explosive sound. I call this sound the '*popcorn popping sound.*' **B.** The initial consonant '**Rr**' is a voiced consonant and the vocal cords vibrate in the throat when it is made. I call this sound '*the dog growling*' sound. **C.** The initial consonant **'Cc'** may be a voiced consonant with a hard sound or a soft voiceless sound that makes the same sound as the consonant'Ss.' As a hard sound I call the letter '**Cc**' *'the coughing sound.'*

Day 1: Introduce the initial consonant '**Pp**' using this sentence. '*Peter Piper picked a peck of pickled peppers and put the peppers in a purple bag.'* What sound do you hear at the beginning of most of the words in the sentence. (Pp) How do we make this sound? Our lips are pressed together at the beginning of the word. Think of other words that make the same sound at the beginning. List the words on a chart. Circle the beginning sounds. What letter makes this sound. (**Pp**) Tell your students that this is the '*popcorn popping'* sound. Distribute the worksheet on page 13 and work with the students to complete it or instruct them to work independently.

Picture Key: Row 1: parrot, bicycle, piano, door Row 2: girl, peanut, pencil, tent Row 3: soap, pot, goat, pear Row 4: puzzle, tie, puppet, leaf

Activity Worksheet: Page 13 Students are to circle and name all the pictures that begin with the letter '**Pp**.'

Day 2: Introduce the initial consonant '**Rr**' by using the following sentence. Listen carefully to this sentence: *Robbie Rabbit ran rapidly across Mr. Rogers' garden and nibbled on some radishes, raspberries, roses, rhubarb, and red peppers*. What is the name of the sound that you hear often at the beginning of the words in the sentence. (**Rr**) How do we make this sound? The mouth is slightly open, the tongue slides forward and the sound comes from the back of the throat. List other words on a chart that begin with the sound that 'Rr' makes. The sound that 'Rr' makes sounds like an *angry dog*. Duplicate the worksheet on page 14 and work with the students to complete it or instruct them to work independently.

Picture Key: Row 1: rope, pot, turtle, raccoon Row 2: button, ring, rooster, seal Row 3: rattle, desk, bus, rainbow Row 4: car, rug, star, roof

Activity Worksheet: Page 14 Students are to circle and name all the pictures that begin with the letter '**Rr**.'

Day 3: Introduce the initial consonant '**Cc**' by using the following sentence. Listen carefully to this sentence: *Carl Cowboy's favourite foods are corn, cake, carrots cookies, cauliflower, and candy.* What is the name of the sound that you hear often at the beginning of the words in the sentence? (***Cc***) How do we make this sound? The mouth is open at the beginning and air comes out from the back of the throat to make a '*cuh*' sound. I call this the coughing sound. Think of other words that begin with this sound. List the words on a chart. Circle the letter '***c***' at the beginning of each one.

Picture Key: Row 1: calendar, net, pencil, can Row 2: bear, camel, fish, cage Row 3: cow, fork, butterfly, candle Row 4: pumpkin, car, turtle, camera

Activity Sheet: Page 15 Distribute the worksheet and work with you students to complete it or instruct them to work independently. Students are to circle and name all of the pictures that begin with the initial consonant '**Cc**.'

Day Four: Review the consonants '**Pp, Rr**, and **Cc**' using the following riddles. 1. I am an animal with quills. (*porcupine*) What letter do I begin with? (*Pp*) 2. I am large, round and orange. (*pumpkin*) What letter do I begin with? (*Pp*) 3. I am a bird that lives on a farm and likes to wake people up in the morning.(*rooster*) What letter do I begin with ? (*Rr*)

Picture Key: Row 1: raccoon, pillow, ring, canoe Row 2. pot, rooster, cow, pencil Row 3: rose, cat, rake, camera Row 4: rope, candle, piano, camel

Activity Sheet: Page 16 Students will circle the initial consonant heard at the beginning of each picture.

Day 5: Use the following instructions for an auditory and visual discrimination test for the consonants '**Pp**, **Rr,** and **Cc**.'

A. Auditory Instructions: Use the following instructions to test the auditory recognition of **Pp**, **Rr**, and **Cc**. Circle the letter that you hear at the beginning of each word that I say. **Instructions:** Point to Box 1. Circle the letter that you hear at the beginning of 1. reindeer 2. pepper 3. moose 4. sand 5. robot 6. roof 7. bottle 8. maple
Answer Key: 1. r 2. p 3. m 4. s 5. r 6. r 7. b 8. m

B. Visual Discrimination: Review the names of the pictures. Instruct students to record the initial consonants on the lines in each box. **Answer Key:** Row 1: C, R, C Row 2: r, c, p Row 3: p, r, p Answer Key: Row 1: c, r, c Row 2: r, c, p Row 3 p, r, p

Name: ______________________________ Day 1 | Week 2

Skill: The sound at the beginning of '**pumpkin**' is made by the letter '**Pp**'

pumpkin

Say the name of each picture. **Circle** and **name** each picture that begins with the sound that '**Pp**' makes in each row.

______	______	______	______
______	______	______	______
______	______	______	______
______	______	______	______

Name: ______________________________ | Day 2 | Week 2 |

Skill: The sound at the beginning of 'rabbit' is made by the letter '**Rr**.'

rabbit

Say the name of each picture. **Circle** and **name** each picture that begins with the sound **'Rr'** makes.

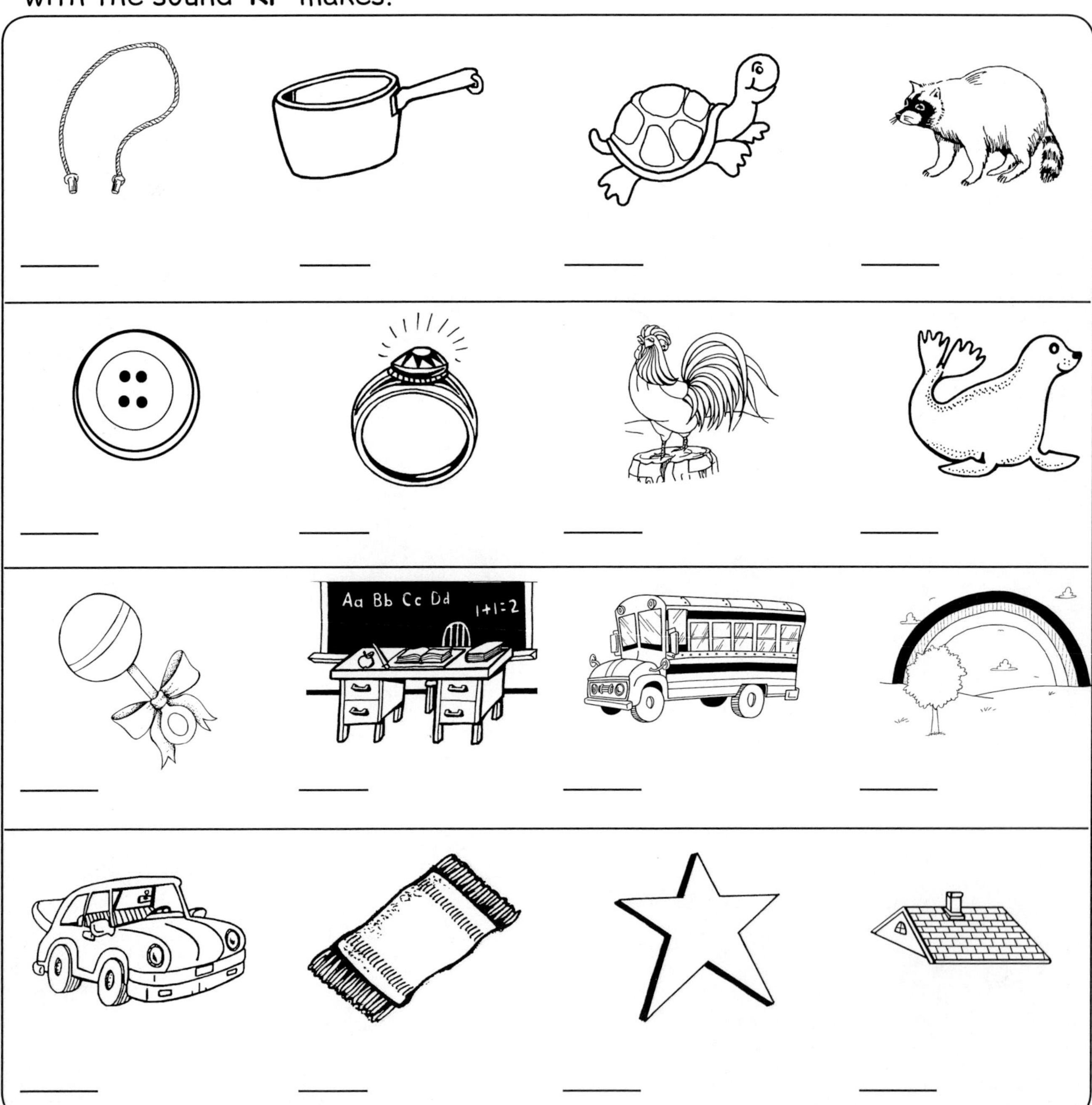

Name: ______________________________

Day 3 | Week 2

Skill: The sound at the beginning of '**cat**' is made by the letter '**Cc**.'

cat

Say the name of each picture. **Circle** and **name** each picture that begins with the sound that '**Cc**' makes in each row.

____ ____ ____ ____

____ ____ ____ ____

____ ____ ____ ____

____ ____ ____ ____

Name: ______________________________ | Day 4 | Week 2 |

Skill: Auditory and visual recognition of the sounds made by the initial consonants '**Pp, Rr,** and **Cc**.'

Circle the letter heard at the beginning of each picture.

 P R C	 p c r	 r c p	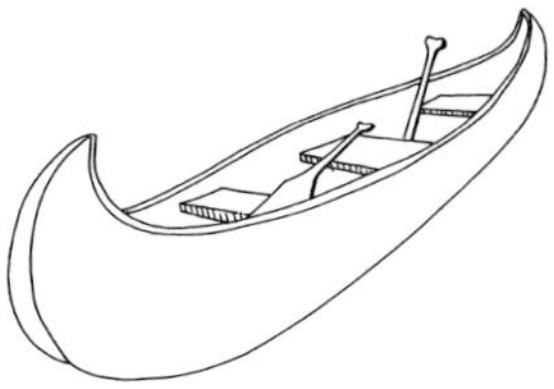 P R C
 R P C	 R p C	 R C P	 p r c
 p r c	 c p r	 P R C	 R P C
 p r c	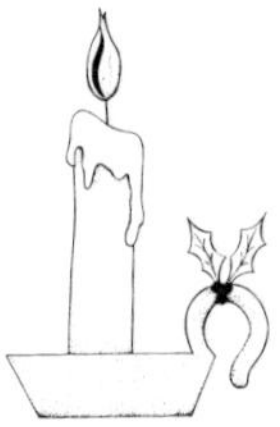 R P C	 b r p	 R C P

Name: ______________________________

Day 5	Week 2

Skill: Auditory/Visual Discrimination Test

A.

1. C P R	2. r p c	3. d p m	4. r s x
5. m r d	6. c r p	7. b p t	8. n m f

B. Visual Discrimination/Auditory Test: Does the picture begin with **Pp**, **Rr**, or **Cc** ?

______	______	______
______	______	______
______	______	______

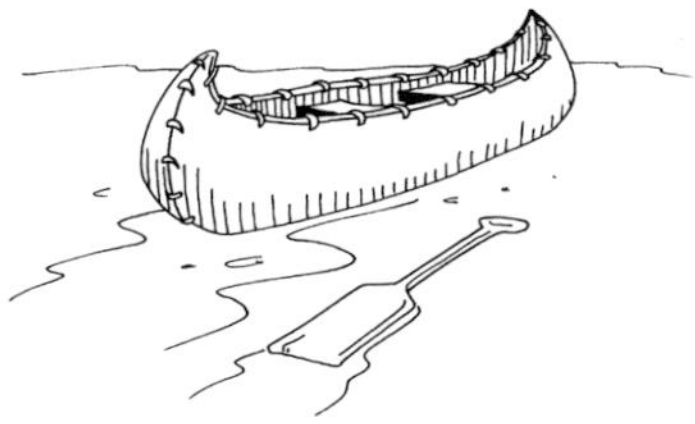

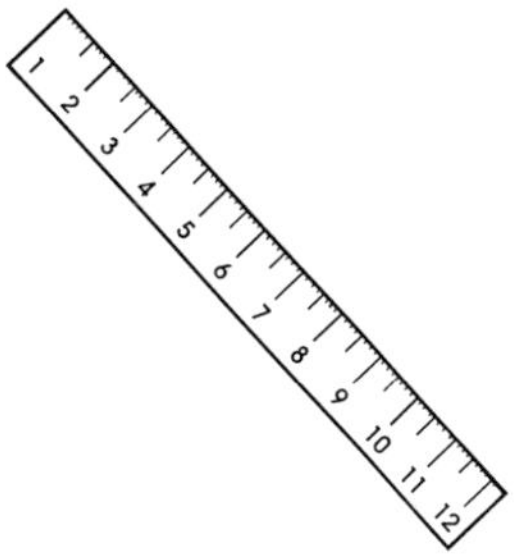

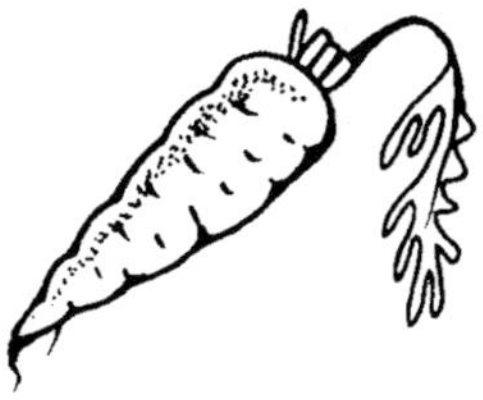

 ISBN: 9781771586863

Week 3: Initial Consonants 'Gg, Hh, and Nn'

Objective: To teach and review the initial consonants 'Gg', Hh, and, Nn'

Teacher Information: The initial consonant 'Gg' is a voiced stopped consonant. It is an explosive sound that passes into the vowel at the beginning of a word as in the word '**gun**.' I call this sound the '**gargling**' sound. **B.** The initial consonant 'Hh' is a voiceless continuant that is made by pushing air from the back of the throat. For example: **hug**, **happy** C. The initial consonant '**Nn**' is a nasal consonant that is made when the tongue pushes the mouth above the teeth. I call this sound the '**nose tickling**' sound. For example **nut**, **noisy**.

Day 1: Introduce the initial consonant '**Gg**' using the following short story. Gabby Goose was always giggling. She giggled at the goats grazing on green grass; at a girl chewing gooey gum and eating gumdrops; at the bears eating garbage at the dump. Discuss the sound heard at the beginning of most of the words and how the letter is made. This sound is a voiceless consonant and comes from the back of the throat. Brainstorm for other '**Gg**' words and record them on a chart. Circle all the initial consonants that are '**Gg**.' Tell your students that the letter '**Gg**' is the '*gargling*' sound. Distribute the worksheet on page 19 and work with your students to complete it or instruct them to finish it independently.

Picture Key: Row 1: goat, jar, game, pear Row 2: dog, gate, tooth, soap Row 3: girl, monkey, pumpkin, garbage Row 4. ball, gum, hen, ghost

Activity Worksheet: Page 19 Students are to circle and name all the pictures that begin with the letter '**Gg**'

Day 2: Introduce the initial consonant '**Hh**' using the following short story about 'Harvey the Horse.' **Story:** Harvey was a huge, heavy horse that lived in a stall in a barn on the Harper's farm. Every day Farmer Harper hauled a huge bale of hay to Harvey's stall. Harvey whinnied happily when he saw the huge bale of hay and munched on it hungrily. Discuss the sound heard at the beginning of most of the words and how the sound is produced. The letter '**Hh**' is a voiceless continuant and the sound comes from the back of the throat while air is released. List the words heard in the story on a chart. Circle all the initial consonants that are the letter '**Hh**.' Brainstorm for other words that begin like '*Harvey the Horse*.' Tell your students that the letter '**Hh**' is the '*out of breath*' sound that you make when you stop running. Distribute the worksheet found on page 20 and work with the students to complete it or instruct them to finish it independently.

Picture Key: Row 1: heart, fox, hat, mitten Row 2: bag, harp, pig, hook Row 3: helicopter, hill, pear, mop Row 4: pencil, hose, pumpkin, house

Activity Worksheet: Page: 20 Students are to circle and name all the pictures that begin with '**Hh**.'

Day 3: Introduce the initial consonant '**Nn**' using the following short story. 'Nancy Nuthatch is a nice little bird who lives in a nest in a tree nine metres tall. Nancy Nuthatch never flies south in the fall as she likes the nasty weather in the north. Nancy Nuthatch eats napping insects under the tree's bark and seeds and nuts. She can walk up and down trees nicely. Discuss the sound heard at the beginning of most of the words and how the sound is made. The letter '**Nn**' is a nasal consonant. It is made when the tongue is placed behind the top teeth to make a '*nuh*' sound. I call this the '*bee buzzing sound*.' Duplicate the worksheet on page 21 and work with the students to complete it or instruct them to work independently.

Picture Key: Row 1: mouse, net, butterfly, nine Row 2: nuts, apple, neck, cow Row 3: peas, nail, nurse, seal Row 4: nose, camel, nest, needle

Activity Sheet: Page: 21 Students are to circle and name all of the pictures that begin with the letter '**Nn**.'

Day 4: Review the consonants '**Gg, Hh**, and **Nn**' using these riddles. 1. I am an animal with two horns and a beard. (goat) What letter do I begin with? (Gg) 2. I am a big jungle animal that likes to play in water. (hippo) What letter do I begin with? (Hh) 3. I am a person who looks after sick people. (nurse) What letter do I begin with? (Nn)

Picture Key: Row 1: neck, game, nose, ham Row 2: horn, needle, house, nail Row 3: guitar, hammer, net, gate Row 4: nest, hand, goat, necklace

Activity Sheet: Page: 22 Students will circle the initial consonant heard at the beginning of each picture.

Day 5: Use the following instructions for an auditory and visual discrimination test for the consonants '**Gg. Hh**, and **Nn.**'

A. Auditory Instructions: Use the following instructions to test the auditory recognition of '**Gg, Hh**, and **Nn**.'
Instructions: Point to Box 1. Circle the letter that you hear at the beginning of 1. napkin 2. hanging 3. polite 4. most 5. double 6. ticking 7. noisy 8. robber **Answer Key:** 1. n 2. H 3. p 4. M 5. d 6. t 7. N 8. r
Visual Discrimination Test: Picture Key: Row 1: hammer, goose, numbers Row 2: needle, gate, hamburger Row 3: girl, nail, goat **Answer Key**: Row 1: h, g, n Row 2: n, g, h Row 3: g, n, g

Name: ______________________________ Day 1 | Week 3

Skill: The sound at the beginning of '**goose**' is made by the letter '**Gg**.'

Say the name of each picture. **Circle** and **name** each picture that begins with the sound that the letter '**Gg**' makes in each row.

Name: ______________________________

Day 2 | Week 3

Skill: The sound at the beginning of '**horse**' is made by the letter '**Hh**.'

horse

Say the name of each picture. **Circle** and **name** each picture that begins with the sound that the letter '**Hh**' makes in each row

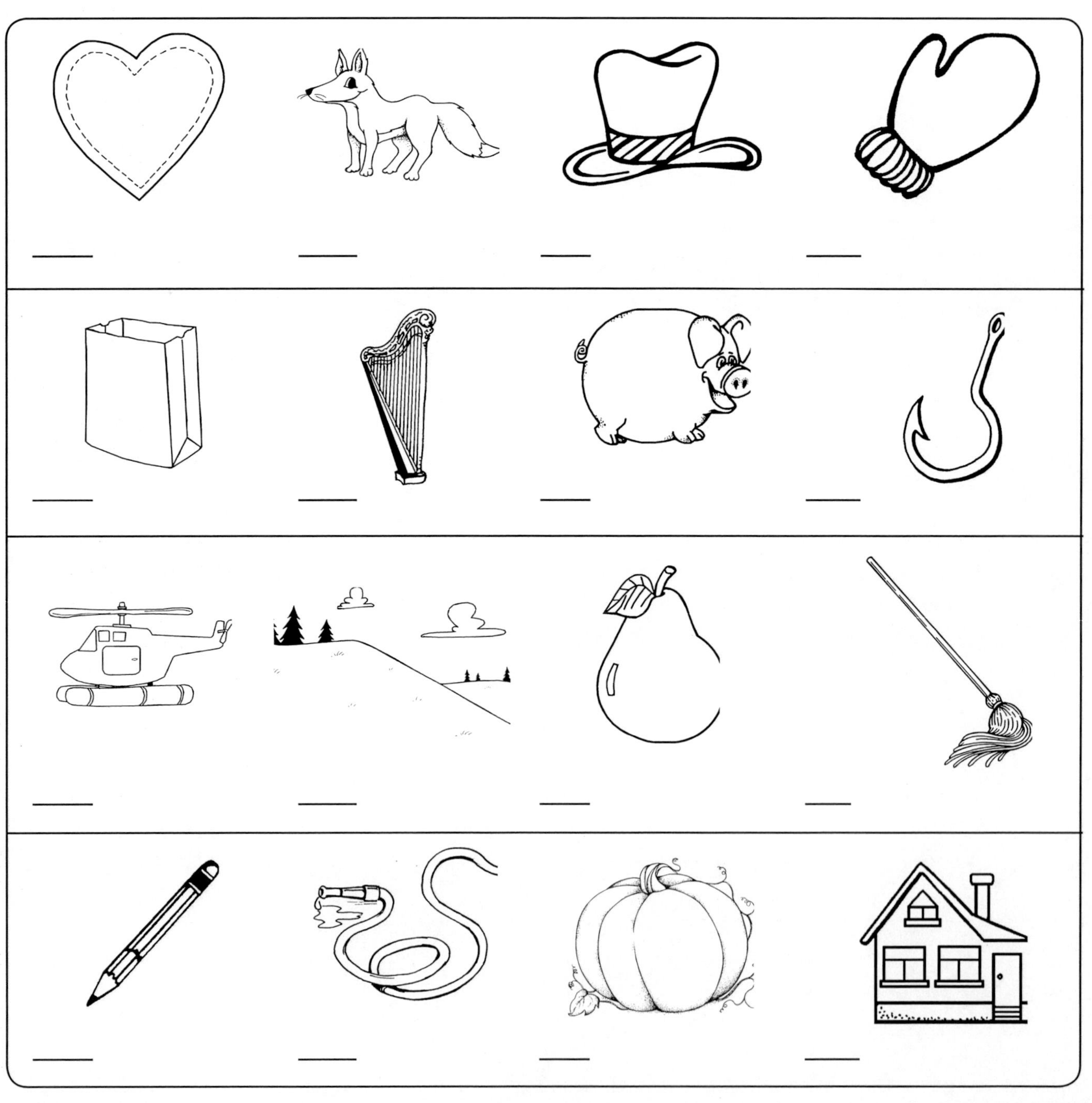

Name: ______________________________ Day 3 | Week 3

Skill: The sound at the beginning of '**nut**' is made by the letter '**Nn**.'

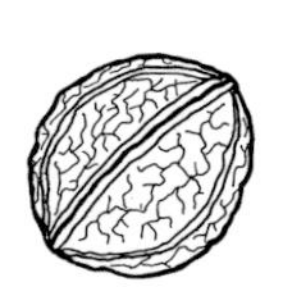
nut

Say the name of each picture. **Circle** and **name** each picture that begins with the sound that '**Nn**' makes in each row.

Name: ______________________________ | Day 4 | Week 3 |

Skill: Auditory and visual recognition of the sounds made by the initial consonants '**Gg**, **Hh**, and **Nn**'

Circle the letter heard at the beginning of each picture.

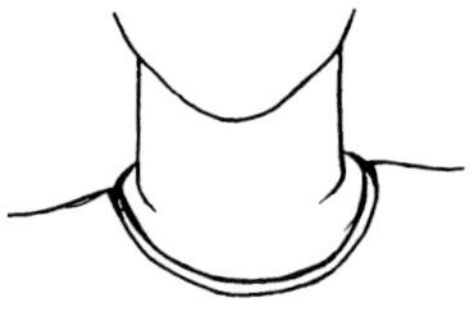 g h n	 h n g	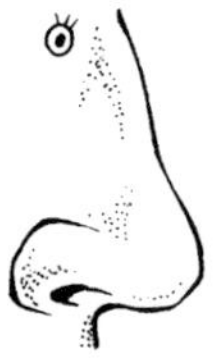 G H N	 n g h
 N G h	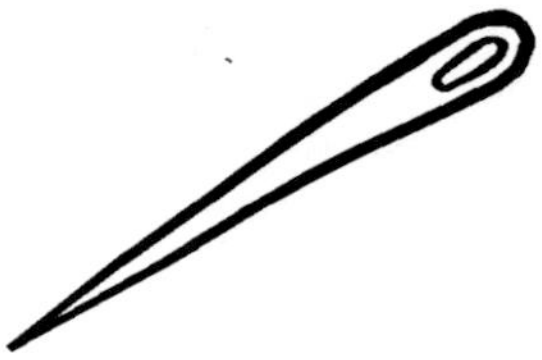 G h n	 g n h	 N H G
 H N G	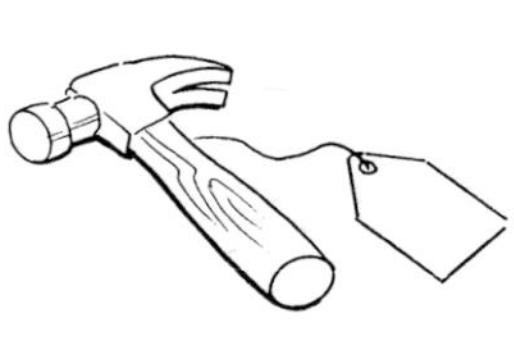 N G H	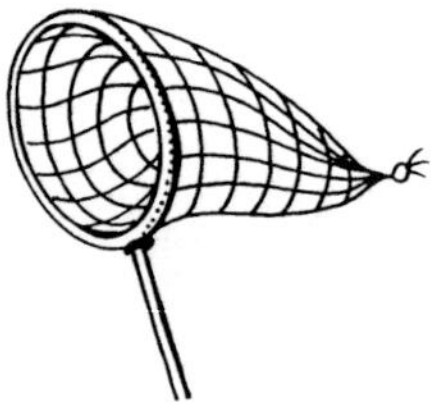 g n h	 H G N
 h n g	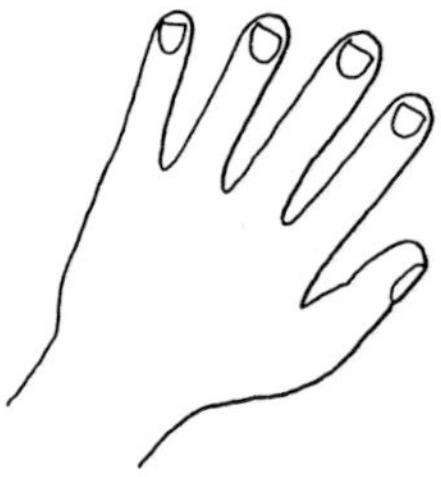 N H G	 H N G	 g n h

SSR1140 ISBN: 9781771586863

Name: ______________________

Day 5	Week 3

Auditory Discrimination Test

A.

1. m n r	2. L H N	3. p b g	4. C D M
5. d p d	6. h f t	7. N M V	8. p r n

B. Visual and Auditory Discrimination: Does the picture begin with '**Gg**, **Hh**, or **Nn** ?'

(Week 4:) Initial Consonants 'Bb, Kk, and Ll'

Objective: To teach and review the initial consonants 'Bb, Kk, and Ll'

Teacher Information: A. The initial consonant '**Bb**' is a voice stopped consonant. Voice stopped consonants are completely obstructed for an instant similar to water being stopped in a hose by a hand causing the water to squirt out in various directions. I call this sound the bubbling sound made by water boiling or running quickly in a creek saying 'buh, buh, buh.' **B**. The initial consonant '**Kk**' is a voiced stopped consonant. In voiceless consonants the vocal cords do not vibrate in the throat. I call this sound the little coughing sound. **C**. The initial consonant '**Ll**' is a voiced consonant. When used the tip of the tongue touches the roof of the mouth behind the front teeth. I call this sound the 'licking the lollipop' sound.

Day 1: Introduce the initial consonant '**Bb**' using the following sentences. "Bucky Bear was a big brown bear who lived in a beautiful forest. One day Bucky Bear saw bunches of bees buzzing in and out of a big hole in a beech tree. Discuss the initial consonant sound frequently heard at the beginning of the words in the sentences. List other 'Bb' words on a chart and circle the initial consonant 'Bb.' Tell your students the letter "Bb' makes a bubbling sound. Distribute the worksheet on page 25 and work with your students to complete it or instruct them to work independently.

Picture Key: Row 1: ball, gun, butterfly, pumpkin Row 2: sun, bicycle, ring, ball Row 3: bat, harp, bus, bone Row 4: bird, nest, bed, hat

Activity Worksheet: Page 25 Students are to circle and name all the pictures that bgin with the letter 'Bb.'

Day 2: Introduce the initial consonant '**Kk**' using the following sentence. Listen to this sentence. 'Katy Kangaroo kicked the kettle full of ketshup and the kitchen soon had a red floor.' Discuss the sound heard at the beginning of most of the words and how the sound is made. The letter 'Kk' is a voiceless stopped consonant and the sound comes from the back of the throat and air is released. List the words found in the sentence on a chart. Circle the consonant 'Kk' at the beginning of each word. Brainstorm for other words that begin like 'Katy Kangaroo' and record them on the chart. Tell your students that the letter 'Kk' makes the little coughing sound. Distribute the worksheet found on page 26 and work with the students to complete it or instruct them to finish it independently.

Picture Key: Row 1: ladder, king, bottle, kitchen Row 2: mask, duck, key, rabbit Row 3: kite, gate, kettle, nose Row 4: butterfly, kitten, house, kleenex

Activity Worksheet: Page 26 Students are to circle and name all the pictures that begin with 'Kk.'

Day 3: Introduce the initial consonant '**Ll**' using the following story. Listen carefully to the words in this story. Loons are birds that mate and live together for life. Lucy and Luke Loon lived on the shore of a large lake. Near the shore the two loons built a large nest. In the nest, Lucy laid three little, light blue eggs. Luke only left Lucy alone when he flew away to look for some food for her. One day when he returned Lucy had a lovely surprise for Luke. In her nest were three little baby loons. Discuss the sound heard at the beginning of 'Lucy' and 'Luke Loon.' Reread the story to have the students locate other words that begin with the same sound. List the words on a chart and discuss the letter and its sound. The initial consonant 'Ll' is a voiced consonant. While making this sound the tongue is raised and presses against the back of the upper front teeth. Tell your students this sound is called the 'licking the lollipop' sound as you move your tongue up to the roof of the mouth the same way that you lick a lollipop. Distribute the worksheet on page 27 and work with your students to complete it or instruct them to complete it independently.

Picture Key; Row 1: gun, lamp, hand, leg Row 2: ladder, nose, leaf, kite Row 4. pig, lettuce, rug, log

Activity Worksheet: Page 27 Students are to circle and name all the pictures that begin with the initial consonant 'Ll.'

Day 4: Review the consonants '**Bb**, **Kk**, and **Ll**.' Use the following riddles. 1. I can fly high in the sky. I begin with the sound that 'Kk' makes. (kite) 2. I may be on a sweater or a shirt. I begin with the sound that 'Bb' makes. (buttons) 3. I am sent in the mail. I begin with the sound that 'Ll' makes. (letter) 4. I am a place to sleep. I begin with the sound that 'Bb' makes. (bed) 5. I am a baby animal. I begin with the sound that 'Kk' makes. (kitten) 6. I am another name for sucker. I begin with the sound that 'Ll' makes. (lollipop)

Picture Key: Row 1: lamp, bat, key, box Row 2: light bulb, king, letter, kitchen Row 3: kite, bell, lobster, bag, Row 4: book, ladybug, bus, kitten

Activity Sheet: Page 28 Students will circle the initial consonant heard at the beginning of each picture.

Day 5: Use the following instructions to test the auditory recognition of '**Bb**, **Kk**, and **Ll**.'
A. Auditory Instructions: Use the following instructions to test the auditory recognition of 'Bb, Kk, and Ll'
Instructions: Point to Box 1. Circle the letter that you hear at the beginning of lizard. Repeat the same instructions for 2. biscuit 3. beaver 4. lay 5. kiss 6. kind 7. loaf 8. box **Answer Key:** 1. l 2. b 3. b 4. l 5. k 6. k 7. l 8. b

B. Visual Discrimination Test: Pictures: Row 1: lamb, bicycle, kitten Row 2: key, leg, bone Row 3: bus, kangaroo, ladder **Answer Key**: Row 1: l, b, k Row 2: k, l, b Row 3: b, k, l

Name: ___________________________

Day 1 | Week 4

Skill: The sound at the beginning of '**bear**' is made by the letter '**Bb**'

Say the name of each picture. Circle and name each picture that begins with the sound that the letter '**Bb**' makes

Name: ______________________________

Day 2 | Week 4

Skill: The sound at the beginning of **'kangaroo'** is made by the letter **'Kk.'**

Say the name of each picture. Circle and name each picture that begins with the sound that the letter '**Kk**' makes in each row.

____	____	____	____
____	____	____	____
____	____	____	____
____	____	____	____

Name: ______________________________ | Day 3 | Week 4 |

Skill: The sound at the beginning of '**loon**' is made by the letter '**Ll**.'

Say the name of each picture. Circle and name each picture that begins with the sound that the letter '**Ll**' makes.

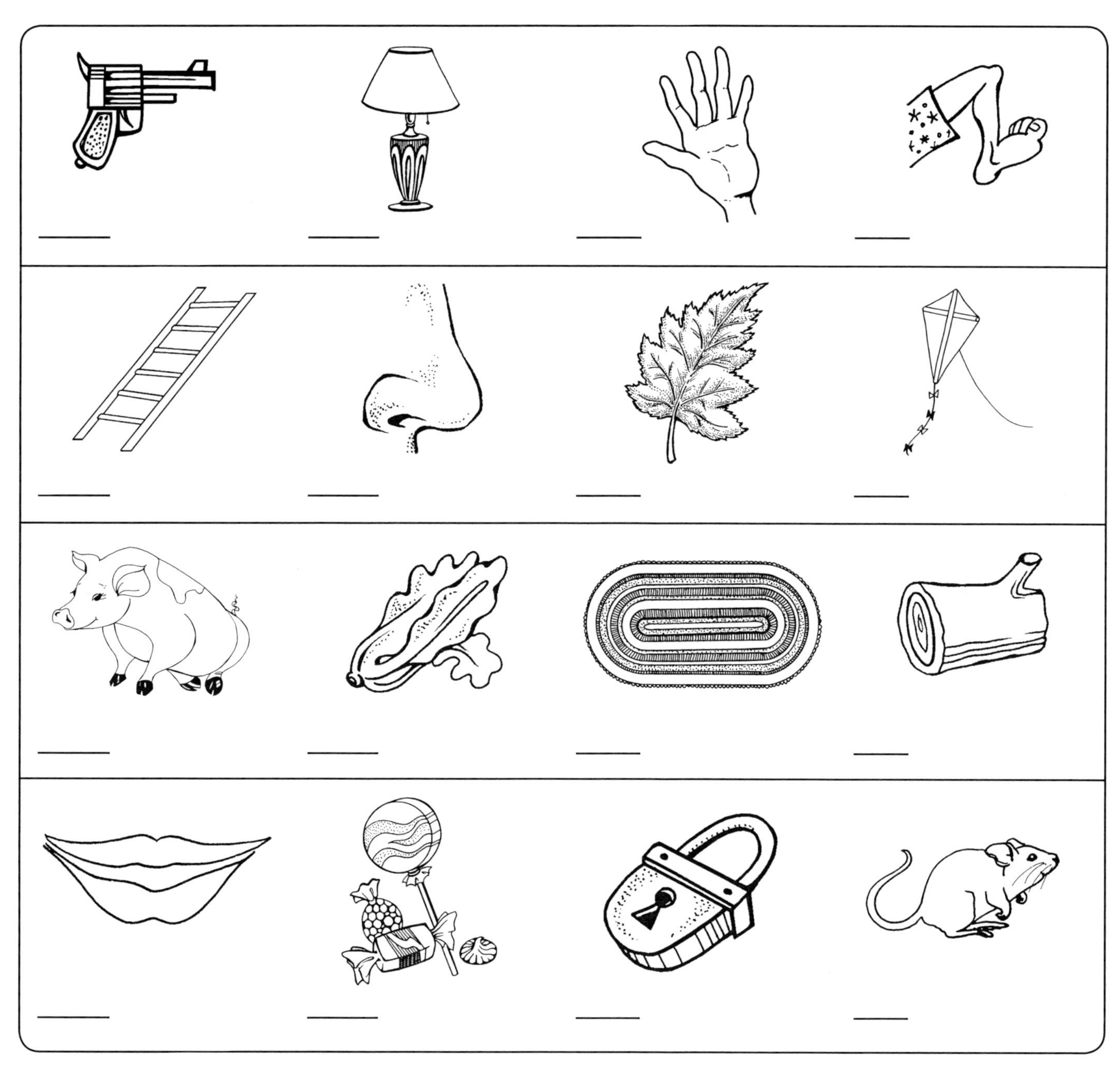

Name: ______________________________ | Day 4 | Week 4 |

Skill: Auditory and visual recognition of the sounds made by the initial consonants '**Bb**, **Kk**, and **Ll**.'

Circle the letter heard at the beginning of each picture.

 B K L	 b l k	 K L B	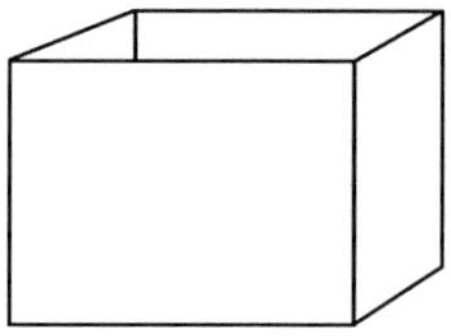 l b k
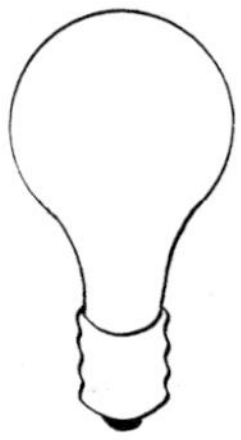 B K L	 b l k	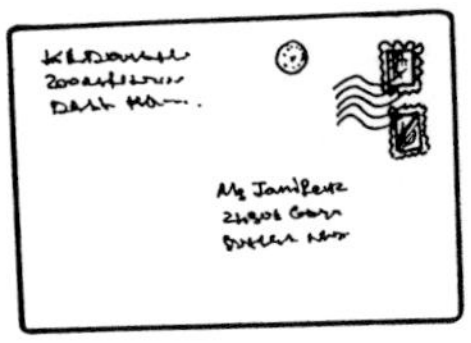 L b k	 k b l
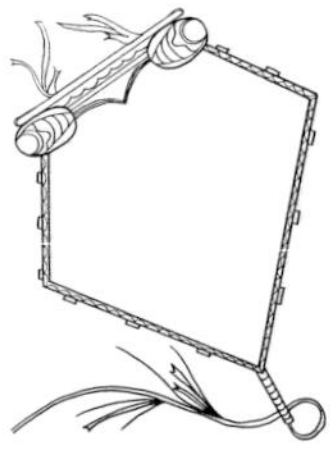 L b k	 k b l	 L B K	 B k l
 K B L	 B K l	 K B L	 b k l

SSR1140 ISBN: 9781771586863

Name: ______________________________

Day 5	Week 4

A. Auditory Discrimination Test

1. b k l	2. L K B	3. P R B	4. l d b
5. K R S	6. n l k	7. L B k	8. P D B

B. Visual Discrimination Test:

Does the picture begin with 'Bb, Ll or Kk.'

____	____	____
____	____	____
____	____	____

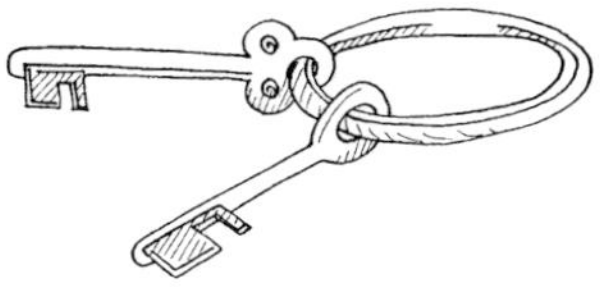

Week 5 : Initial Consonants 'Dd, Ff, Jj'

Objective: To teach and review the initial consonants **'Dd**, **Ff**, and **Jj'**

Teacher Information: A. The initial consonant **'Dd'** is a voice stopped consonant. Stopped consonants are explosive sounds heard at the beginning and ending of a word. Examples: den, nod. I call this sound the machine gun sound when repeated quickly. Example: duh, duh, duh. **B.** The initial consonant **'Ff'** is a voiceless continuant. The top front teeth rest on the inside of the lower lip and air comes out. I call this the angry cat sound. **C.** The initial consonant **'Jj'** is a voiced continuant. It is made with the mouth slightly closed and the tongue pushes out the sound. I call this the teeth chattering sound when said quickly.

Day 1: Introduce the initial consonant **'Dd'** using the following sentences. " One day Diana Duck decided to dig deep holes in her dainty garden. She dug holes and planted daisies and daffodils and dug out all of the dandelions. Diana Duck was delighted with her dazzling display in her garden. Discuss the initial consonant sound heard frequently at the beginning of the words in the sentences. On a chart, list other words that begin with 'Dd' and circle the initial consonant. Tell your students the letter 'Dd' makes a similar sound like machine gun when said quickly. Distribute the worksheet on page 31 and work with the students to complete it or instruct them to work independently.

Picture Key: Row 1: pig, door, ball, dime Row 2: desk, basket, deer, dinosaur Row 3: popcorn, doghouse, doll, duck Row 4: balloon, pencil, dog, pot

Activity Worksheet: Page 31 Students are to circle and name all the pictures that begin with the letter **'Dd**.'

Day 2: Introduce the initial consonant **'Ff'** using the following story. Listen to this story about 'Fanny Fairy' for words that begin like her name. Fanny Fairy flew fast all over the world with her famous magical wand looking to make bad things better. If she saw a sad face she made it into a happy one. If a family was hungry, she gave them food. One fine day she filled a poor farmer's fields with fast growing crops. Another time while flying over a burnt forest, Fanny waved her fairy wand and the forest was suddenly filled with tall fir trees. Fanny was certainly a fantastic fairy.

Picture Key: Row 1: face, deer, foot, rose Row 2: bunny, finger, house, forest Row 3: farm, candle, feather, fish Row 4: key, fox, mushroom, fan

Activity Worksheet: Page 32 Students are to circle and name all the pictures that begin with the initial consonant 'Ff.'

Day 3: Introduce the initial consonant **'Jj'** using the following sentences. Listen carefully to each sentence that I am going to say about 'Jerry the Juggler.' 1. Jerry the Juggler worked at a circus juggling jars of jam. 2. Jerry also juggled juicy ju-jubes, jugs filled with juice and jazzy jack- o'-lanterns. Discuss the sound heard at the beginning of 'Jerry the Juggler.' Reread the sentences and record the words that begin with 'Jj' on a chart. List other words as well. The initial consonant 'Jj' is a voiced consonant. While making this sound the teeth are closed and the tongue moves back from them. Tell your students that this is the 'teeth chattering' sound one makes when feeling cold. Distribute the worksheet on page 33 and work with your students to complete it or instruct them to work independently.

Picture Key: Row 1: door, jet, baby, jar Row 2: jeep, fish, jail, hammer Row 3: mice, jack-o'-lantern, key, jacket Row 4: jungle, jeans, socks, jelly

Activity Worksheet: Page: 32 Students are to circle and name all the pictures that begin with the letter **'Jj**.'

Day 4: Review the consonants **'Dd, Ff**, and **Jj**,' Use the following riddles. 1. I am place where bad people are sent. I begin with the the sound that 'Jj' makes. (jail) 2. I am a home for a pet. I begin with the sound that 'Dd' makes. (doghouse) 3. We cover a bird's body to keep it warm. We begin with the sound that 'Ff' makes. (feathers) 4. I am a little coin. I begin with the sound that 'Dd' makes. (dime) 5. No one likes me growing on their lawns. I begin with the sound that 'Dd' makes. (dandelion) 6. I am large and orange with a scarey face. I begin with the sound that 'Jj' makes. (jack-o'-lantern)

Picture Key: Row 1: deer, finger, jelly, jeep Row 2: fire, jet, dandelion, fork Row 3: doctor, farmer, dinosaur, jam Row 4: jar, doughnut, doll, fox

Activity Worksheet: Page 33 Students are to circle the initial consonant heard at the beginning of each picture.

Day 5: Use the following instructions to test the auditory recognition of 'Dd, Ff, and Jj.'

A. Instructions: Point to Box 1. Circle the letter that you hear at the beginning of 1. jester 2. father 3. juicy 4. famous 5. danger, 6. fix, 7. jerk 8. donkey **Answer Key:** 1. J 2. f 3. j 4. f 5. d 6. f 7. j 8. d

B. Visual Discrimination Test: Pictures: Row 1: door, jungle, daffodil Row 2. fairy, duck, jug Row 3: doctor, forest, feet **Answer Key:** Row 1: d, j, d Row 2: f, d, j Row 3: d, f, f

Name: ______________________________ | Day 1 | Week 5 |

Skill: The sound at the beginning of '**duck**' is made by the letter '**Dd**.'

duck

Say the name of each picture. Circle and name each picture that begins with the sound that the letter '**Dd**' makes.

Name: ______________________________ | Day 2 | Week 5 |

Skill: The sound made at the beginning of '**fairy**' is made by the letter '**Ff**'

fairy

Say the name of each picture. Circle and name each picture that begins with the sound that the letter '**Ff**' makes in each row.

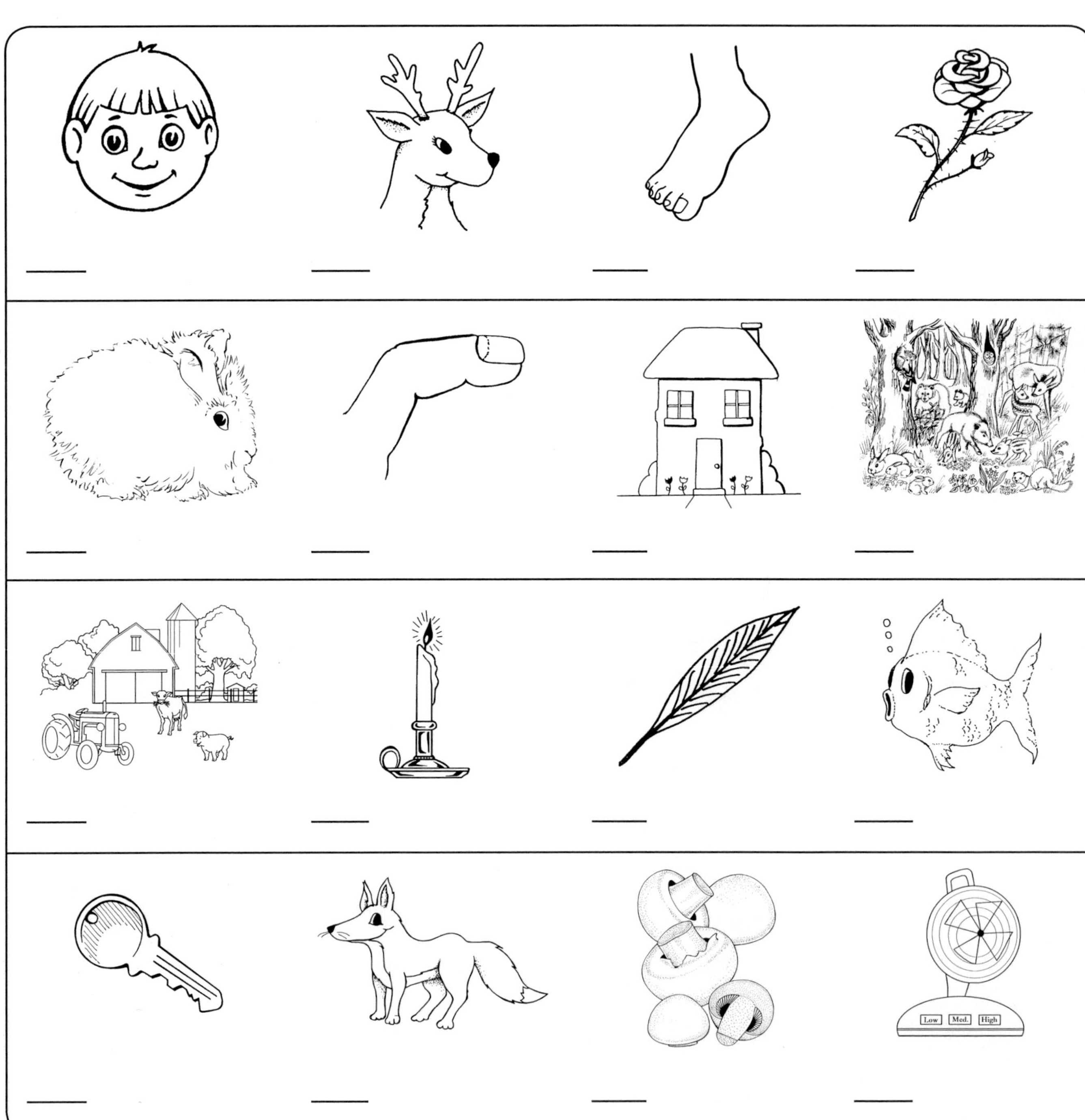

Name: ______________________________

Day 3 | Week 5

Skill: The sound at the beginning of 'juggler' is made by the letter '**Jj**.'

juggler

Say the name of each picture. Circle and name each picture that begins with the sound that the letter '**Jj**' makes.

Name: ______________________________ Day 4 | Week 5

Skill: Auditory and visual recognition of the sounds made by the initial consonants 'Dd, Ff, and Jj'.

Circle the letter that you hear at the beginning of each picture.

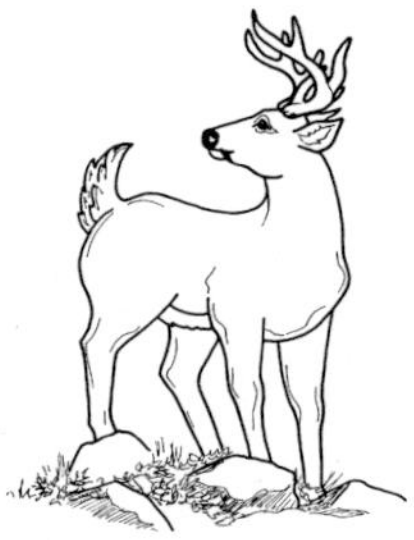 D F J	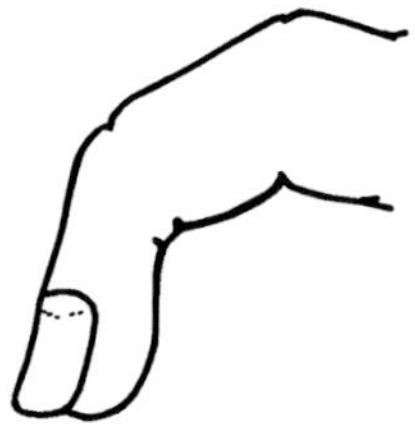 d f j	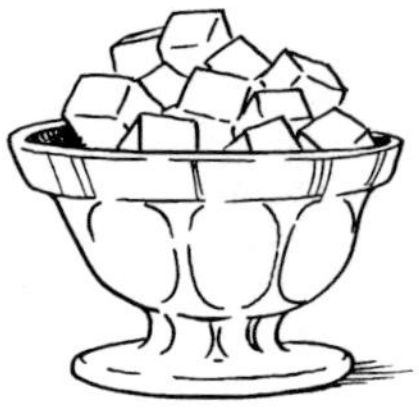 F J D	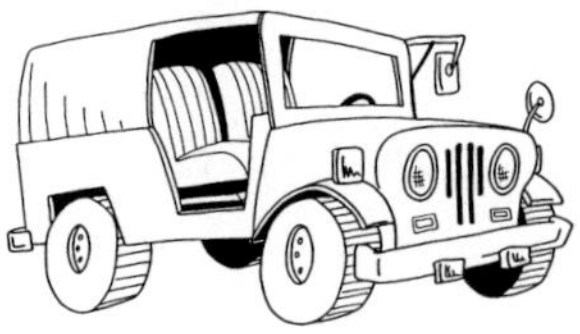 J d F
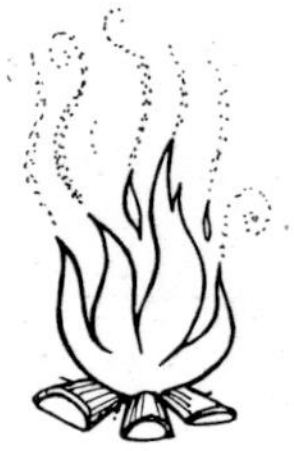 d j f	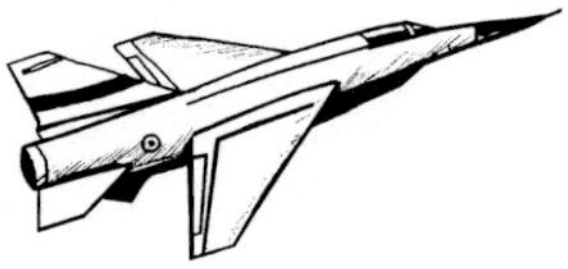 f d j	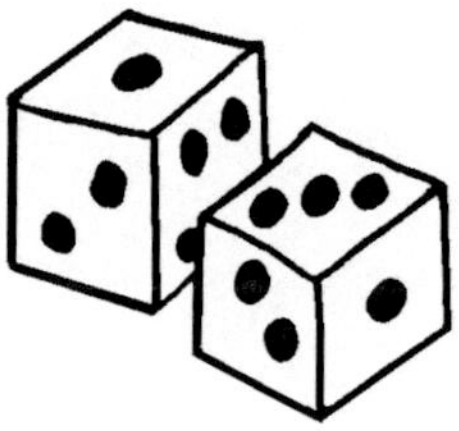 J D F	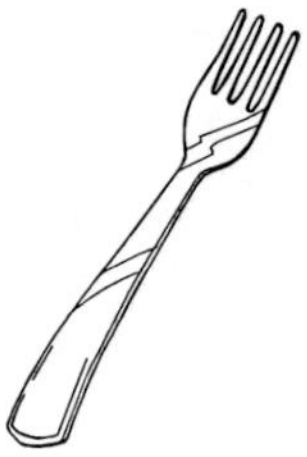 J d f
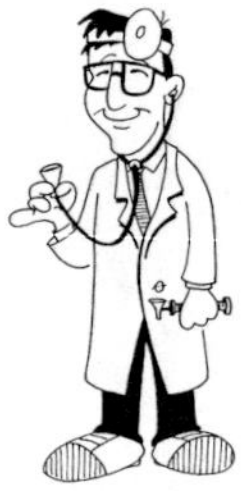 J F D	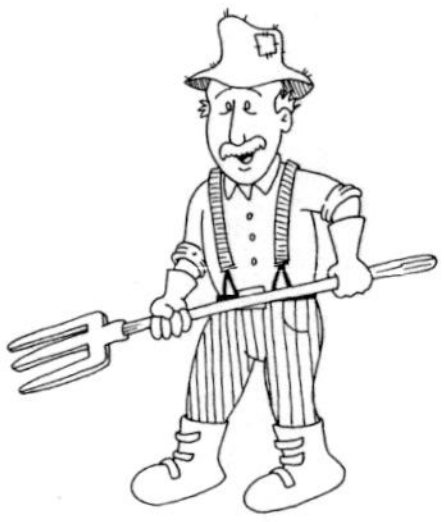 J D F	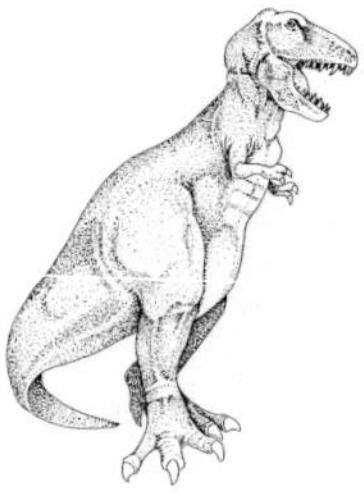 j d f	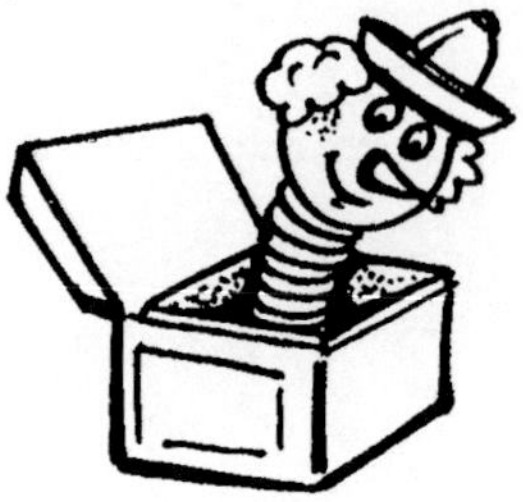 J D F
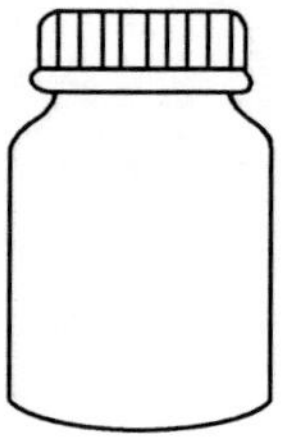 d j f	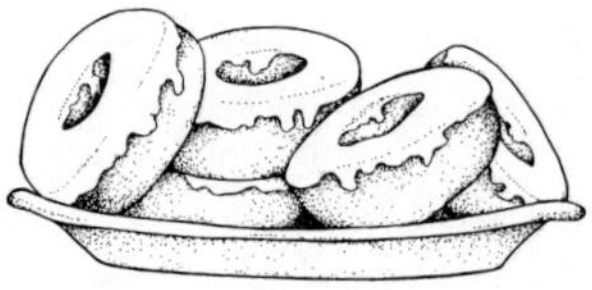 d f j	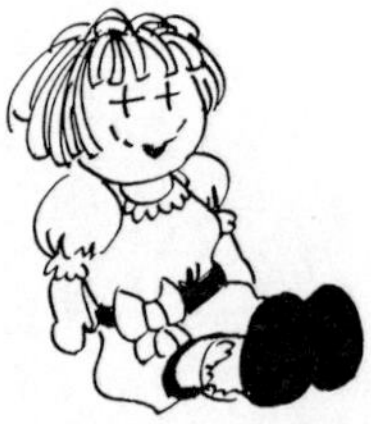 J f D	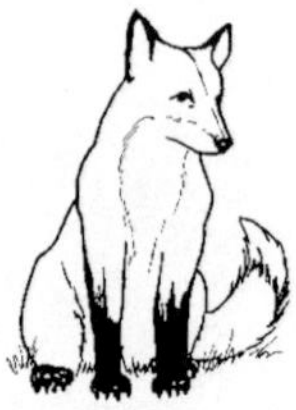 J F D

Name: ______________________________

Day 5	Week 5

A. Auditory Discrimination Test:

1. D J F	2. d j f	3. F J D	4. j d f
5. J d f	6. J D F	7. d f j	8. J f d

B. Visual Discrimination Test:

Does the picture begin with '**Dd**, **Jj** or **Ff**?' Record the correct letter on the line.

____	____	____
____	____	____
____	____	____

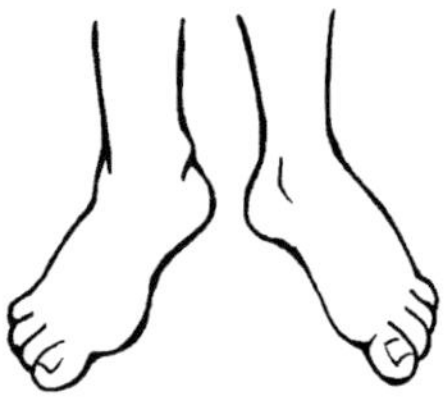

Week 6: Initial Consonants 'Qq, Vv, and Ww'

Objective: To teach and review the initial consonants **'Qq, Vv, and Ww'**

Teacher Information: A. The initial consonant 'Qq' has an unusual sound and is always followed by the letter 'Uu' in words. It makes the same sound as the letters 'kw' make when blended together. I call this sound the 'duck quacking sound' as it sounds like an angry duck making noise. **B.** The initial consonant 'Vv" is a voiced consonant. It is made when the top front teeth rest on the inside of the lower lip and make the lower lip vibrate when air passes through. I call this letter the lip tickling sound. **C.** The initial consonant 'Ww' is a voiced consonant and air is pushed out by the tongue through the lips. I call this letter the windy sound.

Day 1: Introduce the initial consonant '**Qq**' as a blend as the letter '**u**' always follows it in words. Listen to the words in the sentences that I say. 1. The prince asked the queen a quick question. Which words in the sentence begin like '**quilt**?' (queen, quick, question) Record the words on a chart. Do the same for the following sentences. 2. The duck quit quacking and quivering and became quiet when the fox left. 3. On the quiz there were quite a few questions. Ask your students the name of the letter that always follows the letter 'q.' (u) List other words that begin with '**qu**.' Distribute the worksheet for the students to complete.

Picture Key: Row 1: barn, queen, caterpillar, quarter Row 2: quilt, doll, question mark, fence Row 3: quills, gift, quails, jug 4. moose, quiver of arrows, log, duck quacking

Activity Worksheet: Page 37 Students are to circle and name all the pictures that begin with the letters 'Qu.'

Day 2: Introduce the initial consonant '**Vv**' with the following sentence. On **Valentine's** Day, **Victor** sent **Valerie** a beautiful **valentine** and a **vase** of flowers. Which words in the sentence begin with the same sound. List the words on a chart and discuss the sound made. Add other words that begin with the consonant '**Vv**.' The initial consonant 'Vv' is a voiced consonant. The sound is made when the front teeth press on the inside of the lower lip. A buzzing, windy sound is made. I call this sound the lip tickling sound Distribute the worksheet and work with the students to complete or instruct them to finish it independently.

Picture Key: Row 1: vest, jungle, dentist, volcano Row 2: robber, bale, vase, lamp Row 3: van, witch, van, toes Row 4: quilt, volleyball, king, violets

Activity Worksheet: Page 38 Students are to circle and name all the pictures that begin with the letter 'Vv.'

Day 3: Introduce the initial consonant '**Ww**' using the following story. Wanda Witch was a wee woman who had a magic wand. She would wave it while she walked along a winding path through the woods and watched things change. One day Wanda changed a walnut into a watermelon, a worm into a walrus and flowers into weeds. Wanda loved working with her wonderful wand. Discuss the sound made at the beginning of 'Wanda Witch.' Reread the story to have the students locate other words that begin the same way. List the words on a chart and have the students circle the beginning consonant and discuss its sound. Explain to your students that the sound that 'Ww' makes is a windy sound that comes out from the back of the throat. It is called the windy sound. Distribute the worksheet on page 39 and work with the students to complete it or instruct them to work independently.

Picture Key: Row 1: web, mice, worm, kitchen Row 2: pin, walrus, cookies, window Row 3: wall, house, wind, forest Row 4: bus, wool, family, wolf

Activity Worksheet: Page 39 Students are to circle and name all the pictures that begin with the letter '**Ww**.'

Day 4: Review the consonants '**Vv, Qq**, and **Ww**' with this listening activity. What letter do you hear at the beginning of 1. quiet (qu) 2. watch (w) 3. vanish (v) 4. quit (qu) 5. work (w) 6. velvet (v) 7. wagging (w) 8. vinegar (v) 9. quiet (qu) 10. vanish (v)

Picture Key: Row 1: web, quarter, wagon, volleyball Row 2: question mark, waiter, vase queen Row 3: quilt, violin, well, van Row 4: window, vegetables, quail, vine

Activity Sheet: Page: 40 Students will circle the initial consonant heard at the beginning of each picture.

Day 5: Use the following instructions to test the auditory recognition of '**Vv, Qq**, and **Ww**.'

A. Auditory Test Instructions: Use the following instructions to test the auditory recognition of '**Vv, Qq**, and **Ww**.' **Instructions:** Point to Box 1. Circle the letter that you hear at the beginning of 1. quiet 2. vest 3. wobble 4. visit 5. weather 6. quiz 7. weep 8. quack Answer Key: 1. q 2. v 3. w 4. v 5. w 6. qu 7. w 8. qu

Visual Discrimination Test: Pictures: Row 1: van, quills, vegetables Row 2: window, violin, quiver Row 3: watch, quilt, wing **Answer Key:** Row 1: v, qu, v Row 2: w, v, qu Row 3: w, qu, w

,

Name: ______________________________ Day 1 | Week 6

Skill: The sound at the beginning of '**quilt**' is made by the letters '**qu**.'

Say the name of each picture. Circle and name each picture that begins with the sound that '**qu**' makes.

____	____	____	CANADA 25 CENTS 1980 ____
____	____	? ____	____
____	____	____	____
____	____	____	____

Name: ______________________

Day 2 | Week 6

Skill: The sound at the beginning of '**valentine**' is made by the letter '**Vv**.'

valen-

Say the name of each picture. Circle and name each picture that begins with the sound that '**Vv**' makes in each row.

Name: ______________________________

Day 3	Week 6

Skill: The sound at the beginning of 'witch' is made by the letters '**Ww**.'

witch

Say the name of each picture. Circle and name each picture that begins with the sound the **'Ww'** makes.

___	___	___	___
___	___	___	___
___	___	___	___
___	___	___	___

Name: ______________________________ Day 4 | Week 6

Skill: Auditory and visual recognition of the sounds made by the initial consonants '**Vv**, '**Qq**,' and '**Ww**.'

Circle the letter heard at the beginning of each picture.

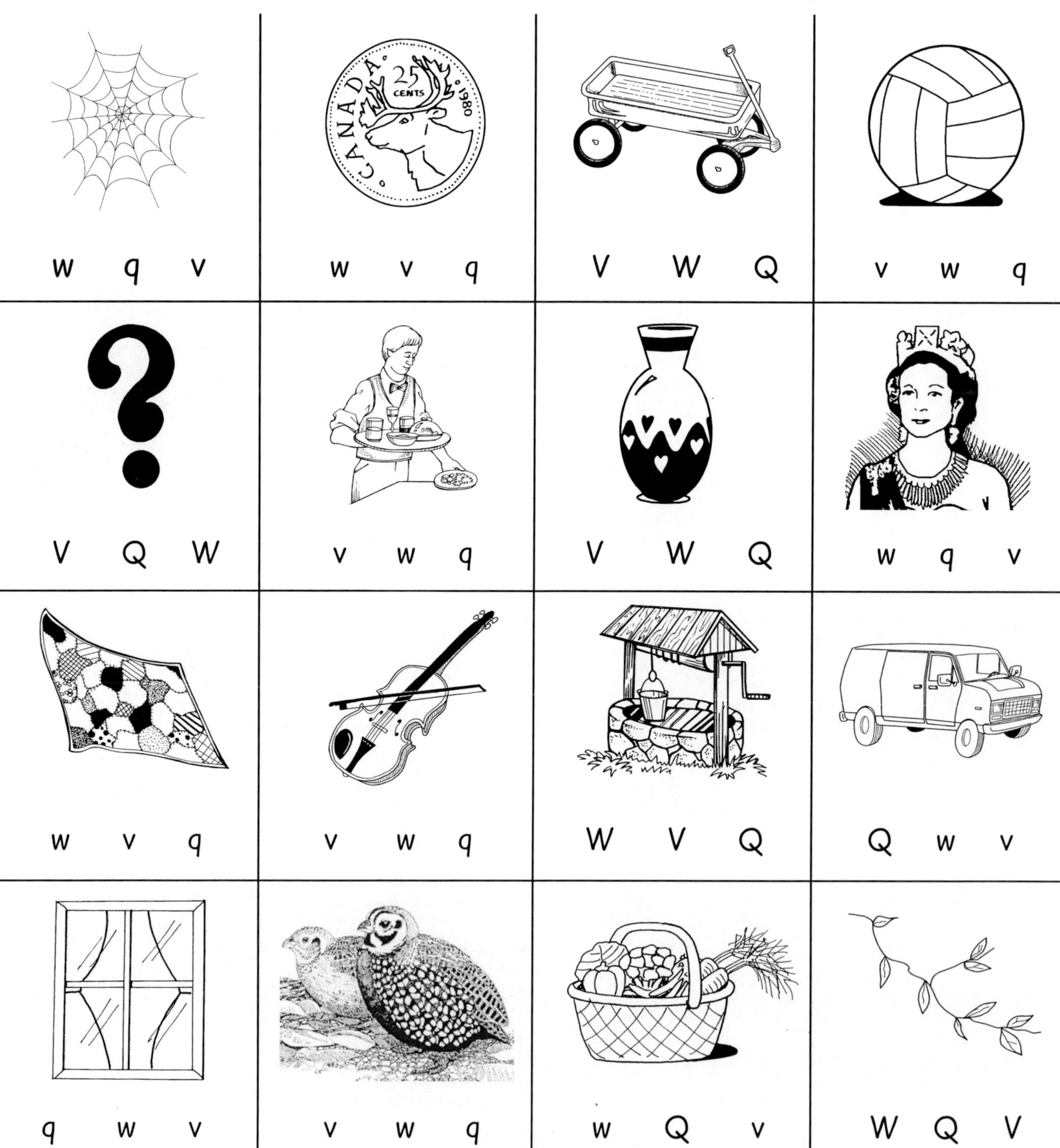

Name: ______________________________ | Day 5 | Week 6 |

A. Auditory Discrimination Test:

1.	2.	3.	4.
v q w	W Q V	v Q w	V W Q
5.	6.	7.	8.
q w v	V W Q	q V w	W Q v

B. Visual Discrimination Test:

Does the picture begin with '**Qq**, **Vv**, or **Ww**?'

___	___	___
___	___	___
___	___	___

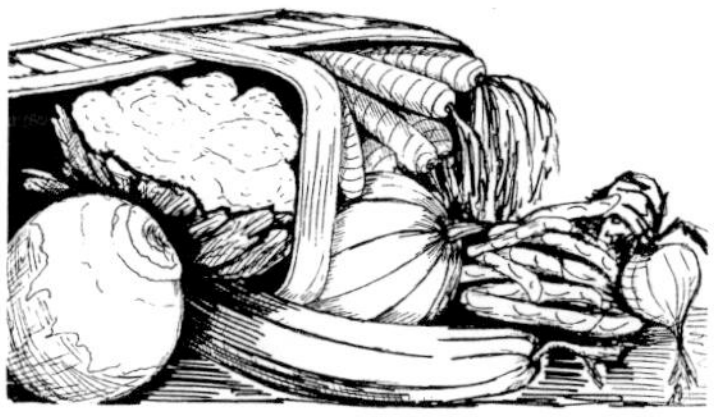

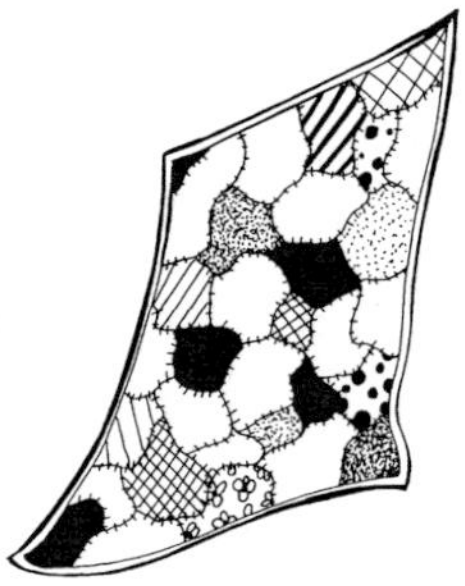

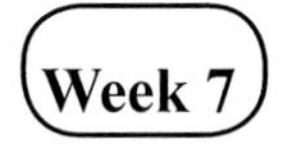

Week 7 Initial Consonants 'Xx, Yy, and Zz'

Objective: To teach and review the initial consonants **'Xx, Yy,** and **Zz'**

Teacher Information: A. The letter **'Xx'** is seldom used at the beginning of words. When it is used it usually says its own name. When it is used at the end of a word it makes a hissing sound. **B**. The letter **'Yy'** makes the lazy way to say yes **'yuh**.' It is made with an open mouth. **C**. The letter **'Zz'** is used at the beginning of some words but is more often heard at the end of a word. It makes a 'buzzing' sound.

Day 1: Introduce the initial consonant **'Xx'** with the following sentences. 1. Johnny had to have an x-ray on his arm. 2. At Xmas gifts are placed under the evergreen tree. 3. The man played the xylophone in the orchestra. Which words in the sentences begin with the sound made by the letter **'Xx**?' (x-ray, Xmas, xylophone) The letter **'Xx'** does make a different sound at the end of words. Listen to these words. 'box, fox' What does the **'Xx'** say in these words? (k-ss) Listen to these words. Is the letter **'Xx'** at the beginning or ending of the word. 1. extra (beginning) 2. box (ending) 3. examine (beginning) 4. wax (ending) 5. excited (beginning) 5. mix (ending) 6. x-ray (beginning) List words on a chart that have the sounds **'Xx'** makes in two columns on a chart. One column for the **'Xx'** at the beginning and one column for the **'Xx'** at the end.

Picture Key: Row 1: wax, Xmas, ax, Row 2: ox, fox, xylophone Row 3: six, mix, fix

Activity Worksheet: Page 43 Students are to record on the correct line where they hear the sound that **'Xx'** makes at the beginning or ending of each picture.

Day 2: Introduce the initial consonant **'Yy'** using the following short story. ' In the far north of a country, animals called 'yaks' live in herds. One of the yaks was quite young and its body was covered with yards of woolly hair. Every year in the spring Yolanda's hair was cut by the people who owned her. They used the hair to make yarn to make clothes. Ask the following questions and record the words on a chart. 1. Who in the story live in herds? (yaks) What was the name of one of the yaks? (Yolanda) How much hair was on Yolanda's body? (yards) What do you notice about the words on the chart? (They all begin with the letter 'Yy.') Listen to the story again for other words that begin with the sound that 'Yy' makes. Add the words to the chart: young, year, yarn. The letter **'Yy'** is made with an open mouth and sounds like the lazy way to say 'yes,' - 'yuh.' Distribute the worksheet on page 44 and work with the students to complete it or instruct them to finish it independently.

Picture Key: Row 1: jeep, yarn, Xmas, yoyo 2. yawn, vine, yard, roof Row 3: yacht, xylophone, yolk, queen Row 4: cap, yell, basket, yes

Activity Worksheet: Page 44 Students are to circle and name all the pictures that begin with the letter 'Yy.'

Day 3: Introduce the initial consonant **'Zz'** using this sentence. 'Zoey Zebra lived in a beautiful zoo where she liked to zip and zigzag all over the green grass playing with the other zebras.' Discuss the sound used at the beginning of 'Zoey Zebra.' Read the sentence again and have the students listen for other words that begin with 'Zz.' List the words on a chart. Discuss the sound that **'Zz'** makes at the beginning of words. Tell your students it makes a buzzing sound similar to the one a bee makes. Distribute the worksheet found on page 45 and work with your students to complete it or have them do the page independently.

Picture Key: Row 1: yard, zoo, yoyo, violin Row 2: Xmas, yarn, zipper, yolk Row 3: zero, worm, vacumn, xylophone Row 4: fox, zuchinni, yogurt, zigzag

Activity Worksheet: Page 45 Students are to circle and name all the pictures that begin with the letter 'Zz.'

Day 4: Review the consonants 'Xx, Yy, and Zz' by having the students listen to groups of words and having them pick out the ones that do not begin the same way. Set 1: yacht, yes, your, going Set 2: fish, zebra, zoo, zoom Set 3: x-ray, extra, exchange, bus Set 4: yellow, you, jar, yarn Set 5: zigzag, zuchinni, zinnia, spagetti

Picture Key: Row 1: Xmas, zuchinni, yacht, zero Row 2: zipper, yarn, zylophone, zigzag Row 3: yolk, zebra, yoyo, yelling Row 4: yak, zoo, yes, yard

Activity Sheet: Page 45 Students will circle the initial consonant heard at the beginning of each picture.

Day 5: Use the following instructions to test your students on the visual and auditory sounds of 'Bb, Cc, Dd, Ff, Gg, Hh, Jj, Kk, Ll. Mm. Nn, Pp, Qq, Rr, Ss, Tt, Vv, Ww, Xx, Yy, Zz.'

A. Auditory Instructions: Point to Box #1. Circle the letter that 'cabin begins with. Repeat the instructions for the following boxes: 2. exclaim (x) 3. quail (q) 4. popcorn (p) 5. nothing (n) 6. dolphin (d) 7. young (y) 8. baseball (b) 9. napkin (n) 10. watch (w) 11. feather (f) 12. kilt (k) 13. jungle (j) 14. zipper (z) 15. happily (h)

B. Visual Discrimination Test: Row 1: hook, kite, jeep, vase Row 2: bell, vine, rain, moon, Row 3: ladder, candy, zebra, gun Row 4: feather, window, top, sock **Answer Key:** Row 1: b, k, j, v Row 2: b, v, r, m Row 3: l, c, z, q Row 4: f, w, t, s

Name: ______________________________ Day 1 | Week 7

Skill: The sound at the beginning of **Xmas** is made by the letter '**Xx**'

Xmas

The sound at the ending of some words is made by the letter '**Xx**.'

box

Say the name of each picture. Record the letter '**Xx**' on the correct line to tell where it is heard.

Name:______________________________ | Day 2 | Week 7

Skill: The sound at the beginning of '**yak**' is made by the letter '**Yy**.'

yak

Say the name of each picture. **Circle** and **name** each picture that begins with the sound that '**Yy**' makes in each row

Name: ______________________________ Day 3 | Week 7

Skill: The sound at the beginning of '**zebra**' is made by the letter '**Zz**.'

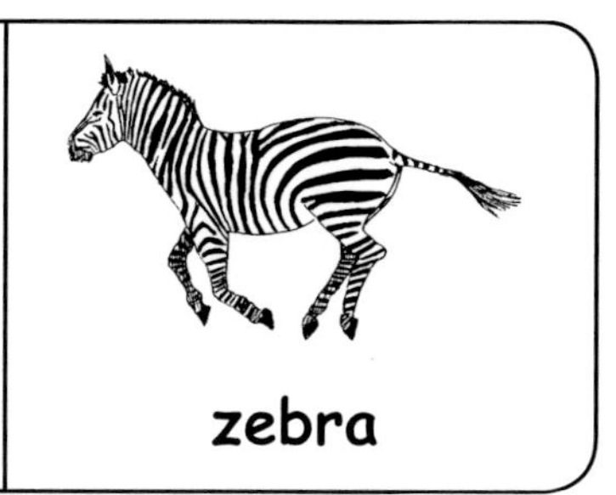

zebra

Say the name of each picture. **Circle** and **print** the letter of each picture that begins with the sound that '**Zz**' makes.

___	ZOO ___	___	___
___	___	___	___
0 ___	___	___	___
___	___	YOGURT ___	___

Name: ______________________________ Day 4 | Week 7

Skill: Auditory and visual recognition of the sounds made by the initial consonants '**Xx, Yy**, and **Zz**.'

Circle the letter heard at the beginning of each picture

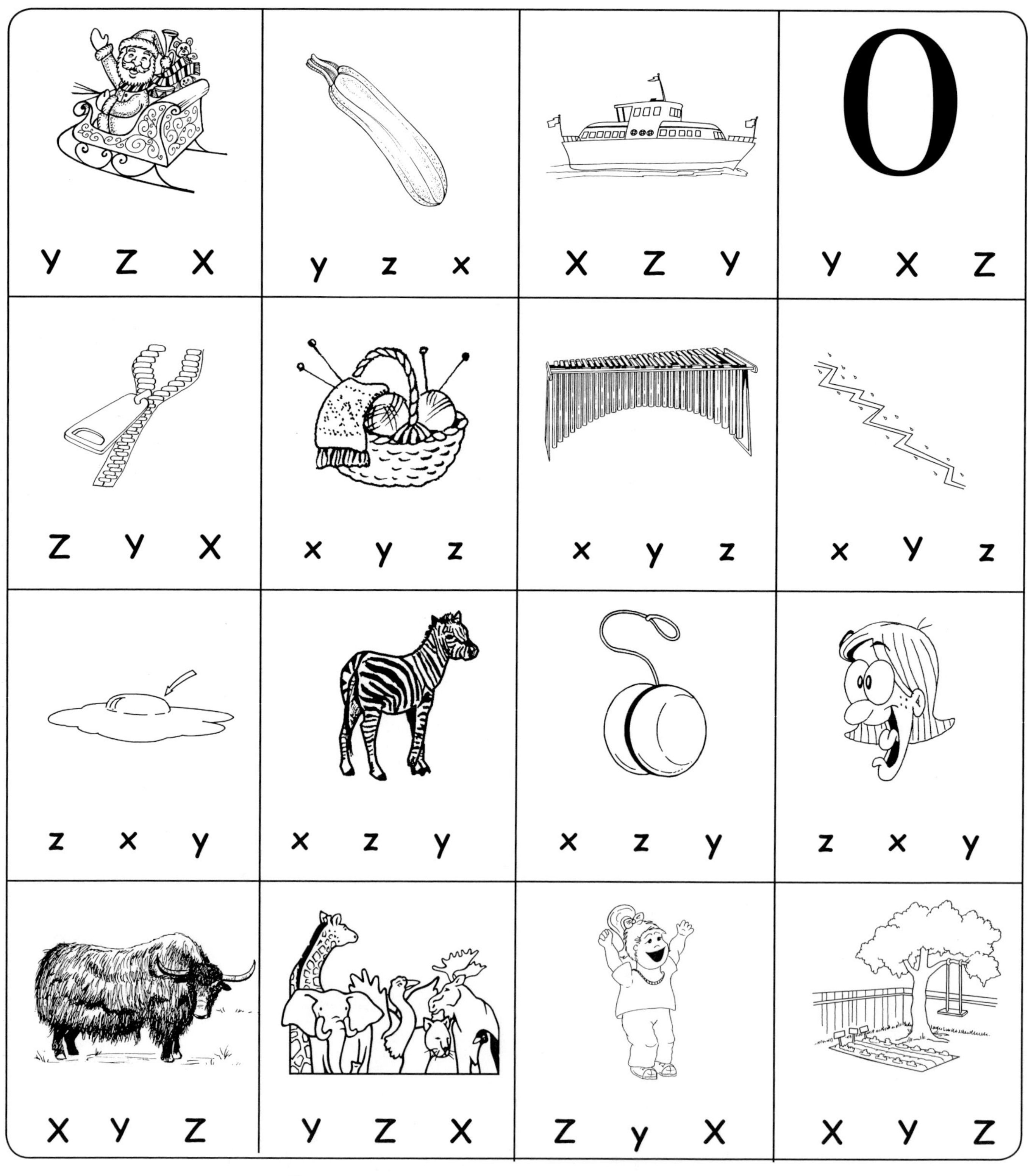

Name: ______________________________ | Day 5 | Week 7 |

A. Auditory Discrimination Test of the Initial Consonants 'Bb, Cc, Dd, Ff, Gg, Hh, Jj, Kk, Ll, Mm, Nn, Pp, Qq, Rr, Ss, Tt, Vv, Ww, Xx, Yy, Zz'

1. B C d	2. x y z	3. O Q P	4. d b p	5. M N V
6. b d p	7. V Y W	8. B P D	9. N M V	10. v w n
11. s f c	12. V d K	13. g p j	14. x y z	15. H F B

B. Visual Discrimination Test of Initial Consonants

___	___	___	___
___	___	___	___
___	___	___	___
___	___	___	___

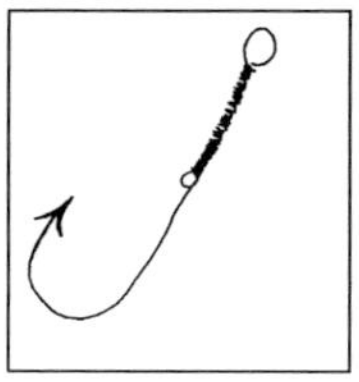

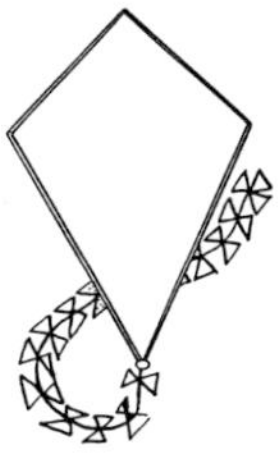

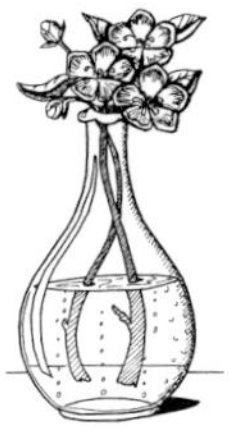

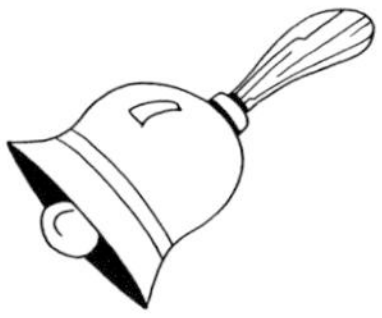

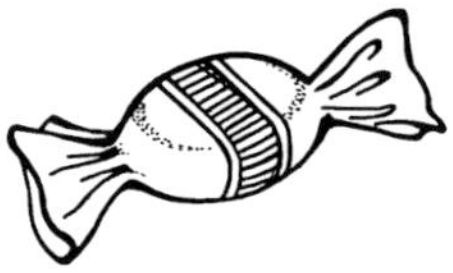

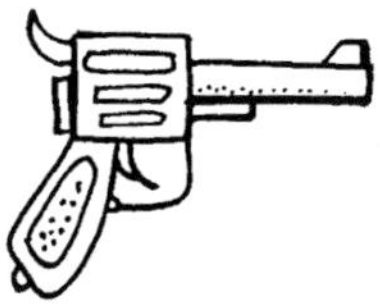

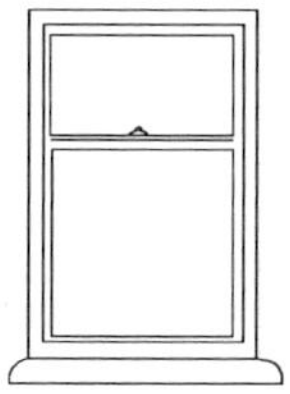

Week 8 Final Consonants 'g, l, d, f, p, n, b, m, t'

Objective: To teach and review the final consonants '**g**, **l**, and **d**'

Teacher Information: Final consonants usually make the same sounds as initial consonants. Some exceptions are 'has, was, because, and cause.' It is important that students look and listen for the final sounds in words. Identifying sounds in three letter words helps students to read and spell them.

Day 1: Review the initial consonant sounds '**g, l, d**' with the following listening exercise. 1. What sound do you hear at the beginning of these words? 1. good, gather, gone (g) 2. leather, listen, large (l) 3. dish, dig, dive (d) This time listen to the end of these words: 1. dog, pig, dug What sound do you hear: (g) 2. Listen to the end of these words: 1. pail, bowl, nail What consonant sound do you hear at the end? (l) 3. Listen to the end of these words: 1. bad, lid, sled What sound do you hear? (d) Draw to your students' attention that words can begin and end with consonants.

Picture Key: Row 1: bag, nail, sad Row 2: sail, log, lid Row 3: tail, head, seal

Activity Worksheet: Page 49 Students are to record the initial and final consonants for each picture to make its name.

Day 2: Review the initial consonant sounds '**f, p, n**' using the following listening activity. Listen to this group of words. 1. fish, 2. funny 3. fat How are these words the same? (They all begin with 'Ff.') Repeat the exercise using 1. pan, pig, pin. (Pp) 2. nurse, nine, never (Nn) This time listen to the end of each word. 1. puff, off, stiff What sound did you hear at the end of each word? (f) 2. cup, nap, lip (p) 3. fun, tan, pen (n)

Picture Key: Row 1: roof, pin, top Row 2: tap, loaf, bun Row 3: wolf, cap, pan

Activity Worksheet: Page 50 Students are to record the initial and final consonants heard for each picture to form the word.

Day 3: Review the initial and final consonants '**m**, **p**, **b**' using the following exercise. What sound do you hear at the beginning of the following words: 1. muffin (Mm) 2. picture (Pp) 3. bike (Bb) 4. magic (Mm) 5. balloon (Bb) 6. pump (Pp) This time I want you to listen to the end of each word for its final sound: 1. tub (Bb) 2. leap (Pp) 3. farm (Mm) 4. club (Bb) 5. top (Pp) 6. ham (Mm)

Picture Key: Row 1: ham, bat, mat Row 2: cat, jam, rat Row 3: tub, cub, hat

Activity Worksheet: Page 51 Students are to record the initial and final consonants for each picture to complete its name

Day 4: Review the final consonants d, b, n, k, f, r, l, x, and z. Which word in each group does not have the same final consonant. 1. bell, wall, <u>talk</u> 2. wood, <u>water</u>, old 3. wolf, <u>pull</u>, calf 4. buzz, fuzz, <u>fox</u> 5. leg, beg, <u>head</u> 6. cook talk <u>lamp</u> 6. <u>rag</u>, tub, rib 7. pan, fin, <u>jam</u> 8. sink, blink, <u>dog</u> 9. <u>far</u>, fat, <u>car</u> 10. <u>wolf</u>, fox, ox

Day 5: Use the following instructions to test students on the visual and auditory sounds of the final consonants 'b, d, f, g, k, l, m, n, p, r, s, t, x, z.' Page 52

A. Auditory Instructions: Point to Box #1. Circle the letter that makes the final sound at the end of 1. head (d) 2. peel (l) 3. hump (p) 4. hug (g) 5. book (k) 6. car (r) 7. rub (b) 8. hum (m) 9. rat (t)

B. Initial and Visual Discrimination Test: The students are to print on the lines the initial and final consonants to make the word that relates to the picture.

Answer Key: Row 1: road, jail, sad Row 2: gas, box, man Row 3: cub, meal, pen

Name: ______________________________ | Day 1 | Week 8 |

Some words end with the sounds that the letters '**d**, **l**, and **g**' make. They are called **final consonants**.

Examples:

mu**d**	pai**l**	do**g**

Say the name of each picture. **Print** the sound that you hear at the **beginning** and **ending** of each picture to make the word.

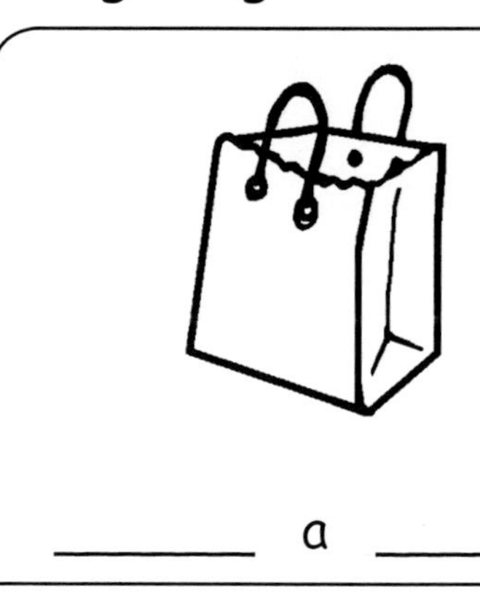		
______ a ______	______ ai ______	______ a ______
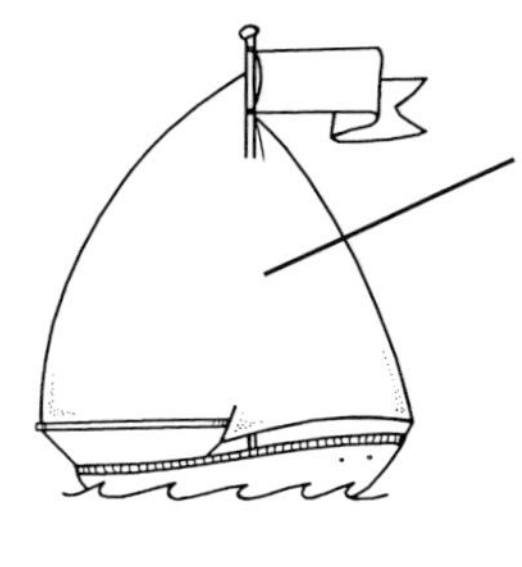	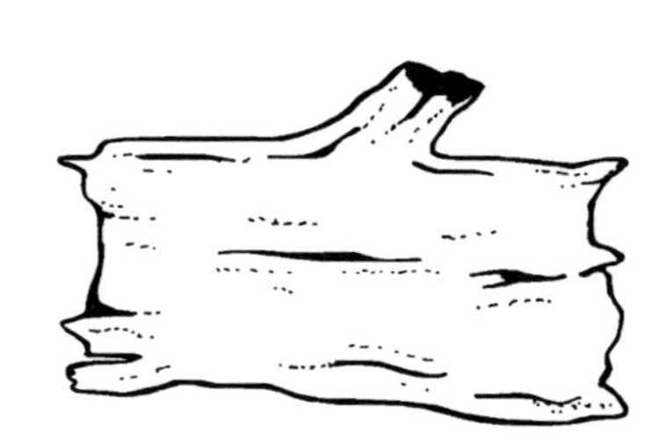	
______ ai ______	______ o ______	______ i ______

______ ai ______	______ ea ______	______ ea ______

Name: ______________________________ | Day 2 | Week 8 |

Some words end with the sounds that the letters **'f, p, and n'** make. They are called **final consonants** and are found at the end of words.

ca**n** ma**p** lea**f**

Say the name of each picture. **Print** the sound that you hear at the **beginning** and **ending** of each picture to make a word.

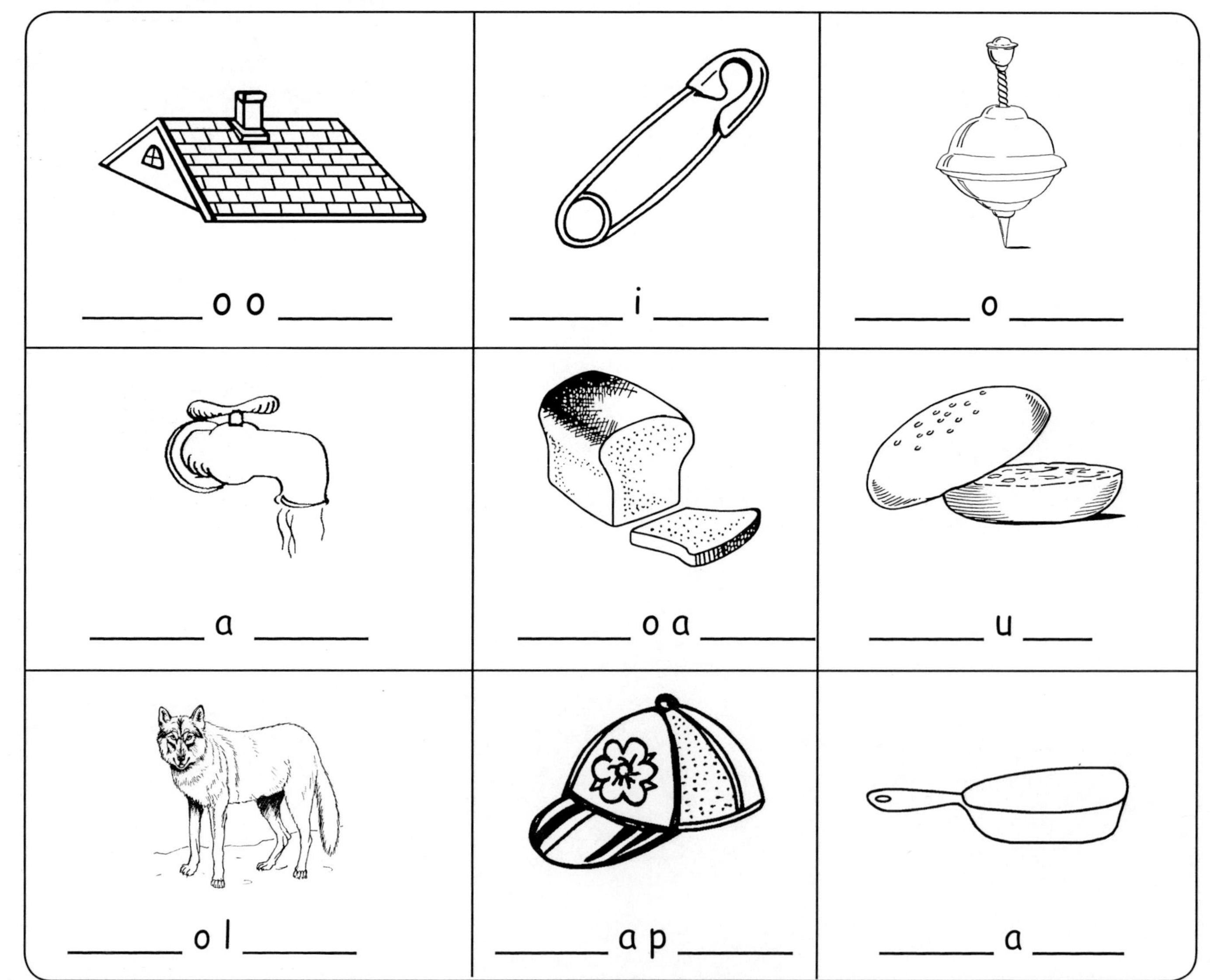

Name: ______________________________

Day 3	Week 8

Some words end with the sounds that the letters '**m**, **t**, and **b**' make. They are called **final consonants** and are found at the end of words.

gum

pot

cob

Say the name of each picture. **Print** the sound that you hear at the **beginning** and **ending** of each picture to make the word.

 ____ a ____	 ____ a ____	 ____ a ____
 ____ a ____	 ____ a ____	 ____ a ____
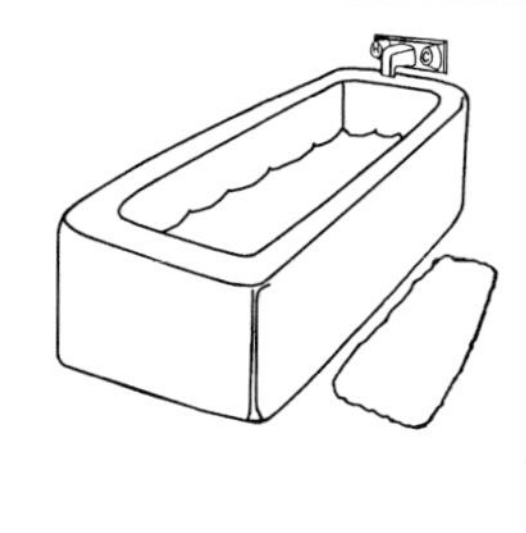 ____ u ____	 ____ u ____	 ____ a ____

Name: ______________________________ | Day 4 | Week 8 |

Skill: Auditory and visual recognition of the final consonants **g, l, d, f, p, n, b, m, t**

What sound do you hear at the end of each picture? **Print** the sound that you hear on the line to complete each word.

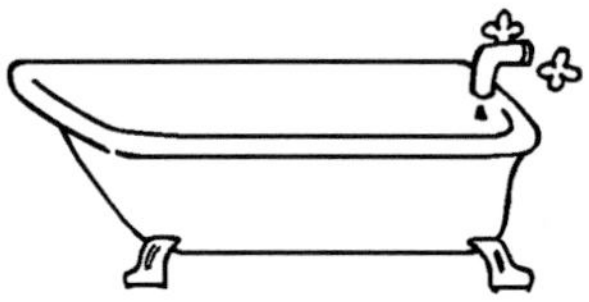

p a i ____	d o ____	t u ____	c a ____
r o o ____	b e ____	b a ____	b a ____
l o a ____	10 t e ____	m a i ____	c a ____
m a ____	t a i ____	c a ____	r o o ____

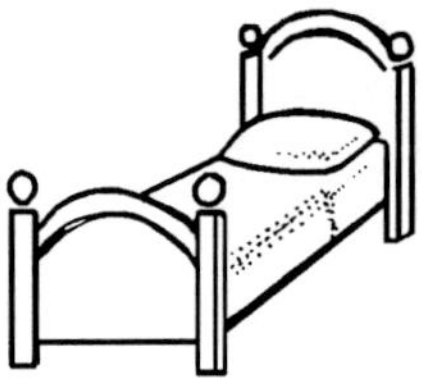

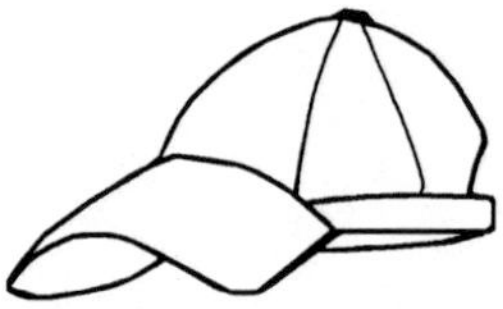

Name: ______________________________ | Day 5 | Week 8 |

A. **Auditory Discrimination Test of the Final Consonants** 'g, l, d, f, p, n, b, m, and t'

1. d b c	2. t h l	3. b p d
4. y j g	5. f k h	6. m r n
7. d b p	8. n w m	9. h t l

B. **Initial and Final Visual Discrimination Test:**

 ______ o d ______	 ______ a i ______	 ______ a ______
 ______ a ______	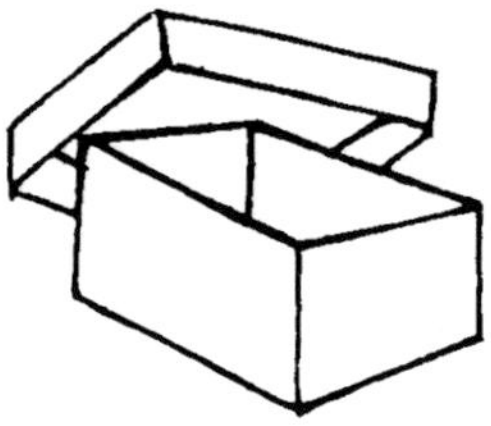 ______ o ______	 ______ a ______
 ______ u ______	 ______ e a ______	 ______ e ______

Week 9: Final Consonants 'd, m, t, l, p, s'

Objective: To teach and review final consonants 'd, m, t, l, p, s'

Teacher Information: Final consonants usually make the same sounds as initial consonants. Some exceptions are 'has, was, because, and cause'. It is important that students look and listen for the final sounds in words. Identifying sounds in three letter words helps students to read and spell them.

Day 1: Review the initial and final consonants 'd, m, t, l, p, s.' Play the game called 'Start and Stop.' Say a word. Ask your students to tell if a certain letter starts or stops a word. Say the word 'thud.' Question: Does the sound that 'd' makes start or stop the word 'thud?' (stops) Continue in the same manner with the following words. Words: 1. (Pp) pop (starts and stops) 2. (Mm) hum (stops) 3. (Tt) talk (starts) 4. (Dd) head (stops) 5. (Mm) munch (starts) 6. (Tt) fat (stops) 7. (Ll) call (stops) 8. (Tt) tent (starts, stops) 9. (Pp) push (starts) 10. (Ss) dress (stops)

Picture Key: Row 1: jail, rain, ham, jeep Row 2: jam, bat, beet, jet Row 3: hill, lip, cap, gun Row 4: nut, sun, tap, pan

Activity Worksheet: Page 55 Students are to record the initial and final consonants for each picture to make its name.

Day 2: Review the initial and final consonants 'd, m, t, l, p, s' with these riddles. 1. I begin with 'l' and end with 'p.' I am a light. (lamp) 2. I end with 'm' and you have two of them on your body. (arm). 3. I begin with 'b' and end with 'd'. I am the opposite to good. (bad) 4. I begin with 'd' and end with 't.' I am small round and black. (dot) 5. I begin with 'h' and end with 'p'. It is done on one foot. (hop) 6. I begin with 'l' and end with 's' and I am the Scottish name for a girl. (lass)

Picture Key: Row 1: dad, nut, mom Row 2: top, pail, gas Row 3: pool, boot, nail Row 4: seal, lamp, tent

Activity Worksheet: Page 56 Students are to record the initial and final consonant for each picture to make its name.

Day 3: Review the following final consonants 'g, l, d, f, p, n, b, m, t, l, p, s' with this listening activity. Listen to the three words that I am going to say. **Words:** 'new, no, nice' Do the words all begin the same way? (Yes) What sound do you hear? (n) Listen to these three words; 'can, in, fan.' Do they begin or end the same way? (end) What sound do you hear? (n) Listen to each group of words that I say and tell how they begin or end. **Groups of Words:** 1. mud, hid, had (F.C. 'd') 2. see, saw, seen (I.C. 's') 3. log, bog, frog (F.C. 'g') 4. call, bell, kneel (F.C. 'l') 5. pig, pie, pop (I.C. 'p') 6. moon, man, mat (I.C. 'm') 7. huff, puff, stuff (F.C. 'f') 8. skip, shop, help (F.C. 'p')

Picture Key: Row 1: jam, run, hand Row 2: seed, jeep, net, Row 3: corn, toad, boat Row 4: bus, jail, rain

Activity Sheet: Page 57 Students are to record the initial and final consonants for each picture to make its name.

Day 4: Review the following initial and final consonant sounds with this listening activity. Example: Listen to this group of words 'pump, bump, lump.' How are these words the same. (They all end with the letter 'p' and rhyme) Listen to each group of words that I say and tell how they are the same of how they are different. **Groups of Words**: 1. bend, band, 2. mail, map 3. lend, hid 4. tent, tail 5. dent, door 6. corn, horn 7. room, drum 8. deep, damp

Picture Key: Row 1: hand, bag, heel Row 2: leaf, cup, barn Row 3: girl, pig, cat Row 4: mad, fan, rat

Activity Sheet: Page 58 Students are to record the initial and final consonants for each picture to make its name.

Day 5: Use the following instructions to test your students on the visual and auditory sounds of the final consonants m, t, l, p, s.

A: Auditory Instructions: Point to Box #1. Circle the letter that makes the sound at the end of the word 'bud' (d) 2. harm (m) 3. pit (t) 4. curl (l) 5. rap (p) 6. pass (s) 7. wool (l) 8. hog (g) 9. plum (m)
Answer Key: 1. d 2. m 3. t 4. l 5. p 6. s 7. l 8. g 9. m

B. Initial and Final Visual Discrimination Test: The students are to print the initial and final consonant sound heard in each picture to complete the word.

Picture Key: Row 1: mud, room, goat Row 2. mat, raft, pup 3. head, mop, peas Answer Key : Row 1. m d, r m, g t Row 2: m t, r t, p p Row 3: h d, m p, p s

SSR1140 ISBN: 9781771586863

Name: ______________________________ | Day 1 | Week 9 |

Most words begin and end with a consonant.
An initial consonant begins a word and a final consonant ends a word.
Example: **cat** The initial consonant '**c**' starts the word and the final consonant '**t**' stops the word.

Start and **stop** the words in the box to match each picture.

____ a i ____	____ a i ____	____ a ____	____ e e ____
____ a ____	____ a ____	____ e e ____	____ e ____
____ i l ____	____ i ____	____ o ____	____ u ____
____ u ____	____ u ____	____ a ____	____ a ____

Name: ______________________________ Day 2 | Week 9

Most words begin and end with a consonant.
Examples: cat, dog, run, his, pal, sap

Start and **stop** each word in the boxes to name each picture.

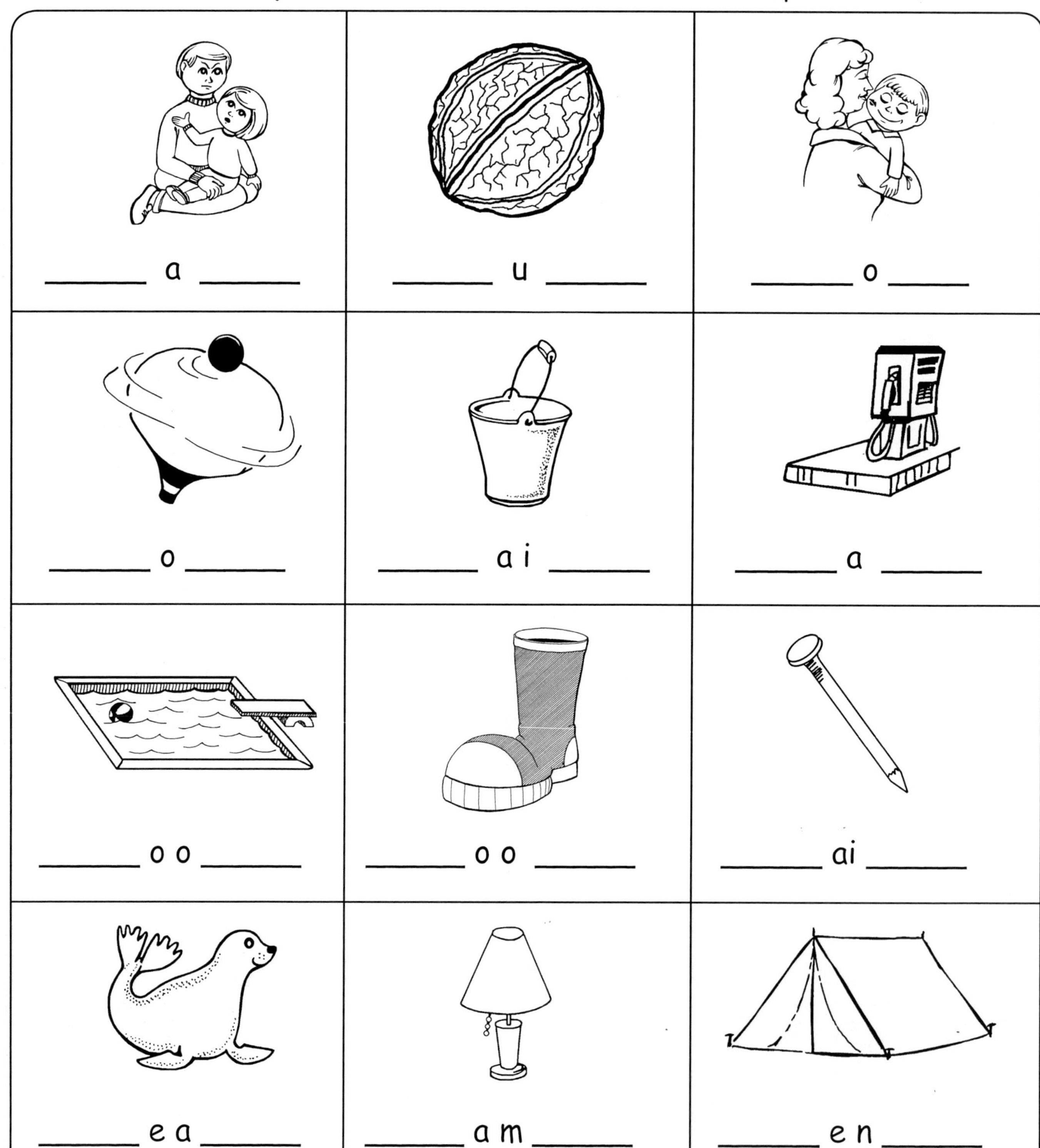

Name: ______________________________

Day 3	Week 9

Most words begin and end with a consonant.
Examples: pig, room, cat, hall, rub

Start and **stop** each word in the boxes to match each picture.

 ___ a ___	 ___ u ___	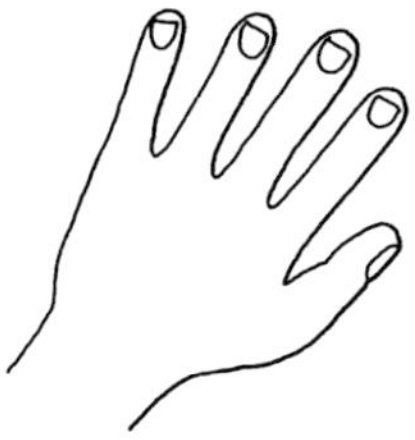 ___ a n ___
 ___ e e ___	 ___ e e ___	 ___ e ___
 ___ o r ___	 ___ o a ___	 ___ o a ___
 ___ u ___	 ___ a i ___	 ___ a i ___

 ISBN: 9781771586863

Name: ________________________________

Day 4 | Week 9

Most words begin and end with a consonant.

Examples: bad, rail, ham, sat, nap, dig, feel

Start and **stop** each word in the boxes to match the picture

______ a n ______	______ a ______	______ o o ______
______ e a ______	______ u ______	______ a r ______
______ i r ______	______ i ______	______ a ______
______ a ______	______ a ______	______ a ______

Name: ______________________________ | Day 5 | Week 9 |

A. Auditory Discrimination Test of the final consonants 'd, m, t, l, p. s'

1. b d g	2. N R M	3. t k f
4. K P L	5. b q p	6. S C Z
7. f l k	8. P C G	9. m n r

B. Initial and Final Consonant Visual Discrimination Test:

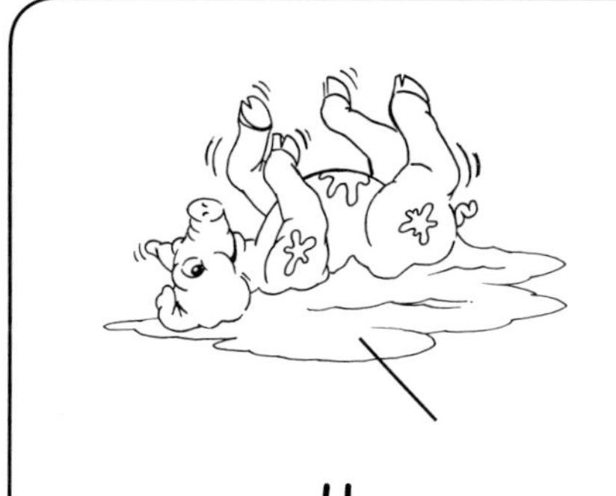 ____ u ____	 ____ o o ____	 ____ o a ____
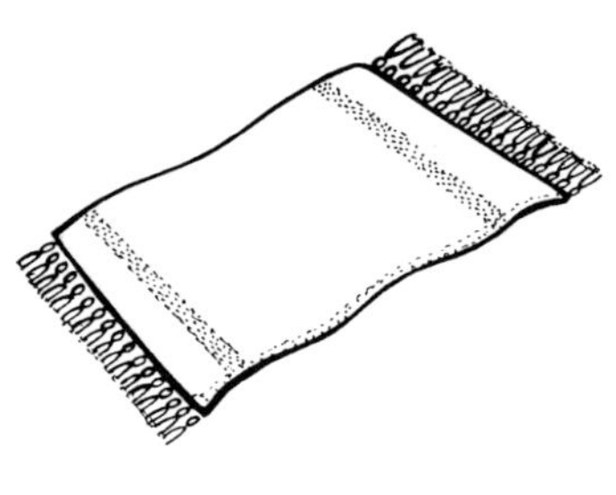 ____ u ____	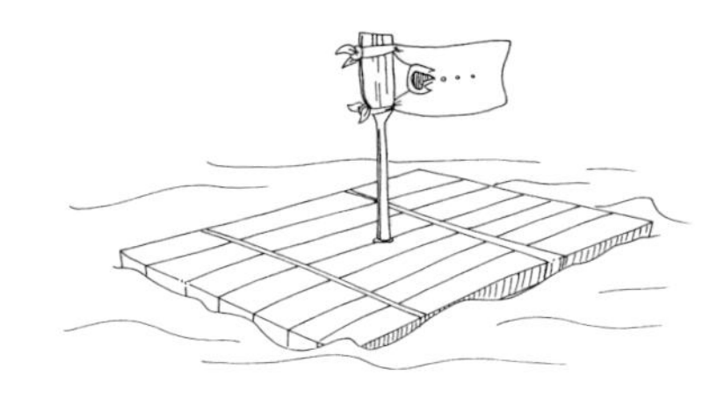 ____ a f ____	 ____ u ____
 ____ e a ____	 ____ o ____	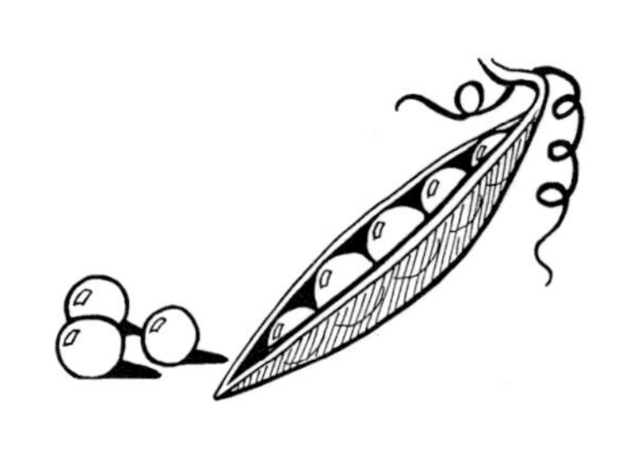 ____ e a ____

Week 10: Final Consonants 'd, b, n, k, f, r, z, x'

Objective: To teach and review the final consonants d, b, n, f, r, l, x, z

Teacher Information: Final consonants usually make the same sound as initial consonants. Some exceptions are 'has, was, because, and cause.' It is important that students look and listen for the sounds in words. Identifying sounds in three letter words helps students to read and spell them.

Day 1: Review the initial consonant sounds 'd, b, and n' with the following exercise. What sound do you hear at the beginning of these words? 1. door, dig, deer (d) 2. beans, birds, bags (Bb) 3. new, nice, near (n) This time listen to the end of these words: 1. head, slid, paid. What sound do you hear at the end of these words? (d) Now listen for the sound at the end of these words. "had, could, wood' What sound do you hear? (d) Listen to the end of each group of words for its final sound. 1. had did, hold (d) 2. fan, tin, can (n) 3. cob, bib, hub (b)

Picture Key: Row 1: cob, bed, pin Row 2: fan, tub, lid Row 3: pen, cab, bead

Activity Worksheet: Page 61 Students are to record the initial and final consonants for each picture to complete its name.

Day 2: Review the initial and final consonants '**k**, **f**, and **r**' with the following listening exercise. Listen to the beginning of these three words 1. kill, kind, king. What sound do you hear? (k) 2. fine, funny, foot (f) 3. robin, rose, rest (r) This time listen to the end of the words. 1. flick, snack, luck What sound do you hear at the end of each word? (k) Listen to each group of words for its final sound. 1. leaf, off, puff (f) 2. pop, hop, peep (p) 3. fun, fan, fin (f) What sound do you hear at the end of 1. rug (g) 2. pail (l) 3. laid (d) 4. huff (f) 5. map (p) 6. ran (n)

Picture Key: Row 1: kick, jar, leaf, car Row 2: roof, book, calf, door Row 3: bank, pear, hair, back

Activity Worksheet: Page 62 Students are to record the initial and final consonants for each picture to make its name.

Day 3: Review the initial consonant sounds '**b**, **m** and **t**' with the following listening exercise. Tell how this group of words are the same. 1. butter, button, barn (begin with Bb) 2. mouse, monkey man (begin with Mm) 3. tie, tiger, top (begin with Tt) Now listen to the following groups of words and tell me how they are all the same. 1. tub, rub, shrub (end with Bb) 2. arm, room, gum (end with Mm) 3. rat, hit, not (end with Tt),

Picture Key: Row 1: ham, bat, mat Row 2: cob, jam, rat Row 3. tub, cub, hat

Activity Worksheet: Page 63 Students are to record the initial and final consonants for each picture to make its name.

Day 4: Review the initial and final consonants previously taught. Use the following groups of words to review the initial and final sounds taught. Listen to each group of words. Do they begin or end with the same sound. What is the sound called? Groups of Words: 1. had, land (Final Dd) 2. puff, leaf (Final Ff) 3. puppet, purple (Begin with Pp) 4. pin, wagon (Final Nn) 5. bed, bath (Begin with Bb) 6. arm, jam, (Final Mm) 7. rat, tent (End with Tt) 8. ghost, gas (Begin with (Gg) 9. stuff, stiff (Final Ff) 10. live, long (Begin with Ll)

Picture Key: Row 1: pail, dog, tub, can Row 2: room, bed, bat, bag Row 3: bread, ten, mail, cat Row 4: map, tail, cap, roof

Activity Worksheet: Page 64 Students will record the final consonant to complete each word

Day 5: Use the following instructions to test your students on the visual and auditory sounds of the final consonants 'g, l, d, f, p, n, b, m, t.' Page 65

A. Auditory Test Instructions: Point to Box#1. Circle the letter that makes the sound at the end of the word cup (p) Repeat the instructions for the following boxes: 2. well (l) 3. lad (d) 4. hug (g) 5. huff (f) 6. sun (n) 7. stub (b) 8. harm (m) 9. nut (t)

B. Initial and Final Visual Discrimination Test: The students are to print the initial and final sound heard in each picture to complete each word

Picture Key: Row 1: soap, jail, sad Row 2: log, leaf, man Row 3: cub, meal, pen

Answer Key: Row 1: s p; j l; s d Row 2: l g; l f; m n Row 3: c b; m l; p n

Name: ______________________________ | Day 1 | Week 10 |

Some words end with the sounds that the letters '**d**, **b**, and **n**' make. They are called final consonants.
Examples:

m u d

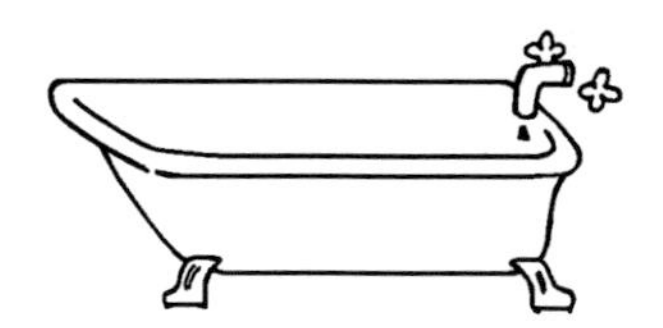

t u b

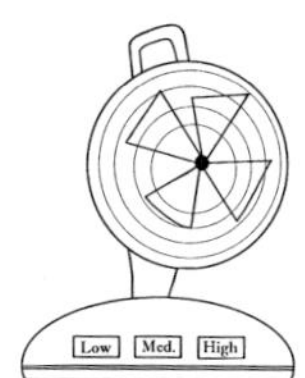

f a n

Say the name of each picture. **Print** the sound that you hear at the beginning and ending of each picture to make the word.

____ o ____	____ e ____	____ i ____
____ a ____	____ u ____	____ i ____
____ e ____	____ a ____	____ e a ____

Name: ___________________________

Day 2	Week 10

Some words end with the sounds that the letters '**k**, **r**, and **f**' make. They are called **final consonants**.

m i l **k**

d e e **r**

w o l **f**

Say the word for each picture. **Print** the sound that you hear at the beginning and ending of each picture to make the word.

____ i c ____	____ a ____	____ a ____	____ e a ____
____ oo ____	____ oo ____	____ al ____	____ oo ____
____ an ____	____ ea ____	____ ai ____	____ ac ____

Name: ______________________________

Day 3	Week 10

Some words end with sounds that the letters '**x, z** and **l**' make
They are called **final consonants**.

fix

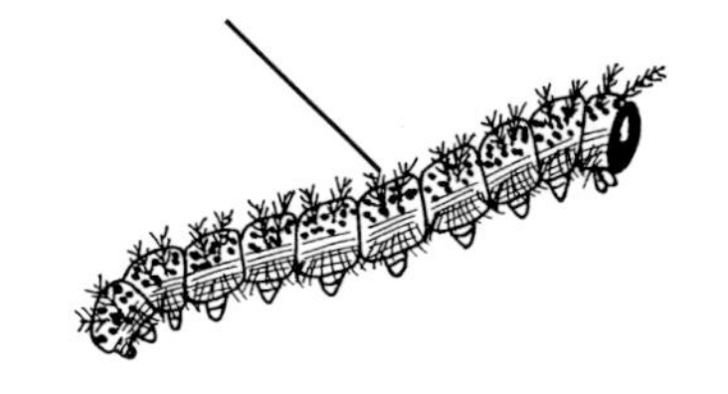

fuzz

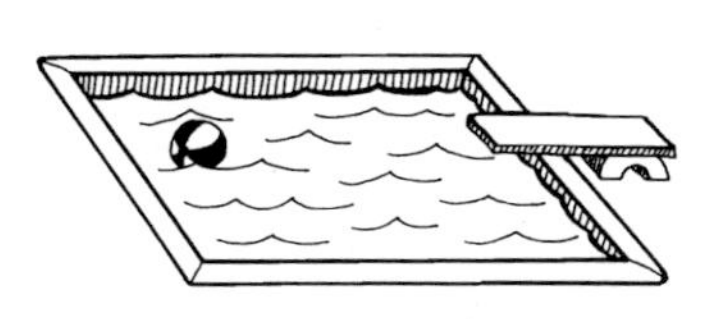

pool

Say the name of each picture. **Print** the sound that you hear at the beginning and ending of each picture to make the word.

6 _____ i _____	_____ u z _____	_____ e a _____
_____ a i _____	_____ i _____	_____ o _____
_____ o _____	_____ a _____	_____ i z _____

Name: ______________________________

Day 4 | Week 10

Skill: Auditory and visual recognition of the final consonants 'd, b, n, k, f, r, z, x'

What sound do you hear at the end of each picture? **Print** the letter that makes the final sound on the line to complete each word.

h e a ____	s i n ____	c a ____	s p o o ____
f o ____	c l u ____	s t a ____	s a c ____
t i g e ____	b o ____	s h e l ____	c h a i ____
b u z ____	w o l ____	b e a ____	h e ____

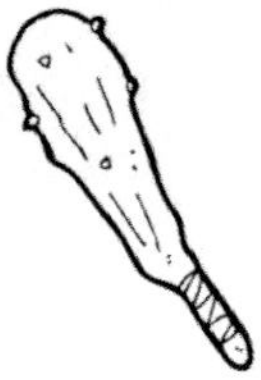

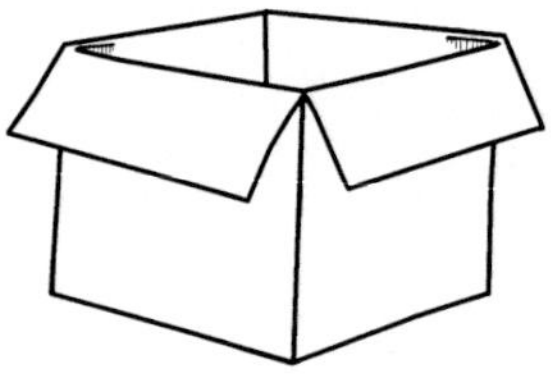

SSR1140 ISBN: 9781771586863

Name: ______________________________ | Day 5 | Week 10 |

A. Auditory Discrimination Test of the final consonants 'd, m, t, l p, s, g, b, n, f, k, and x

1. d g b	2. s n f	3. g p d	4. m n r
5. p f g	6. t f b	7. z w x	8. n v m
9. c t s	10. l k f	11. p b d	12. d g b

B. Initial and Final Discrimination Test

 ____ e e ____	 ____ a c ____	 ____ a l ____	 ____ o ____
 ____ e a ____	 ____ e a ____	 ____ i r ____	 ____ o ____
 ____ u ____	 ____ o ____	 ____ a r ____	 ____ a n ____

Week 11: Short Vowel 'a'

Objective: To teach the recognition of the **short vowel** ă in words.

Teacher Information: Short Vowel sounds are issued from the back of the throat when isolated. In most words they blend with the initial and final sounds. Introduce the symbol ˘ that sometimes appears over short vowels in words.

Day 1: Introduce the short vowel ă using the following format. I am going to say words which begin like 'apple.' When you hear a word that doesn't begin with ă like in apple raise your hand. Words to be given: at, an, me, attention, action, act, fall, Annie, Alice, on, as, attic, Amy. Sometimes the â sound is heard inside a word. Listen to these words. When you hear an ă sound inside a word raise your hand.
Words: skip, can bed, tin, bad, sea, pig, bag, pond, wig, fan, up, hand, set, hit, hat

Picture Key: Row 1: apple, sock, bear, bag Row 2: fox, bat, bell, hand Row 3: ant, sun, ax, ham Row 3: ant, sun, ax, ham Row 4: cab, top, cup, mask

Activity Sheet: Page 67 Students are to circle and colour all the pictures with the short ă vowel sound. Pictures to be circled and coloured are: apple, sack, bag, bat, hand, ant, ax, ham, cab, mask

Day 2: Review the short vowel ă sound with this listening game. Listen to the three words that I am going to say. Which one has the short ă sound? 1. ape, toe, tan 2. top, tip, tap 3. lump, lamp, limp 4. cob, cub, cap 5. bug, big, bag 6. pat, bit, but 7. bad, bed, bud 8. set, sit, sat

Picture Key: Row 1: man, cup, bat, candle Row 2: bed, sack, lamp, sock Row 3: rain, nest, hat, candy Row 4: cat, pig, rock, sand

Activity Worksheet: Page 68 Students are to print the short vowel â on the lines provided correctly and then colour the pictures. **Answer Key:** man, bat, candle, sack, lamp, hat, candy, cat, sand

Day 3: Using the chalkboard or a chart print the following three letter words with the short vowel ă sound. Words: cat, pad, tap, bat, tab, dad, fan, bag Have the students name each word.

Picture Key: Row 1. pan, man, ham, jam Row 2. bag, tag, bat, cat 3. rat, hat, fan, man 4. cap, map, bag, bat

Activity Worksheet: Page 69 Students are to draw a line from the word to the picture it names.

Day 4: Print eight of the 'an' word endings down a chart. Example: ___ an Explain to your students that you are going to make words that have the short ă sound. Give a clue for each of the words. Example: It is made of metal and is also called a tin. Record the correct letter at the beginning of the word. Example: can Do the same for the words Dan, fan, man, pan, ran, tan, and van

Activity Worksheet: Page 70 The students are to circle and print the correct word in each sentence.

Answer Key: 1. fan 2. bat 3. van 4. cat 5. bat 6. sand 7. man 8. hat

Day 5: Use the following instructions to test your students ability to recognize the short vowel ă.

A. Auditory Instructions : Listen to each word that I say. If the word has the short vowel ă sound circle the word 'yes' in each box. If the word doesn't have the short â vowel sound circle the word 'no.'

Words: 1. pan 2. pig 3. ran 4. pen 5. bun 6. mash 7. cap 8. bug 9. bag 10. sap

Answer Key: 1. Yes 2. No 3. Yes 4. No 5. No 6. Yes 7. Yes 8. No 9. Yes 10. Yes

B. Visual Discrimination Test: Print the letter 'a' on the lines if the pictures have the short ă sound.

Picture Key: Row 1: cat, cake, cone, sack Row 2: flag, bell, snake, apple Row 3: dime, hat, cup, tap

Answer Key: cat, sack, flag, apple, hat, tap

Name: ______________________________ Day 1 | Week 11

cat

In the word cat we hear the **short 'a'** sound.

This sound is usually spelled by the letter **'a.'**

Say the name of each picture. **Circle** and **colour** all the pictures that have the short 'a' vowel sound.

Name: ______________________________

Day 2 | Week 11

The short vowel **'a'** is found in many words. Examples: c**a**n, p**a**t, h**a**nd

Listen to the names of the pictures. **Print** the letter **'a'** on the line below each picture whose name has the **short 'a'** sound.

 __________	 __________	 __________	 __________
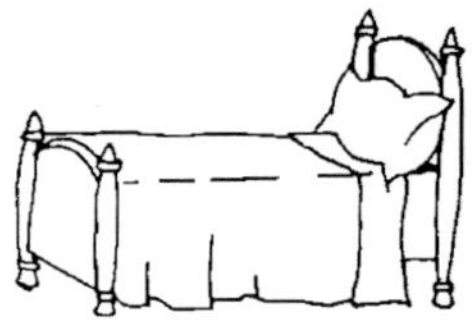 __________	 __________	 __________	 __________
 __________	 __________	 __________	 __________
 __________	 __________	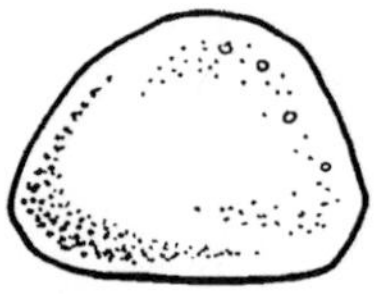 __________	 __________

Name: ______________________________ Day 3 | Week 11

The short vowel 'a' is heard at the beginning or inside many words.
Examples:

apple

can

Read the words carefully in each box and **name** the pictures. **Draw** a **line** from each word to the picture that it names.

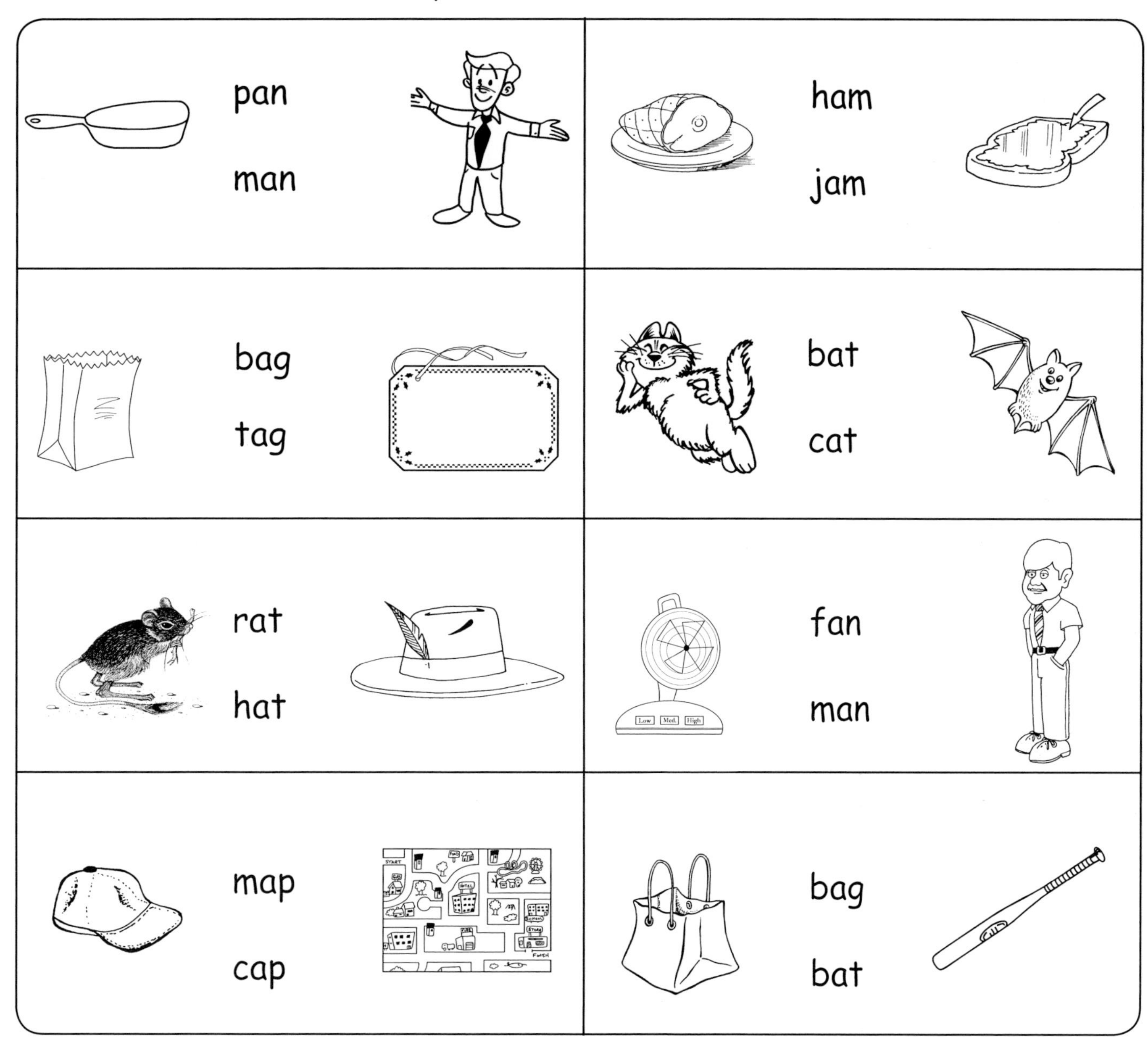

Name: ______________________________

Day 4 | Week 11

Read the sentence and the words in each box.
Print the word from the box that makes a good sentence on the line in each one.

See the big **fan**. (tan, **fan**, ran)

1. The ________________ is big. (tan, fan, ran)

2. Jack can ________________ the ball. (cat, sat, bat)

3. The ________________ is big and red. (can, fan, van)

4. The ________________ is big and black. (sat, cat, fat)

5. See the little ________________ fly. (bat, mat, hat)

6. I can play in the ________________. (hand, land, sand)

7. The ________________ is Sam's dad. (can, ran, man)

8. Pat has a big, blue ________________. (sat, hat, fat)

Name: ______________________________

Day 5 Week 11

A. Auditory Test on Short Vowel 'Aa':

1. Yes No	2. Yes No	3. Yes No	4. Yes No	5. Yes No
6. Yes No	7. Yes No	8. Yes No	9. Yes No	10. Yes No

B. Visual Discrimination Test

 ________	 ________	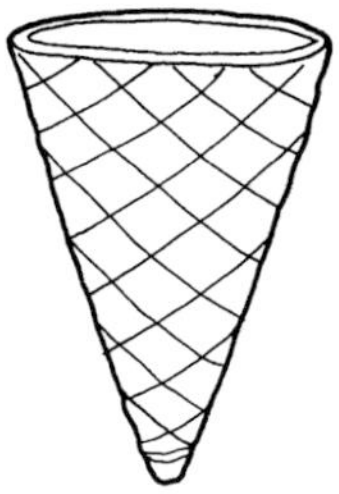 ________	 ________
 ________	 ________	 ________	 ________
 ________	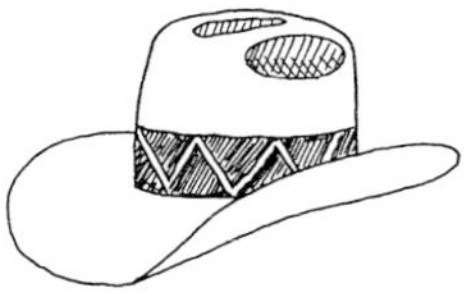 ________	 ________	 ________

Week 12 Short Vowel 'e'

Objective: To teach the recognition of the **short vowel 'e'** in words.

Teacher Information: Short vowel sounds are issued from the back of the throat when isolated. In most words they blend with the initial and final sounds. Introduce the symbol ˘ that sometimes appears over short vowels in words.

Day 1: Introduce the short vowel **'e'** using the following format. Listen to the beginning of each word that I say. 'egg, echo, edge' What sound did you hear at the beginning of each one. (eh) The sound at the beginning is the short vowel 'e'. Sometimes you hear it at the beginning of words or in the middle. Listen to these words and tell where you hear the short 'e' sound. Is it at the beginning or inside the word? **Words:** 1. egg (B) 2. bell (M) 3. elbow (B) 4. neck (M) 5. head (M) 6. empty (B) 7. nest (M) 8. engine (B) 9. shell (M) 10. echo (B)

Picture Key: Row 1: tent, cat, pen, shell Row 2: feet, bat, bed, bell Row 3: apple, elephant, leaf, web Row 4: rake, jet, meat, fence

Activity Worksheet: Page 73 Students are to circle and colour all the pictures that have the short **'e'** sound. Pictures to be coloured are tent, pen, shell, bed, elephant, web, jet, fence.

Day 2: Review the short vowel **'e'** using the following story. The students are to raise one hand every time they hear the short 'e' vowel sound. Story: At the edge of a jungle lived a group of elephants. One of the elephants was called Ed. During very hot days Ed went to a nearby river to get cool. He enjoyed playing in the water when the weather was extra hot. Sometimes he would fill up his extra long trunk with water and blow it over his head and back. Sometimes he would spray his elephant friends with water as well. Have the students dictate words from the story that have the short 'e' sound so the teacher can print them on a chart. Have them circle the short **'e'** heard in each word.

Picture Key: Row 1: nest, van, tent, nail Row 2: raft, shell, pot, leg Row 3: well, neck, bee, kite Row 4: clock, vest, fish, net

Activity Worksheet: Page 74 The students are to print the letter **'e'** on the lines below each picture with the short **'e'** sound.

Day 3: Using the chalkboard, a white board, or chart paper, print the following three letter words: pet, net, pen, leg, men, beg, led, set. Have the students locate the short 'e' words that answer each clue given. **Clues:** 1. It is used for catching fish and butterflies. (net) 2. Boys grow up to become them. (men) 3. It is an animal kept in a home. (pet) 4. It is used for writing letters. (pen) 5. It is part of your body. (leg) 6. Dogs do this when they are hungry. (beg) 7. To take someone somewhere (led) 8. To put dishes on a table (set)

Picture Key: Row 1: well, bell, nest, vest Row 2: jet, net, peg, leg Row 3. pen, ten, men, hen Row 4: bed, valentine, eggs, legs

Activity Worksheet: Page 75 Students are to match the word to its picture in each box.

Day 4: Using the following riddles review the auditory recognition of short 'a' and short 'e'.
Riddles: 1. You can ride on me in the snow. (sled) What vowel sound do you hear in the word? (Short 'e') 2. Eggs and meat are often fried in one. (pan, short 'a') 3. Some people wear one on their faces on Hallowe'en. (mask, short 'a') 4. It is a warm and soft place to sleep. (bed, short 'e') 5. I am the part of your body that holds up your head. (neck, short 'e') 6. You can build castles with it. (sand, short 'a') 7. A spider spins one to catch bugs. (web, short 'e') 8. A bird lays eggs in it. (nest, short 'e')

Activity Worksheet: Page 76 Students are to select the missing word and print it in the sentence.
Answer Key: 1. pen 2. bed 3. hen 4. jet 5. pet 6. fed 7. vest 8. bell

Day 5: Use the following instructions to test your students' ability to recognize the short vowel **'e'** sound.
A. Auditory Instructions: Listen to each word that I say. If the word has the short **'e'** vowel sound circle the word 'yes' in each box. If the word does not have the short **'e'** sound circle the word 'no'. **Words**: 1. hat 2. yell 3. web 4. can 5. pen 6. hand 7. neck 8. elf 9. pan 10. belt **Answer Key:** 1. No 2.Yes 3.Yes 4. No 5. Yes 6. No 7. Yes 8. Yes 9. No 10. Yes

B. Visual Discrimination Test: Students are to print the letter **'e'** on the line if the picture has the short 'e' sound.
Picture Key: Row 1: can, desk, eggs, flag Row 2: tent, bat, head, fish Row 3: web, jet, clock, well
Answer Key: desk, eggs, tent, head, web, jet, well

Name: ______________________________ Day 1 | Week 12

In the word '**bell**' we can hear the **short 'e'** sound.

This sound is spelled by the letter '**e**'.

Say the name of each picture. **Circle** and **colour** all the pictures that have the **short 'e' vowel** sound.

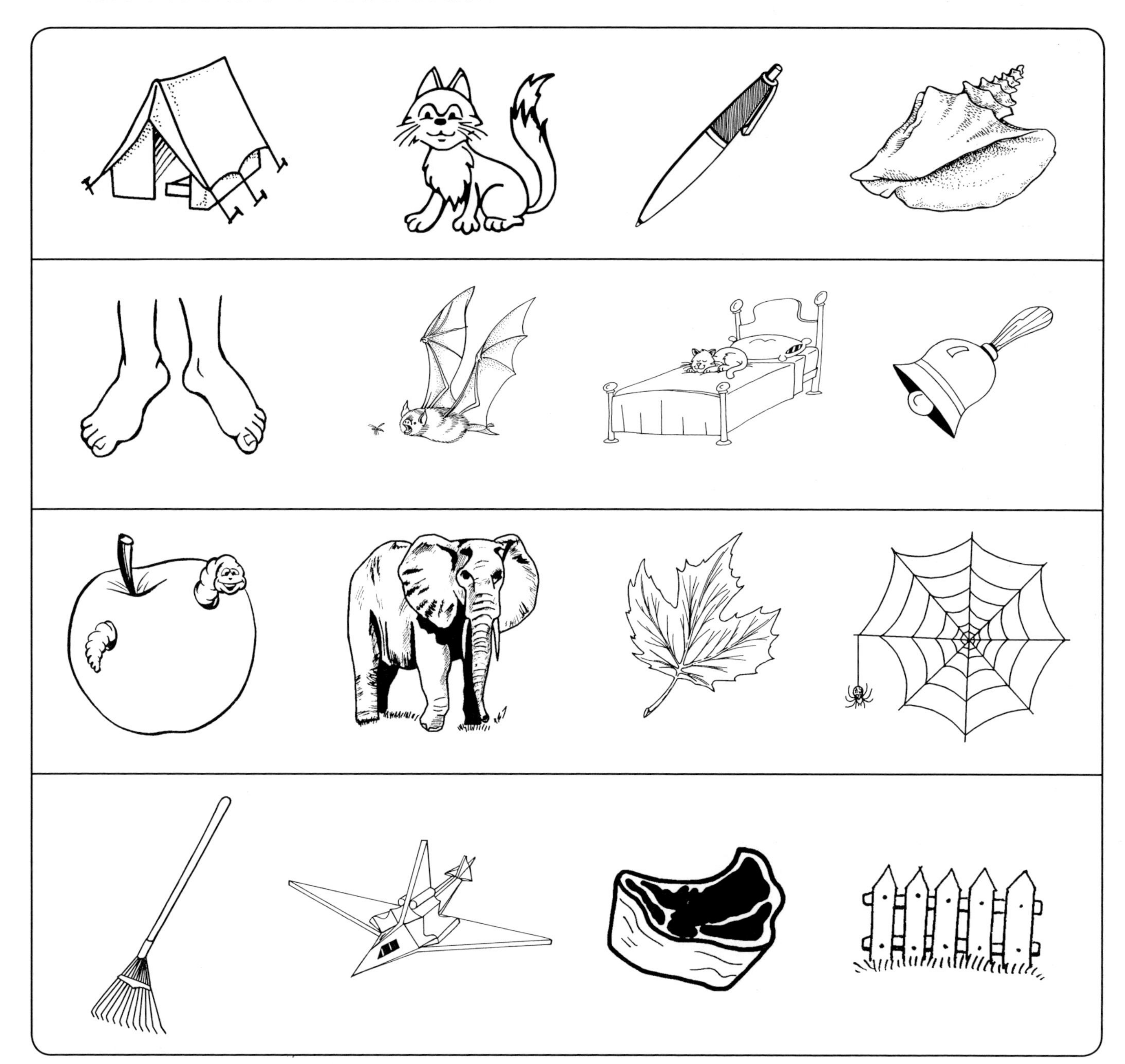

Name: ______________________________

Day 2 | Week 12

The **short vowel 'e'** is found in many words.

Listen carefully to the names of the pictures. **Print** the letter **'e'** on the line below each picture whose name has the short 'e' sound.

 ______	 ______	 ______	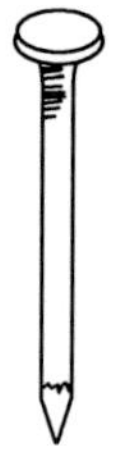 ______
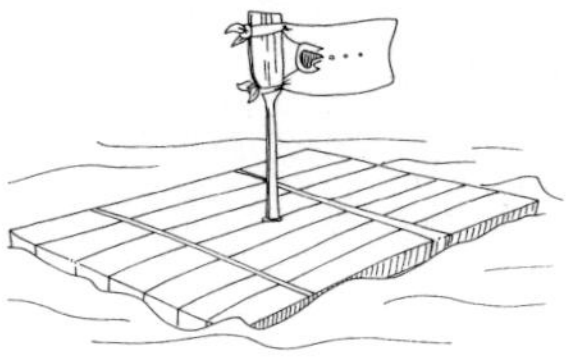 ______	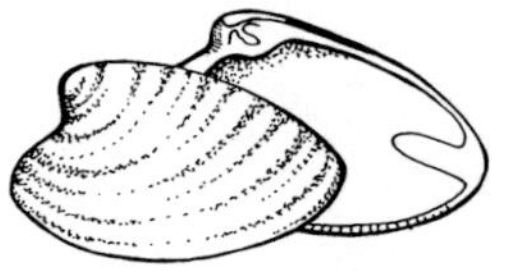 ______	 ______	 ______
 ______	 ______	 ______	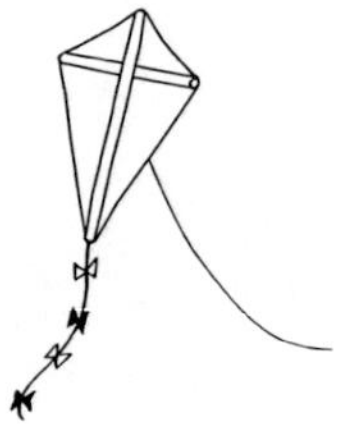 ______
 ______	 ______	 ______	 ______

Name: ______________________________ Day 3 | Week 12

The short vowel **'e'** is heard at the beginning or inside many words.
Examples:

eggs 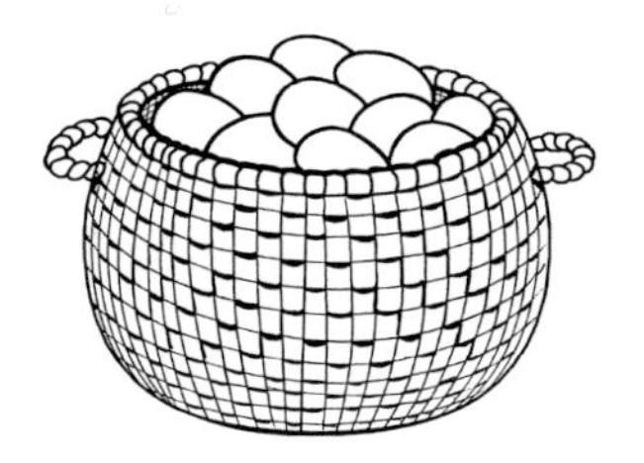

hen 

Read the words carefully in each box and **name** the pictures. **Draw** a line from each word to the picture that it name.

bell well	nest vest
jet net	leg peg
pen ten 10	hen men
bed red	eggs legs

Name: ______________________________

Day 4 | Week 12

Read the sentence and the words in each box.
Print the word from the box,that fits the sentence, on the line in it.
Example:
The boy fell in the well. (tell, bell, well)

1. The pig is in the big ______________. (well, web, pen)

2. My ______________ is big. (bed, fed, fed)

3. The ______________ is in her nest. (pen, pig, hen)

4. The men in the ______________ are set to go. (bat, net, jet)

5. I like to ______________ my dog. (mat, pet, set)

6. Kim ______________ the dog. (red, fed, bed)

7. Ben had on a red ______________. (test, nest, vest)

8. Did you hear the ______________ ring? (tell, bell, sell)

Name: ______________________________

Day 5 | Week 12

A. Auditory Test on Short Vowel 'Ee':

1. Yes No	2. Yes No	3. Yes No	4. Yes No	5. Yes No
6. Yes No	7. Yes No	8. Yes No	9. Yes No	10. Yes No

B. Visual Discrimination Test:

 ISBN: 9781771586863

Week 13 Short Vowel 'Ii'

Objective: To teach the recognition of the short vowel **'Ii'** in words.

Teacher Information: Short vowels sounds are issued from the back of the throat when isolated. In most words they blend with the initial and final sounds. Introduce the symbol ˘ that sometimes appears over short vowels in words.

Day 1: Introduce the **short vowel 'i'** sound by having the students answer the following clues. Record each answer on a chart, white board or chalkboard. Clues: 1. I am a farm animal that lives in a pen and loves to roll in the mud. Who am I? (pig) 2. I am a rich man who wears a crown on my head. Who am I? (king) 3. People and cars use me to travel across water. (bridge) 4. I am a healthy drink. (milk) 5. A baby sleeps in this kind of bed. (crib) Discuss with your students how these words are similar. (They all have the letter 'i' inside.) What sound does the letter 'i' say? (ih) Review the short vowels 'a' and 'e' and their sounds.

Picture Key: Row 1: fish, fan, kick, tent Row 2: raft, dish, brick, bed Row 3: bell, mask, lips, mix Row 4: king, well, elf, ship

Activity Worksheet: Page 79 Students are to colour all the pictures with a short 'i' sound. Pictures to be coloured are: fish, kick, dish, bricks, lips, mix, king, ship

Day 2: Review the short vowels '**a**, **e**, and **i**.' Record the following beginnings of words on a chart ' sa, se, si, fa, fi, fe, da, de, di, ga, ge, gi.' Review the sound that the short vowels 'a, e, and i' make. Then have the students add final consonats to make words. Examples: sat, set, sit, fat, fit, fed, dad, den, did, gas, get, gill Have the students pronounce each word.

Activity Worksheet: Page 80 The students are to print the letter **'i'** on the lines below each picture with the short vowel 'i' sound.

Day 3: Review the position of the short vowel 'i.' Have the students listen for it and tell whether it is heard at the beginning or inside the following words: 1. itchy (B) 2. wind (I) 3. sick (I) 4. ink (B) 5. kiss (I) 6. whip (I) 7. inch (B) 8. inn (B) 9. stick (I) 10. pit (I) After completing the listening activity have the students complete the worksheet.

Picture Key: Row 1: whip, web, flag, pen Row 2: wig, stamp, egg, bridge Row 3: bed, chick, sing, cap Row 4: sink, hadn, wing, shell

Activity Worksheet: Page 81 The students are to draw a line from each word to its picture in each box.

Day 4: On a chalkboard, white board or a chart print the letters 'a, i, and e.' Review their names and their short vowel sounds. Have your students listen and locate the vowel sound heard in each of the following words. Words: west (short e), in (short i) ask (short a), end (short e), tan (short a), ten (short e), wind (short i), ask (short a), itch (short i)

Activity Worksheet: Page 82 Students are to underline the correct words in each box and then print them on the lines in the sentences. **Answer Key:** 1. pig 2. kick 3. bit 4. hill 5. hit 6. fill 7. fix 8. lid

Day 5: Use the following to test your students' ability to recognze the short vowel 'i.'

A. Auditory Instructions: Listen to each word that I say. If the word has the short vowel **'i'** sound, **circle** the word **'yes'** in each box. If the words does not have the short 'i' sound, circle the word **'no'**
Words: 1. stick 2. shell 3. grin 4. safe 5. list 6. pit 7. safe 8. bent 9. sit 10. neck
Answer Key: 1. Yes 2. No 3. Yes 4. No 5. Yes 6. Yes 7. No 8. No 9. Yes 10. No

B. Visual Discrimination Test: Print the letter **'i'** on the line if the picture has the short vowel 'i' sound.
Picture Key: Row 1: grin, nest, king, ant Row 2: lips, tent, bag, swing Row 3: pen, mitt, apple, wig
Answer Key: Row 1: grin, king Row 2: lips, swing Row 3: mitt, wig

Name: ______________________________ | Day 1 | Week 13 |

In the word '**hill**' we hear the **short 'i'** sound.
This sound is spelled by the letter '**i.**'

Say the name of each picture. **Circle** and **colour** all the pictures that have the **short 'i'** vowel sound.

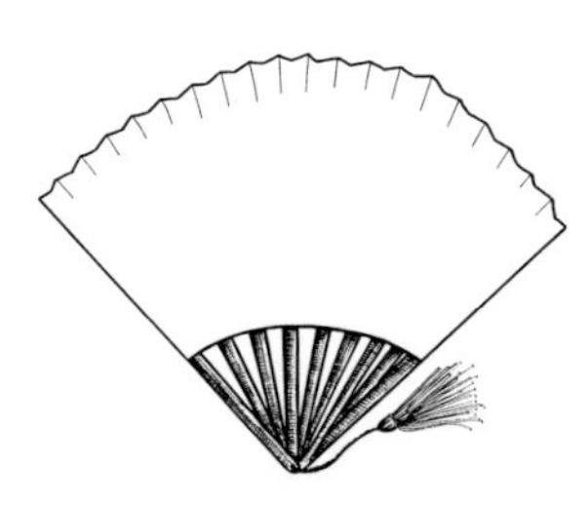

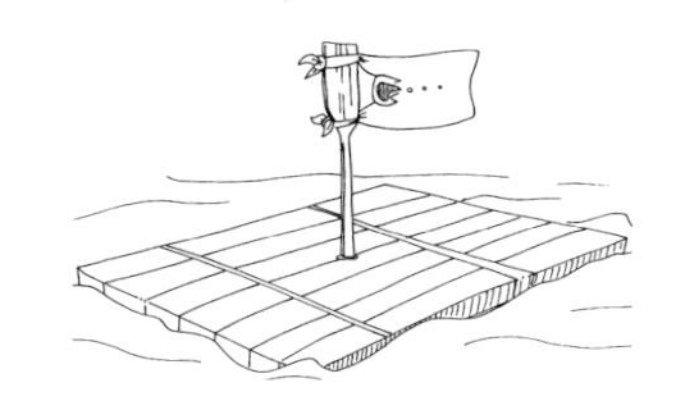

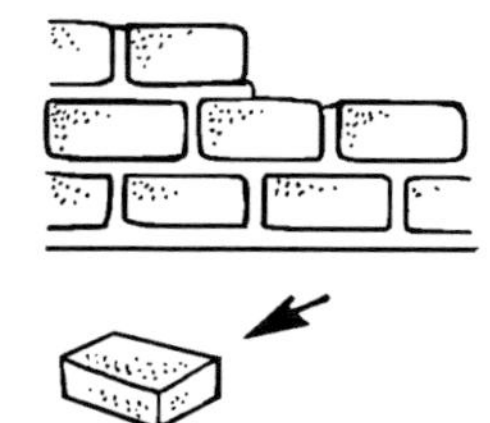
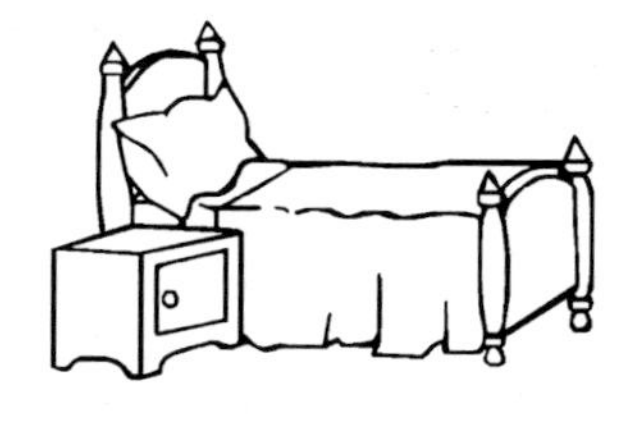

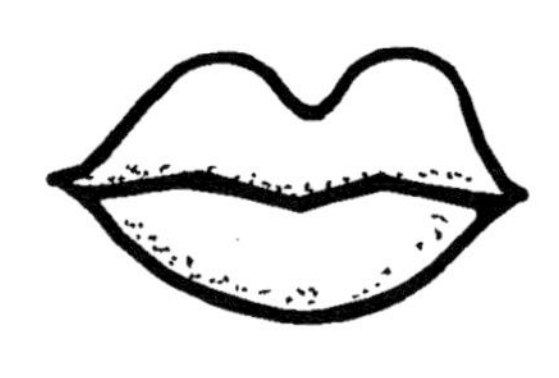

Name: ______________________________

Day 2	Week 13

The **short vowel 'i'** is found in many words.

Listen carefully to the names of the pictures. **Print** the letter **'i'** on the line below each picture whose name has the short 'i' sound.

________	________	________	________
________	________	________	________
________	________	________	________
________	________	________	________

Name: ________________________________ | Day 3 | Week 13 |

The **short vowel 'i'** is heard at the beginning or inside many words.

Examples:

i n k

f i s h

Read the words carefully in each box and **name** the pictures. **Draw** a line from each word to the picture it names.

whip web	pin flag
stamp wig	bridge egg
bed chick	cap ring
hand sink	wing shell

Name: ______________________________ | Day 4 | Week 13 |

Read the sentence and the words in each box.

Print the word from the box that fits the sentence on the line in it.

Example: The boy fell in the <u>well</u> . (web, will, well)

1. The fat ________________ is in the pen. (fit, did, pig)

2. Bill can ________________ the ball. (win, kick, fix)

3. The dog ________________ the man. (bin, ten, bit)

4. The ________________ is too big. (hall, hid, hill)

5. Jim ________________ the ball with a bat. (hat, hot, hit)

6. Did you ________________ the car with gas? (wig, his, fill)

7. The man will ________________ the bike. (fox, fat, fix)

8. Put a ________________ on the pot. (did, lid, lad)

Name: ______________________________ | Day 5 | Week 13 |

A. Auditory Test on the Short Vowel 'i':

1. Yes No	2. Yes No	3. Yes No	4. Yes No	5. Yes No
6. Yes No	7. Yes No	8. Yes No	9. Yes No	10. Yes No

B. Visual Discrimination Test:

Week 14 Short Vowel 'Oo'

Objective: To teach the recognition of the short vowel **'Oo'** in words.

Teacher Information: Short vowel sounds are issued from the back of the throat when isolated. In most words they blend with the initial and final sounds. Introduce the symbol ˘ that sometimes appears over short vowels in words.

Day 1: Introduce the short vowel '**o**' using the following format. **Story:** Otto was a little green frog with black spots on his body. He lived in a little pond. Otto often sat on a rock waiting for insects to fly by. When one flew close to Otto out he would pop his long tongue to catch it. Explain to your students that this vowel sound say 'aw' like in 'Otto' and 'frog.' Read the story again and have the students identify words that have the same sound. Record them on a chart

Picture Key: Row 1: clock, belt, king, log Row 2: elephant, dog, hill, box Row 3: fox, eggs, block, pond Row 4: top, pen, lamp, mop

Activity Worksheet: Page 85 Students are to circle and colour all the pictures that have the short **'o'** sound. **Pictures to be coloured are:** clock, log, dog, box, fox, block, pond, top, mop

Day 2: Review the short **'o'** sound by using the following exercise. Students are to listen for the word in each group that doesn't have the short 'o' vowel sound. Words: 1. stop, hot, cat, doll 2. mop, tip, pop, dot 3. snow, block, pond, stop 4. fog, frog, log, pick 5. pop, pan, cob, shop 6. cross, rod, doll, pet

Picture Key: Row 1: log, web, doll, chin Row 2: bag, frog, pig, rock Row 3: pot, neck, dog, fish Row 4: box, well, bat, fox

Activity Worksheet: Page 86 Students are to print the short vowel sound heard in each picture on the lines provided. **Answer Key:** Row 1: log, doll Row 2: frog, rock Row 3: pot, dog Row 4: box, fox

Day 3: Using the chalkboard, a white board or a chart, record the following three letter words with the short vowel 'o.' **Words:** pop, hop, fox, box, hot, cot, log, dot, rod, dog, top Have the students locate the short 'o' word that matches each clue. **Clues**: 1. It is the opposite to cold. (hot) 2. It is used for fishing. (rod) 3. It is a wild animal. (fox) 4. It can spin around quickly. (top) 5. It is part of a tree. (log) 6. A bunny moves this way. (hop) 7. It is a pet. (dog) 8. It is a kind of drink. (pop) 9. It is a kind of bed. (cot) 10. It comes at the end of a sentence. (dot) 11. It is made of cardboard and carries something inside it. (box)

Picture Key: Row 1: pot, pop, box, fox Row 2: sock, block, log, dog Row 3: pop, pond, doll, dot Row 4: mop, top, rod, pod

Activity Worksheet: Page 86 Students are to match each picture with a line to its word.

Day 4: Using the following sentence clues, review the auditory recognition of short a, e, i and o. Clues: 1. This animal likes to fly at night. (bat) What vowel sound do you hear? (short a) 2. I live in water and eat insects. (frog, short o) 3. In the winter I sleep in one. (den, short e) 4. It is a healthy drink. (milk, short i) 5. You can build a castle with it. (sand, short a) 6. You place it on a pot. (lid, short i) 7. It is a place where you can buy things. (shop, short o) 8. You can do this with a shovel. (dig, short 1)

Activity Worksheet: Page 87 Students are to print the correct word in each sentence. **Answer Key:** 1. pet 2. bell 3. bat 4. hot 5. bed 6. set 7. fell 8. hat 9. ten 10. pet

Day 5: Use the following instructions to test your students ability to recognize the short vowels a, e, i, and o.

A. Auditory Test Instructions: Listen to each word that I say. Circle the vowel sound that you hear in the word.1. itchy 2. block 3. deck 4. safe 5. fist 6. game 7. cob 8. desk 9. wax 10. dock **Answer Key:** Circled letters are: 1. i 2. o 3. e 4. a 5. i 6. a 7. o 8. e 9. a 10. o

B. Auditory/Visual Discrimination Test: Circle the vowel sound that you hear in each picture. **Picture Key:** Row 1: block, vest, fan, pig Row 2: mitt, raft, jet, cross Row 3: fox, nest, sack, swing **Answer Key:** Row 1: o, e, a, i Row 2: i, a, e, o Row 3. o, e, a, i

Name: ______________________________ | Day 1 | Week 14 |

frog

In the word '**frog**' we hear the **short 'o'** sound.

This sound is spelled by the letter **'o'**.

Say the name of each picture. **Circle** and **colour** all the pictures that have the **short 'o' vowel** sound.

Name: ______________________________

Day 2	Week 14

The short vowel **'o'** is found in many words. Examples: p**o**t, h**o**p, st**o**p, c**o**b

Listen carefully to the names of the pictures. **Print** the letter **'o'** on the line below each picture whose name has the **short 'o'** sound.

______	______	______	______
______	______	______	______
______	______	______	______
______	______	______	______

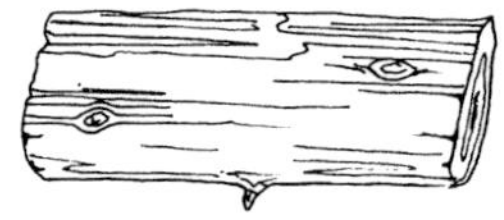

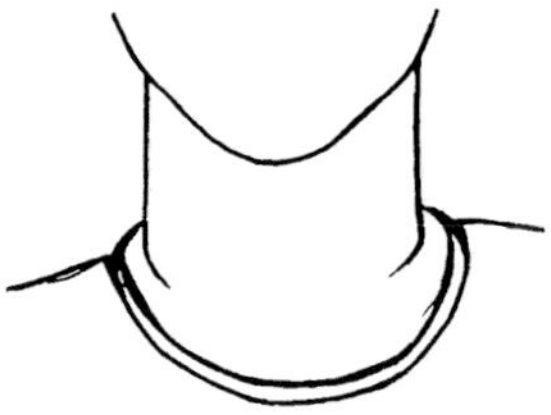

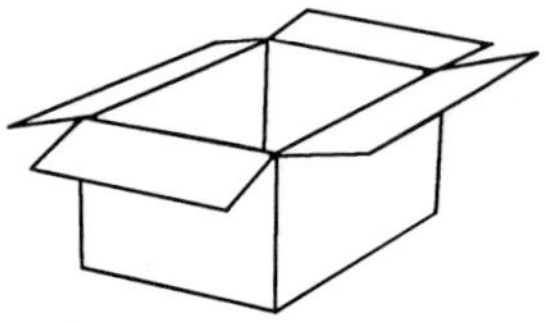

SSR1140 ISBN: 9781771586863

Name: ______________________________ Day 3 | Week 14

The short vowel **'o'** is heard at the beginning or inside many words.

Examples:

ŏlives

frŏg

Read the words in each box carefully and **name** the pictures.

Draw a line from each word to the picture that it names.

pot **pop**	**box** **fox**
block **sock**	**log** **dog**
pop **pond**	**doll** **dot**
mop **top**	**rod** **pod**

Name: ______________________________ | Day 4 | Week 14 |

Read the sentence and the words in each box.

Print the word from the box that fits the sentence on the line in it.

Example: I will dig a hole. **(den, dig, dog)**

1. I can ____________ my dog. (pot, pit, pet)

2. Did you hear the ______________ ring? (ball, bill, bell)

3. I hit the ball with a big ______________ . (bit, bat, bet)

4. The sun can be very _______________. (hat, hit, hot)

5. The boy in the _______________ is sick. (bid, bad, bed)

6. _______________ the book on the table. (set, sat, sit)

7. Jack _______________ down the hill. (fill, fall, fell)

8. Jill has a red _______________ . (hit, hot, hat)

9. Tim has _______________ little fish in his pail. (tin, ten, tan)

10. Ted has a cat for a _______________. (pit, pat, pet)

Name: ______________________________

Day 5	Week 14

A. Auditory Discrimination Test on the short vowels ' a, e, i, o'

1. a e i o	2. a e i o	3. a e i o	4. a e i o	5. a e i o
6. a e i o	7. a e i o	8. a e i o	9. a e i o	10. a e i o

B. Visual Discriminaton Test

 o a e i	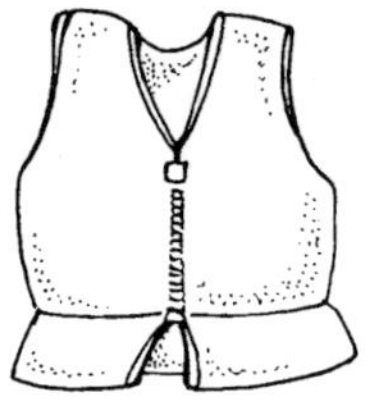 a e i o	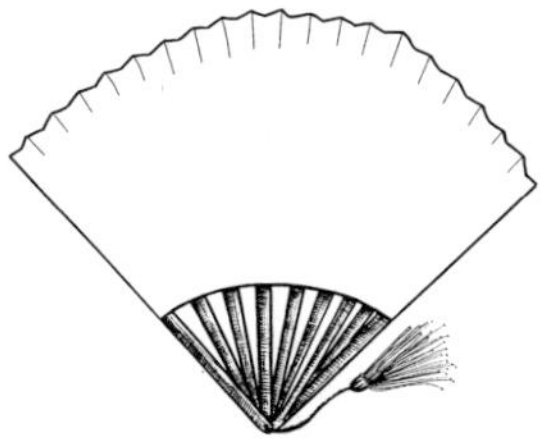 e i o a	 a e i a
 e o a i	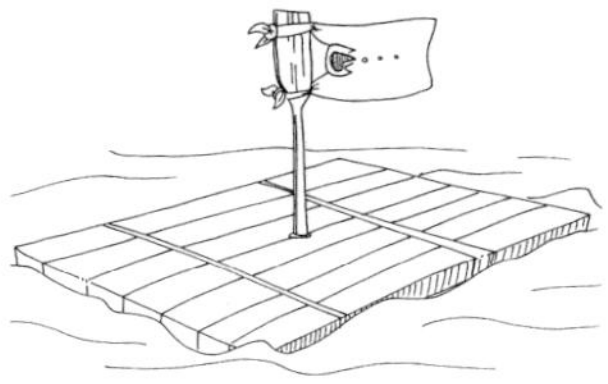 o e i a	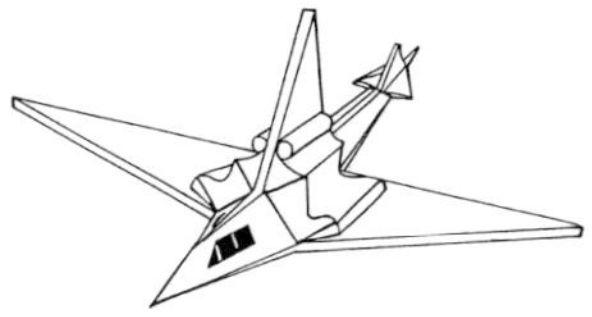 o i e a	 a e i o
 a e i o	 i o e a	 o e a i	 i a e o

Week 15 Short Vowel u

Objective : To teach the recognition of the **short vowel 'u'** in words.

Teacher Information: Short vowel sounds are issued from the back of the throat when isolated. In most words they blend with the initial and final sounds. Introduce the symbol ˘ that sometimes appears over short vowel words.

Day 1: Introduce the short vowel **'u'** using the following story. " Gus is a grumpy camel who lives in a very sunny desert. He has brown hair and a big hump on his back. In his hump fat is stored to help him to walk in the hot sun when there is no water. Gus is able to lug heavy loads on his back. Sometimes he runs but most of the time he walks." Record the short vowel **'u'** at the top of a chart. Explain to your students that the short vowel **'u'** says 'uh' like in 'Gus.' Read the story again and have the students identify words that have the same sound as in Gus. Record them on the chart.

Picture Key: Row 1: pump, pan, mug, pen Row 2: mask, puck, jug, fish Row 3: bus, frog, gun, net Row 4: pig, fox, sun, rug

Activity Worksheet: Page 91 Students are to circle and colour all the pictures that have the short vowel 'u' sound. **Pictures to be coloured:** pump, mug, puck, jug, bus, gun, sun, rug

Day 2: Review the short **'u'** sound by using the following exercise. Students are to listen for the word in each group that has the short vowel 'u' sound. Tell them to listen carefully: 1. cap, cop, cup 2. fan, fun, fin 3. gun, gas, gag 4. dug, dig, dog 5. lamp, limp, lump 6. cob, cub, cab 7. jig, jog, jug 8. bed, bud, bad

Picture Key: Row 1: apple, tub, lips, top Row 2: nest, pond, duck, lamb Row 3: bus, milk, hose, cap Row 4: box, six, cub, bed

Activity Worksheet: Page 92 Students are to print the short vowel sound heard in each picture on the lines provided. Answer Key: Row 1: a, o, i, u Row 2: e, o, u, a 3. u, i, o, a Row 4: o, i, u, e

Day 3: Using a chalkboard, white board or chart record the following three letter words that contain the short 'u' vowel sound. **Words:** nut, rug, mug, bun, tub, tug, gum, cub, mud, bus Have the students locate the short 'u' word that matches each clue. **Clues:** 1. It is found in a hotdog and a hamburger. (bun) 2. It is used for drinking coffee or tea. (mug) 3. Pigs often roll in it. (mud) 4. It can carry many people. (bus) 5. It lies on the floor. (rug) 6. It is used to blow bubbles. (gum) 7. It is a place to get clean. (tub) 8. It is the name given to a young bear. (cub) 9. To pull or carry something (lug) 10. It is eaten by people and some animals. (nut)

Picture Key: Row 1: cub, hug, Row 2: run, bug Row 3: mug, cup Row 4: bus, gun

Activity Worksheet: Page 93 Students are to circle the word in each box that matches each picture. **Words to be circled:** Row 1: cub, hug Row 2: run, bug Row 3. mup, cup Row 4: bus, gun Row 4: bus, gun

Day 4: Review the short vowels with this listening game. Listen to the two words that I say for the vowel sound that you hear. Words: 1. sap, fan (short a) 2. run, up (short u) 3. hop, dot (short o) 4. leg, nest (short e) 5. hill, kiss (short i) This time listen for the word that doesn't belong in each group and tell why. 1. rug, cup, pig (short i) 2. fix, cob, stick (short o) 3. bug, apple, cap (short u) 4. pin, peg, dig (short e) 5. hand, leg, men (short a)

Activity Worksheet: Page 93 Students are to print the correct word in each sentence. **Answer Key:** 1. bell 2. bug 3. sack 4. full 5. beg 6. sick 7. fell 8. hot

Day 5: Use the following instructions to test your students ability to recognize the short vowels 'a,e,i,o,u.

Auditory Instructions: Listen to each word that I say. Circle the vowel sound that you hear in each word.
Words: 1. hump 2. picnic 3. otter 4. match 5. fence 6. swim 7. bottle 8. pump 9. plan 10. peck
Answer Key: Circled letters: 1. u 2. i 3. o 4. a 5. e 6. i 7. o 8. u 9. a 10. e

B. Visual Discrimination Test: Circle the vowel sound heard in each picture.
Picture Key: Row 1: ship, frog, web, candle Row 2: match, fence rock, quilt Row 3: truck, block whistler, brush **Answer Key:** Letters to be circled: Row 1: i, o, e, a Row 2: a, e, o, i Row 3: u, o, i, u

Name: ______________________________

Day 1 | Week 15

In the word '**sun**' we hear a short vowel sound.

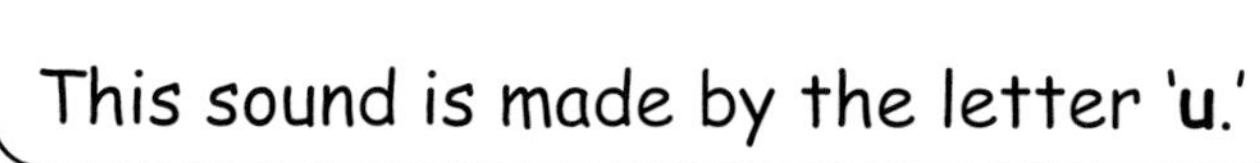

This sound is made by the letter '**u**.'

Say the name of each picture. **Circle** and **colour** all the pictures that have the short '**u**' sound

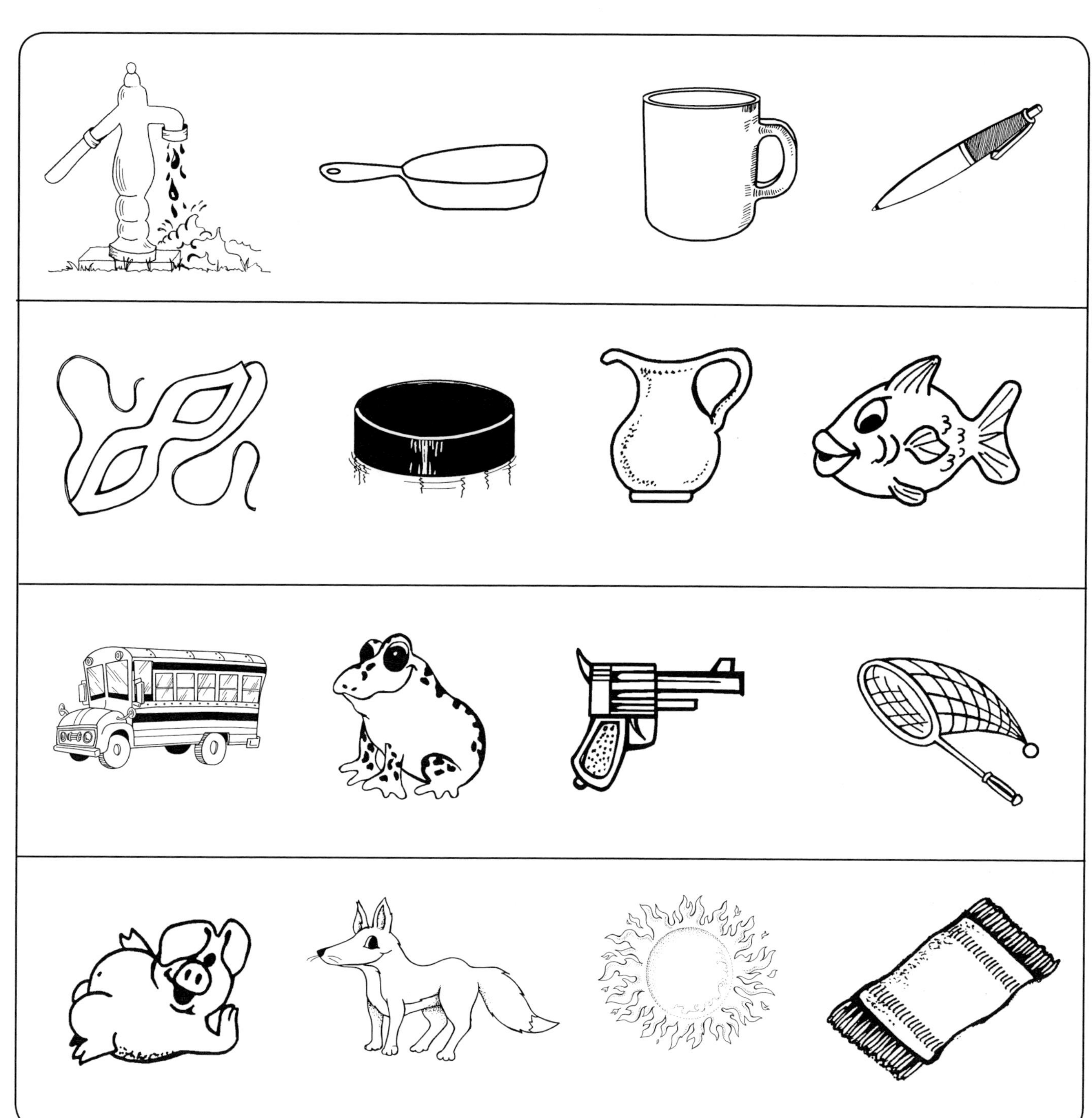

Name: ______________________________ | Day 2 | Week 15 |

The short vowel **'u'** is found in many words.

Listen carefully to the names of the pictures. **Print** the short vowel sound heard in each picture on the line below it.

____	____	____	____
____	____	____	____
____	____	____	____
6 ____	____	____	____

Name: ______________________________ | Day 3 | Week 15 |

The short vowel **'u'** is heard inside many words.

Examples:

tr**u**ck

br**u**sh

Read the words carefully in each box. **Circle** the word that matches the picture.

cup cub cut	hut hug hum
rub rug run	bun bud bug
mud mug muff	cut cub cup
bus bun bud	gum gun gull

Name: ______________________________

Day 4 | Week 15

Read the sentence and the words in each box.

Print the word from the box that fits the sentence on the line in it.

Example: We had fun at school. (fun, fan, fin)

1. Did you hear the ______________ ring. (bill, ball, bell, bull)

2. I saw a yellow ______________ on the wall. (big, bag, bug, beg)

3. Put the apples in the big ______________ . (sick, suck, sack, sock)

4. The well is ______________ of water. (fill, full, fall, fell)

5. My dog likes to ______________ for food. (big, bug, beg, bag)

6. The boy is ____________ and is in his bed. (sack, sock, sick, suck)

7. Jack ______________ down the big hill. (fill, fall, full, fell)

8. The sun can make you feel ______________. (hit, hat, hot, hug)

Name: ______________________________ | Day 5 | Week 15 |

A. Auditory Test on the Short Vowels 'a, e, i, o, u'

1.	2.	3.	4.	5.
a e i o u	a e i o u	a e i o u	a e i o u	a e i o u
6.	7.	8.	9.	10.
a e i o u	a e i o u	a e i o u	a e i o u	a e i o u

Visual Discrimination Test:

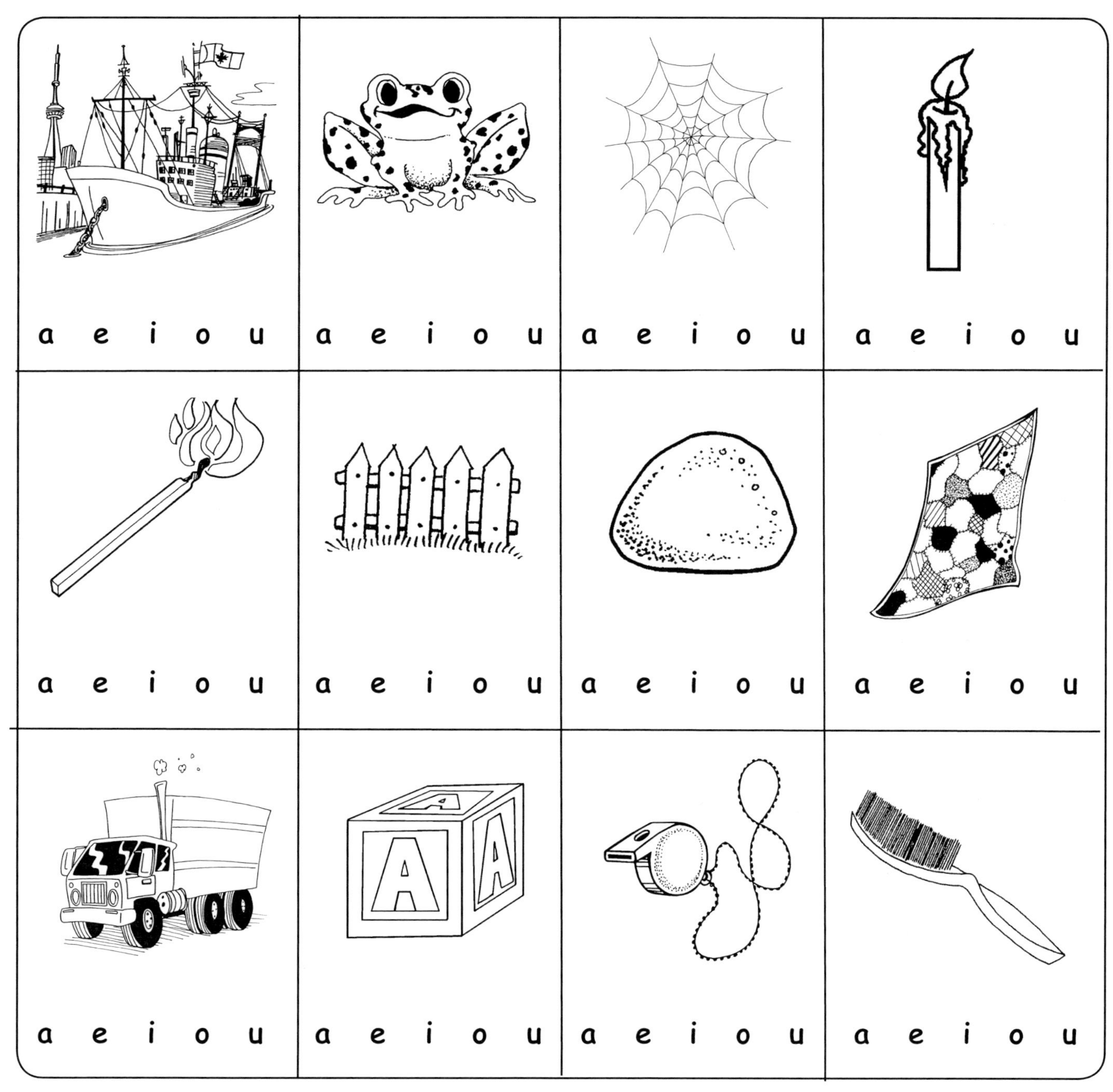

Week 16 Long Vowel 'Aa'

Objective: To teach the recognition of the long vowel '**o**' in words.

Teacher Information: The long vowel '**Aa**' has the same sound as its name in the alphabet. It is made when the mouth is slightly open and comes from the back of the throat. Introduce the symbol ˉ that sometimes appears over the letter '**a**' to indicate that it has a long sound.

Day 1: Introduce the long vowel '**a**' with the following story: In a hot place called a jungle lived a brave ape called Amy. She had long black hair all over her body except on her face. which was covered in black skin. Her arms were long and hairy which helped her to swing from branch to branch. She did not have a tail. Amy loved to race through the jungle trees by swinging from branch to branch using her long hairy arms and hands. Amy was fast and often won the race. Read the story again and have the students listen for **long a** words. Have them clap their hands each time they hear a word with the long '**a**' vowel sound.

Picture Key: Row 1: pail, can, tape, kite Row 2: rake, cat, glass, game Row 3: lamp, lake, cane, sack Row 4: cage, fan, mask, gate

Activity Worksheet: Page 97 Students are to circle and colour all the pictures with the long '**a**' sound

Day 2: Review **long 'a'** and **short 'a'** vowel sounds. Record the words cab, bake, cane on a chart. Draw your students attention to the vowel sound heard and the silent '**e**' at the end of the word. Use the following saying "If a word ends with a silent '**e**', it is because it pinches the first vowel so hard that it makes the vowel shout out its own name.

Picture Key: Row 1: can, cane, cave, rake Row 2: man, lake, tap, gate Row 3: tape, mane, bat, cap Row 4: game, cat, cake, hat

Activity Worksheet: Page 98 Students are to spell the **long 'a'** and **short 'a'** words for the pictures correctly on the line.

Day 3: Review long and short vowel **'a'**. Play the following game. If the word has the **short 'a'** sound, clap your hands. If the word has the **long 'a'** sound, raise your hand. **Words:** apple, game, cave, whale, bag, hand, hair, glass, wax, lamb, wave, pan

Picture Key: Row 1: tap, tape; cap, cape; can, cave Row 2: rake, cake; gate, game; man, mane Row 3: ape, ant; cane, cape; face, fan Row 4: cane, case; pan, pane; cage, ct

Activity Worksheet: Page: 99 Students are to draw a line from the word to its picture in each box.

Day 4: Review the short vowels **'a, e, i, o, u'** and the long vowel **'a'** using this listening exercise. Name the vowel sound that you hear in each word. Words: 1. rain (long a) 2. tag (short a) 3. peg (short e) 4. jug (short u) 5. chair (long a) 6. pet (short e) 7. jump (short u) 8. sit (short i) 9. face (long a) 10. top (short o)

Activity Worksheet: Page 100 Students are to complete each sentence with the correct word. Answers: 1. cape 2. gas 3. tape 4. pan 5. hay 6. lake 7. bat 8. mat

Day 5: Use the following instructions to test your students' ability to recognize the short and long **'a'** in words.

Auditory Instructions: Listen to each word that I say for its vowel sound. Circle the sound that you hear. 1. apple 2. baby 3. map 4. lay 5. rap 6. lamp 7. safe 8. page 9. wax 10. grapes Answer Key: Circled Words: 1. short a 2. long a 3. short a 4. long a 5. short a 6. short a 7. long a 8. long a 9. short a 10. long a

B. Visual Discrimination: Circle the vowel sound heard in each picture's name. **Pictures:** Row 1: cane, cap, cage, gate Row 2: bag, cave, lamp, hay Row 3: mask, chain, sack, game **Answer Key**: Row 1: long a, short a, long a, long a Row 2: short a, long a, short a, long a Row 3: short a, long a, short a, long a

Name: ______________________________ | Day 1 | Week 16 |

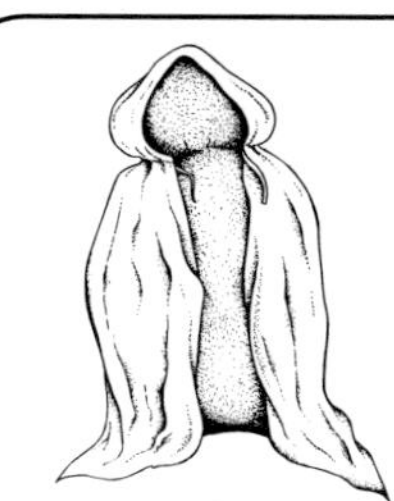

Cape has the long 'a' vowel sound.

It says its own name in words cape

Say the name ofeach picture. **Circle** and **colour** all the pctures with the **long 'a'** vowel sound.

Name: ______________________________ | Day 2 | Week 16 |

Name each picture. **Print** the letter or letters to complete each picture's name.

Examples:

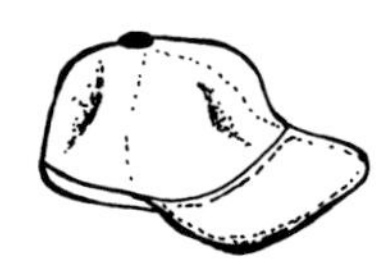 cap

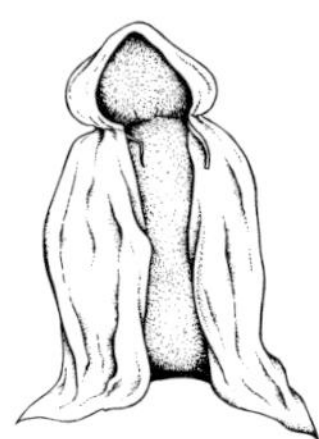 cape

 c ___ n ___

 c ___ n ___

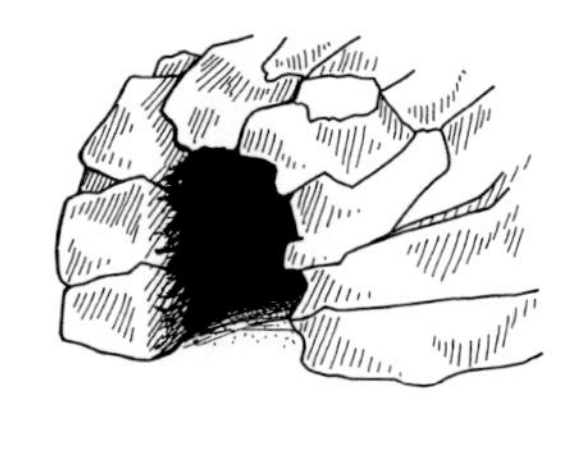 c ___ v ___

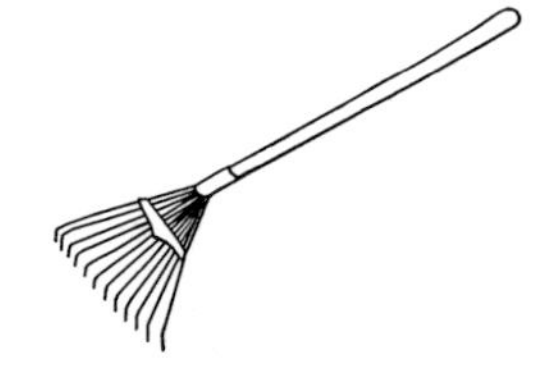 r ___ k ___

 m ___ n ___

 l ___ k ___

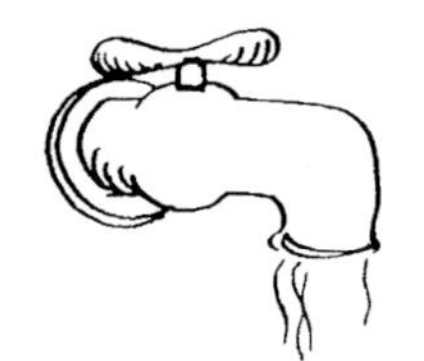 t ___ p ___

 g ___ t ___

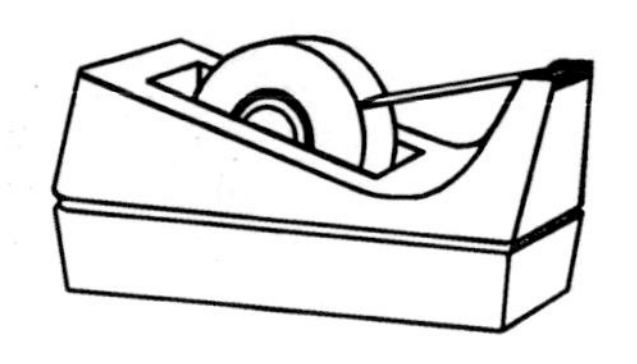 t ___ p ___

 m ___ n ___

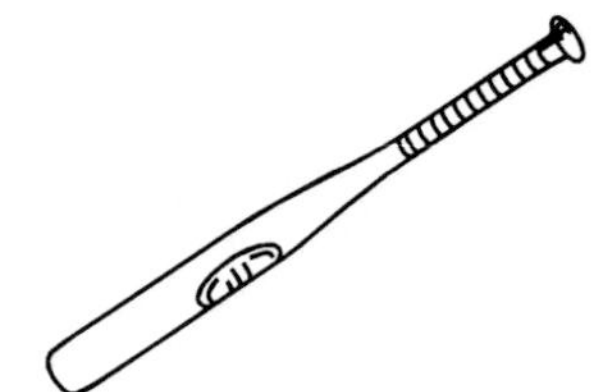 b ___ t ___

c ___ b___

g ___ m ___

c ___ t ___

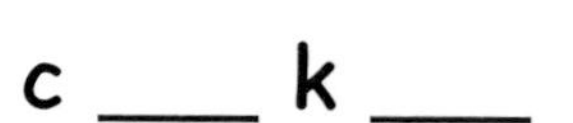
c ___ k ___

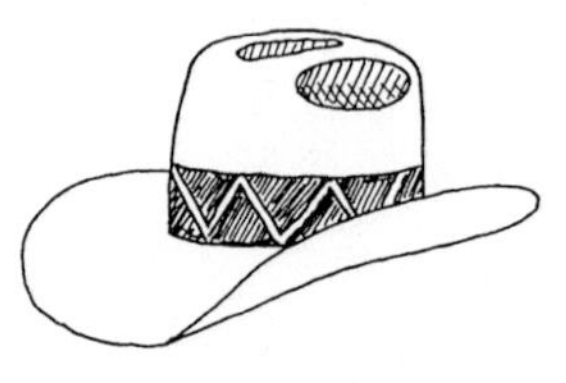 h ___ t ___

Name: ______________________________ | Day 3 | Week 16 |

Read the words and **name** the pictures. **Draw** a **line** from its name to its picture.

Example:

 man

 mane

tap	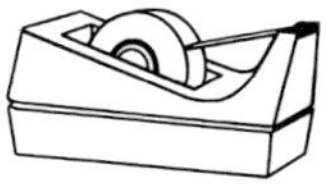 cap	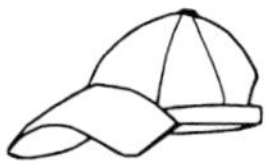 can 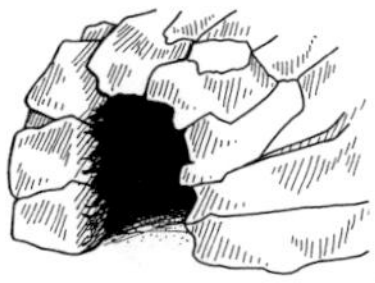
tape	 cape	 cave 
rake	 gate	 man 
cake	 game	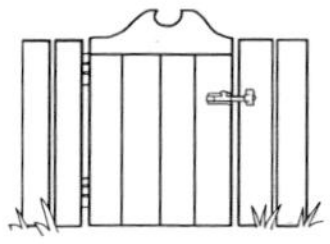 mane 
ape	 cane	 face 
ant	 cape	 fan 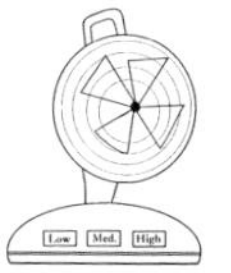
case	 pan	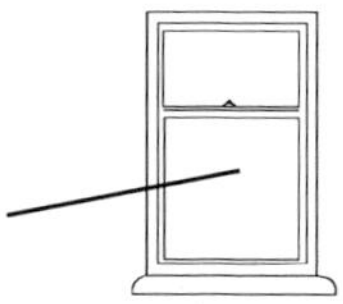 cage 
cane	 pane	 cat 

Name: ______________________________ | Day 4 | Week 16 |

Read each sentence and the words in the box beside it. **Print** the word from the box that will complete each sentence.

Example:

The bear is in the <u>cave</u>. (cat, **cave**, can)

1. Jane has a red ____________. (cat, cape, can)

2. Father will fill the car with ____________. (gas, game, gate)

3. Bill will fix the book with some ____________. (tan, tap, tape)

4. Mother will bake the cake in a ____________. (pane, pad, pan)

5. The horse will eat all the ____________. (ham, hay, hat)

6. You can swim in a ____________. (lamp, lake, lad)

7. The ____________ comes out at night to fly. (back, bag, bat)

8. The cat lay on the ____________. (mad, made, mat)

Name: ______________________________ | Day 5 | Week 16 |

A. Auditory Test on the long and short vowel 'a'

1.	2.	3.	4.	5.
Long a Short a	Long a Short a	Long a Short a	Long a Short a	Long a Short a
6.	7.	8.	9.	10.
Long a Short a	Long a Short a	Long a Short a	Long a Short a	Long a Short a

B. Visual Discrimination Test:

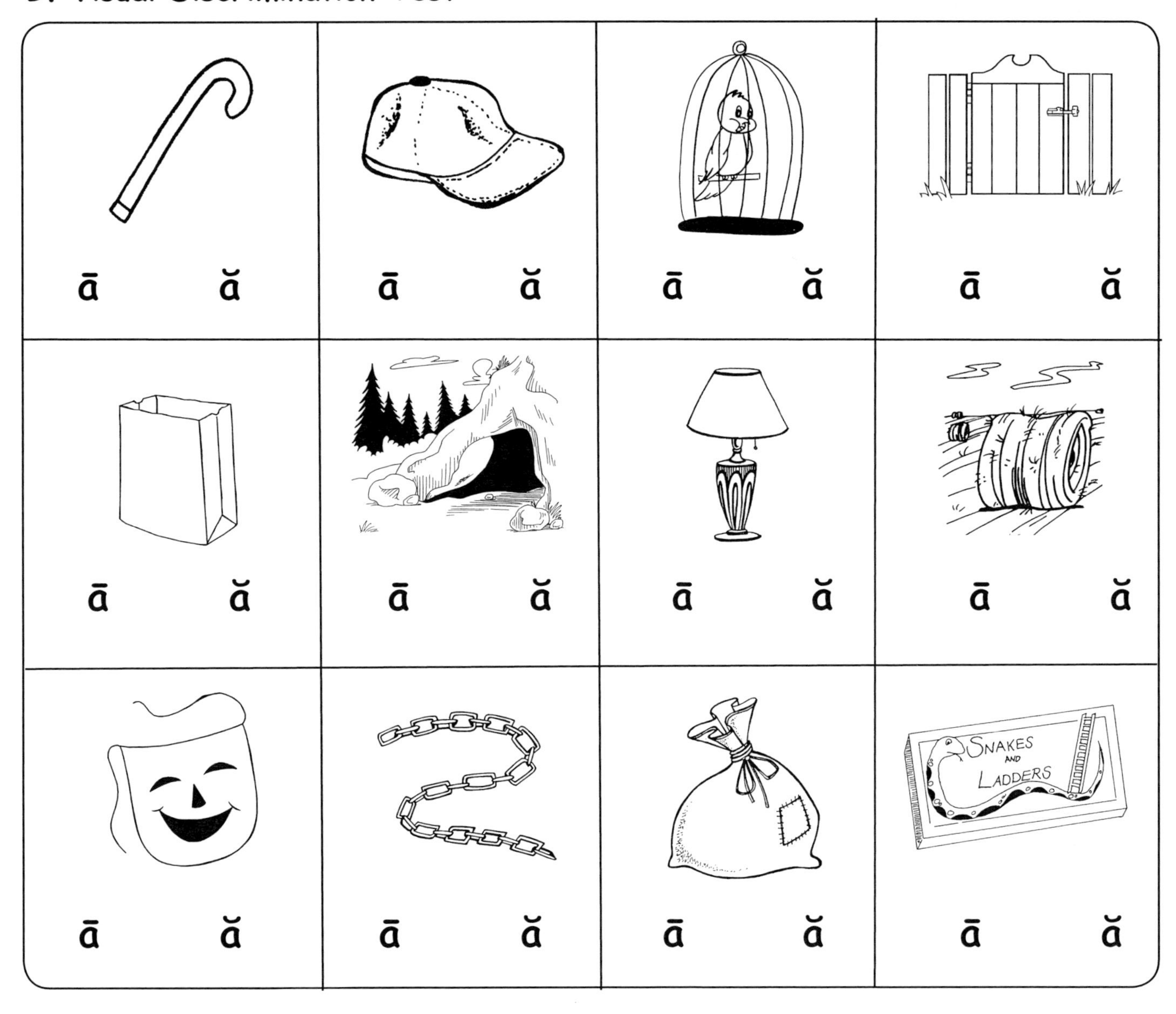

ā ă	ā ă	ā ă	ā ă
ā ă	ā ă	ā ă	ā ă
ā ă	ā ă	ā ă	ā ă

Week 17 Long Vowel 'Ee' Sound

Objective: To teach the recognition of the long vowel 'ē' in words.

Teacher Information: The long vowel ē has the same sound as its name in the alphabet. It is made when the mouth is partially open and comes from the back of the throat. Introduce the symbol ˉ that sometimes appears over the letter 'e' to indicate that it has a long vowel sound.

Day 1: Have your students listen to the following expressions. Have you ever seen any of the following: a <u>sheep</u> driving a <u>jeep</u>; a <u>bee</u> stinging an <u>eel</u>; a <u>deer</u> with sharp <u>teeth</u>; an <u>eagle</u> <u>eating</u> <u>peanuts</u>; a <u>beaver</u> chewing on <u>seeds</u>? Discuss the expressions. List the words that have similar sounds on a chart.
Words: sheep, jeep, bee, eel, deer, teeth, eagle, eating, peanuts, beaver, seeds Discuss how the words are similar. (All the words have the long 'e' sound.) Explain to your students that often when two vowels are seen together in a word, the first vowel does all the talking and has the long vowel sound.

Picture Key: Row 1: neck, ear, bee, jet Row 2: elf, teeth, deer, bell Row 3: jeep, bed, neck, seal Row 4: seeds, peanut, sled, sheep

Activity Worksheet: Page 103 The students are to **circle** the pictures with the **long e** sound and **underline** the pictures with the **short e** sound. **Answer Key:** Pictures to be circled: neck, jet, elf, bell, tent, sled Pictures to be coloured: ear, bee, teeth, deer, jeep, seal, seeds, peanut, leaf

---

Day 2: Review long a, short a, long e, and short e using the following listening activity. What vowel sound do you hear in each word that I say? 1. lamp (short a) 2. ear (long ear) 3. safe (long a) 4. eat (long e) 5. head (short e) 6. cage (long a) 7. shell (short e) 8. leaf (long e) 9. wave (long a),10. beak (long e)

Picture Key: Row 1: rake, ear, cat, leaf Row 2: eagle, fan, leg, hay Row 3: bean, game, bag, nest Row 4: deer, web, well, seal

Activity Worksheet: Page 104 The students are to complete each word with the correct vowel sound.

Answer Key: Row 1: cat, tree, bell, cane Row 2: ear, map, seal, jeep Row 3: nail, feet, cab, flag 4. cake, van, desk, beak

---

Day 3: Review the **long** and **short 'a'** an **'e'**. Record the following headings on a chart: Long a, Short a, Long e, Short e. Say each of the following words and have the students tell you which heading it should be printed under. **Words:** 1. eel 2. desk 3. bank 4. wave 5. nest 6. seat 7. grass 8. rain

Picture Key: Row 1: neck, ear; bee, bed; cave, cab Row 2: men, man; leaf, leg; egg, eat Row 3: cage, cat; pen, pan; pig, peg

Activity Worksheet: Page 105 Students are to match each word to its picture in each box with a line.

Day 4: Record the following words on a chart: bell, sack, gate, deer, web, lake, sap, peas. Have the students locate the word that answers each riddle. **Riddles:** 1. I am a home for an insect. I have the short e sound. (web) 2. I stop animals from walking out of a field. I have the long a sound. (gate) 3. I am a round, green vegetable. I have the long e sound. (pea) 4. You can put things inside me to carry. I have the short vowel a sound. (sack) 5. I can have a lot of water. I have the long vowel a. (lake) 6. I am found inside trees. I have the short vowel a. (sap) 7. I live in a forest. I have the long vowel e. (deer) 8. I can ring loudly in a church tower. I have the short vowel e. (bell)

Activity Worksheet: Page 106 Students are to select the correct word and print it in the sentence.

Answer Key: 1. van 2. bell 3. well 4. pet 5. eat 6. hay 7. hay 7. jail 8. cave

---

Day 5 Use the following instructions to test your students ability to recognize the short vowels a, e, i, o, u and the long vowels a and e

A. Auditory Instructions: Listen to each word that I say. Circle the vowel sound that you hear in each word that I say. **Words:** 1. men 2. cake 3. eat 4. pan 5. tub 6. aim 7. Easter 8. sock 9. rub 10. rain
Answer Key: 1. short e 2. long a 3. long e 4. short a 5. short u 6. long a 7. long e 8. short o 9. short u 10. long a

B. Auditory and Visual Discrimination Test: Circle the vowel sound that you hear in each picture.
Picture Key: Row 1: hat, tree, sled Row 2: tub, pin, nail Row 3: well, block, sheep

Answer Key: Row 1: short a; long e; short e Row 2: short u; short i; long a Row 3: short e, short o; long e

Name: ______________________________ Day 1 | Week 17

sheep

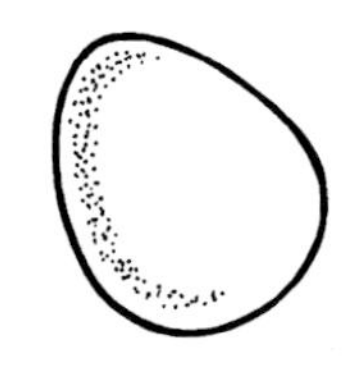

egg

The letter '**e**' can make two sounds.

It has the **long e** sound in sheep and the **short e** sound in **e**gg.

Circle all the pictures that have the **short** 'e' sound and **colour** all the pictures with the **long** 'e' sound

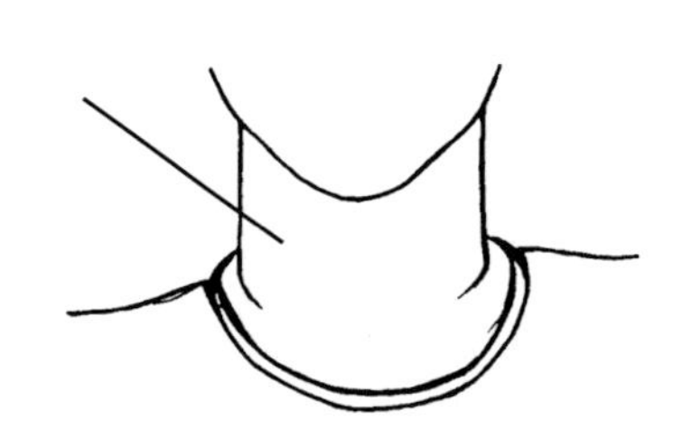

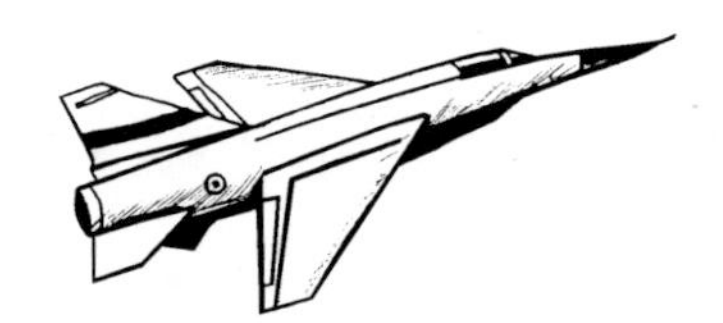

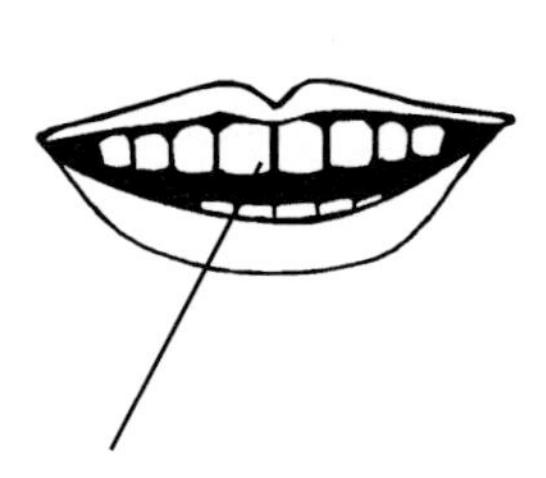

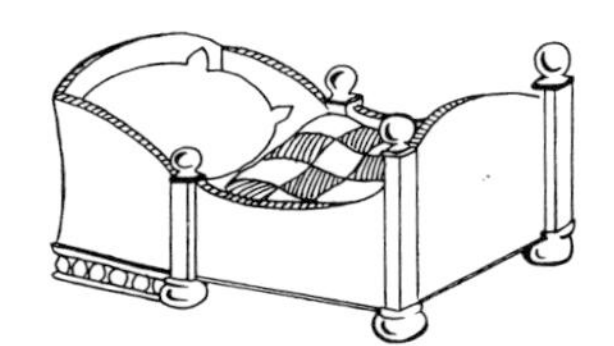

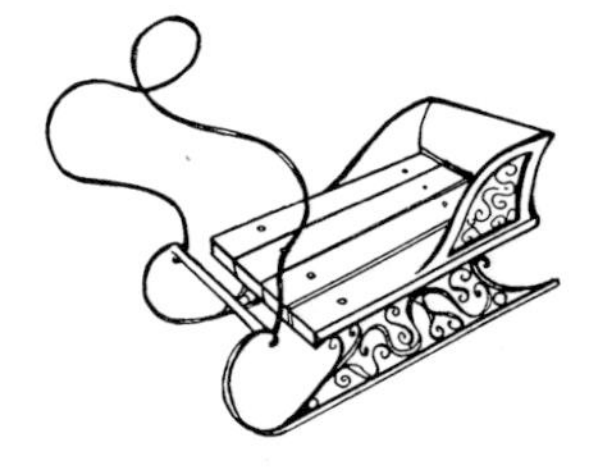

Name: ______________________________ | Day 2 | Week 17

Name each picture. **Print** the missing vowel to complete each picture's name.

Examples:

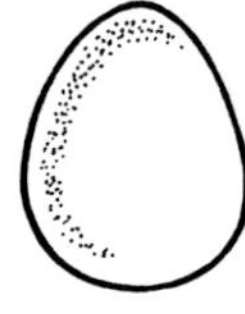

egg

bee

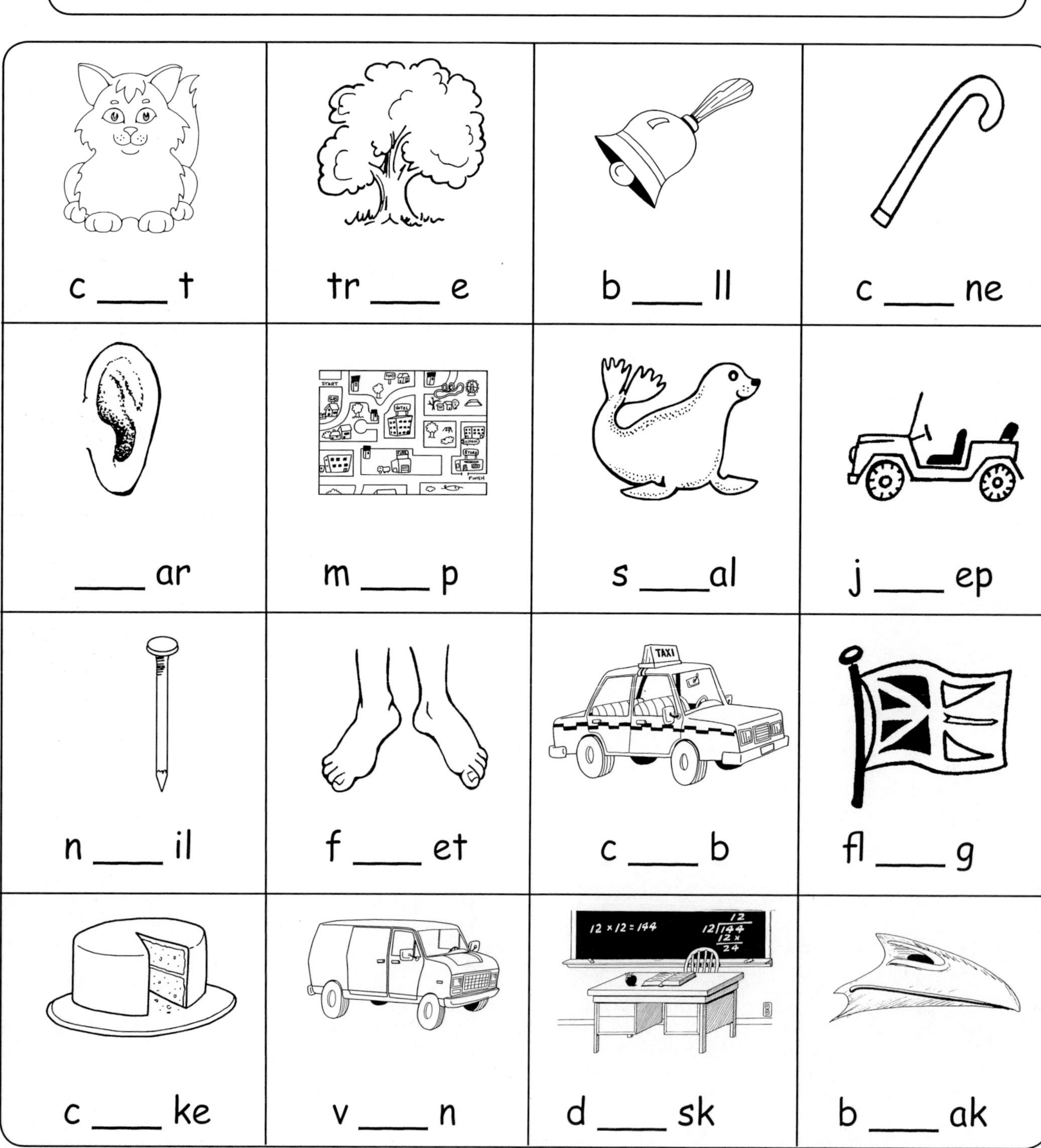

Name: ______________________________

Day 3	Week 17

Long vowels say their own names.

Short vowels make different sounds.

Examples:

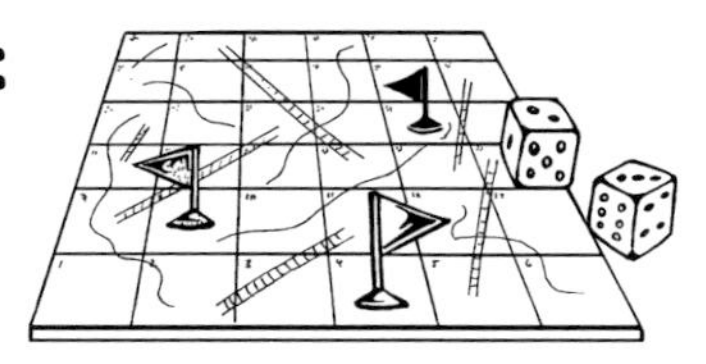

game

can

Match the words to their pictures. **Draw** a line from each word to its picture in each box.

neck	 bee	 cave 
ear	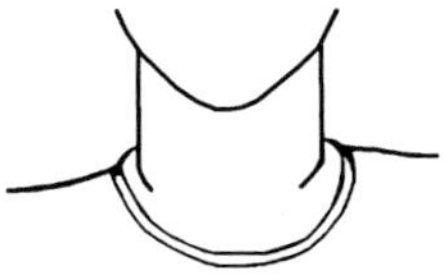 bed	 cab 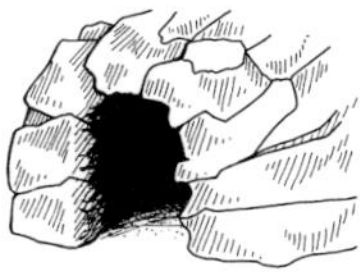
men	 leaf	 egg 
man	 leg	 eat 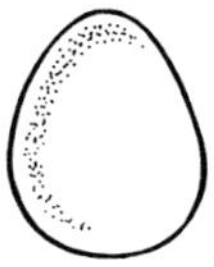
cage	 pen	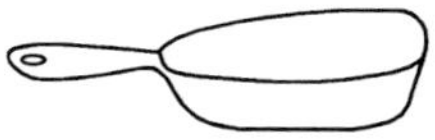 pig 
cat	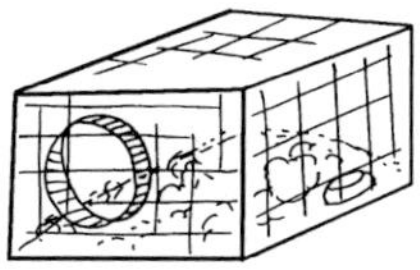 pan	 peg 

ISBN: 9781771586863

Name: ______________________________

Day 4	Week 17

The **long** and **short** vowels '**a**' and '**e**' are found in many words.

Examples:

cave	mask	bee	nest
Long a	Short a	Long e	Short e

Print the correct word in each sentence.

1. I like to ride in our ____________. (vane, van, vet)

2. Can you hear the ____________ ring? (ball, bell, bill)

3. The cat fell down the ____________. (wall, well, will)

4. A dog is a good ____________ to have. (pit, pat, pet)

5. I like to ____________ candy. (elf, egg, eat)

6. The horse ate all of the ____________. (hay, hat, ham)

7. The bad man was put in ____________. (tail, jail, fail)

8. The bats like to sleep in a ____________. (cane, mane, cave)

Name: ____________________________

Day 5	Week 17

A. Auditory Test on the Long Vowels ‘a, e and the Short Vowels a,e,i,o,u’

1. ĕ ă ĭ	2. ē ā ŏ	3. ā ă ē	4. ē ĕ ă	5. ă ĭ ŭ
6. ē ā ĕ	7. ō ē ā	8. ă ĕ ŏ	9. ă ŭ ŏ	10. ā ē ă

B. Auditory and Visual Discrimination Test of Long and Short Vowels

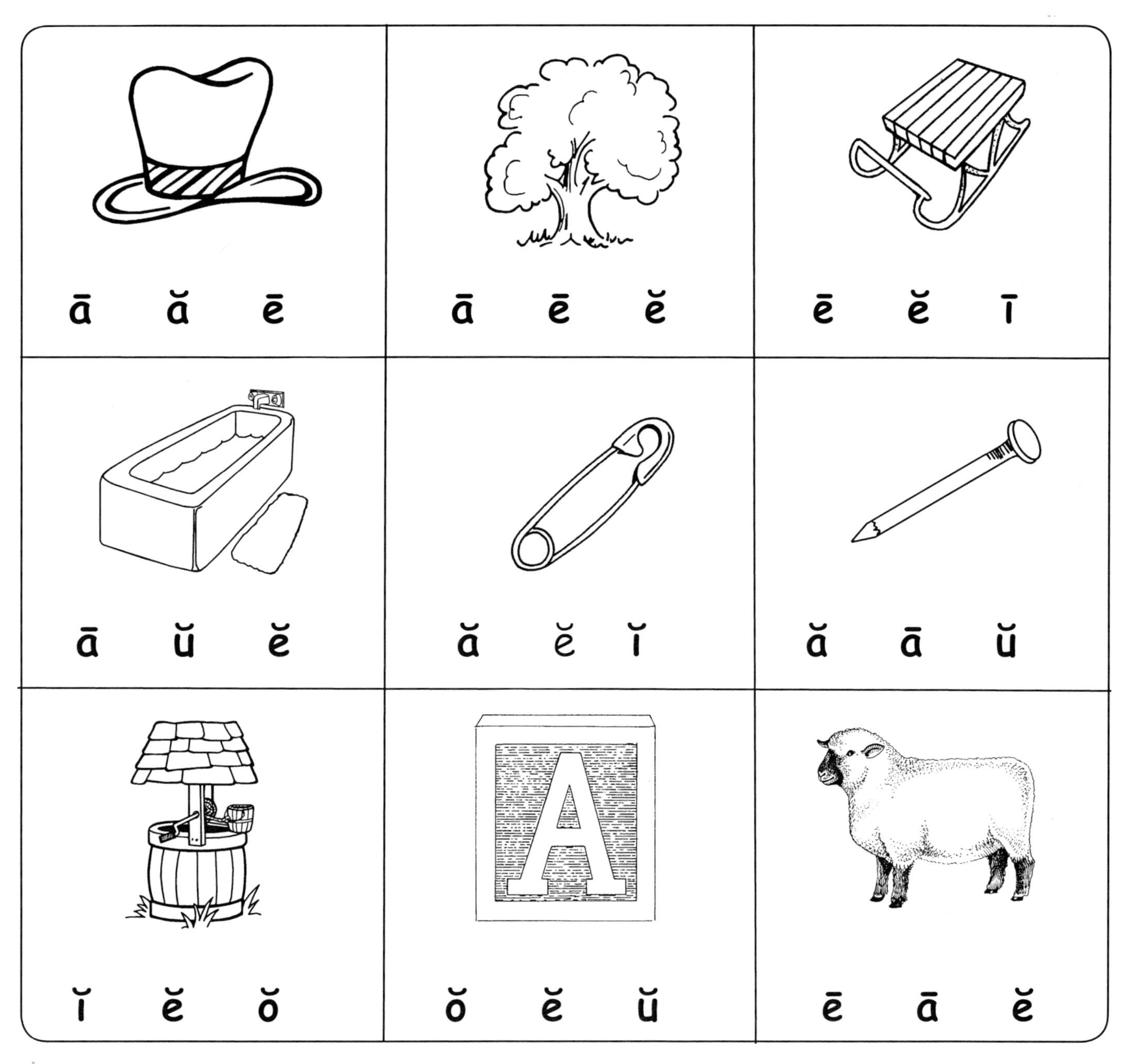

Week 18 Long 'I i' Vowel Sound

Objective: To teach the recognition of the long vowel 'Ii' in words

Teacher Information: The long vowel '**Ii**' has the same sound as its name in the alphabet. It is made when the mouth is partially open and comes from the back of the throat. Introduce the symbol ' ¯ ' that some times appear over the letter 'i' to indicate that it has a long sound.

Day 1: Have your students listen for words in the following story that have the long 'i' sound.
Story: Issac, a little mouse, lived in a big white house with his five brothers and sisters. During the day the mice would hide inside the walls of the house until it was night. Then the mice would dive out of their hole in the wall and head for the nice kitchen. They liked to eat the crumbs of pie, rice, and icing from cakes that were left all over the floor. List the long 'i' words heard in the story on a chart and discuss them.

Picture Key: Row 1: ice, brick, dime, swing Row 2: knife, chick, bib, vine Row 3: mix, dice, pills, slide Row 4: nine, fire, milk, pig

Activity Worksheet: Page 109 The students are to circle the pictures with the long 'i' sound and underline the pictures with the short 'i' sound. **Answers:** Pictures to be circled are: ice, dime, knife, vine, dice, slide, nine, fire. Pictures to be underlined are: brick, swing, chick, bib, mix, pills, milk, pig

Day 2: Review the long and short 'a, e, and i.' Say one of the following words and have the students tell the name of the vowel sound heard in it. Words: 1. chick (short i) 2. match (short a) 3. pile (long i) 4. weed (long e) 5. race (long a) 6. stamp (short a) 7. vine (long i) 8. check (short e) 9. inch (short i) 10. spice (long i)

Picture Key: Row 1: kite, mat, fish, ear Row 2: ice, bee, leg, cat Row 3: cane, bed, fan, hill, Row 4: seal, dime, dish, bell

Activity Worksheet: Page 110 The students are to record the long and short vowels 'a, e, or i' on the line to complete each word. **Answer Key:** Row 1: i, a, i, e Row 2: i, e, e, a Row 3: a, e, a, i Row 4: e, i, i, e

Day 3: Use the following listening activity with your students. Listen to each word that I say carefully. Name the vowel sound heard in each one. 1. neck (short e) 2. yak (short a) 3. teeth (long e) 4. grass (short a) 5. left (short e) 6. dig (short i) 7. pail (long a) 8. bite (long i) 9. kick (short i) 10. rent (short e)

Picture Key: Box 1: wing, mice, fire Box 2: tire, tin, fish Box 3: bike, kick, vine Box 4: fist, lips, hill Box 5: lid, five, kite Box 6: wind, wig, dime

Activity Worksheet: Page 111 The students are to draw a line from each word to its picture in each box.

Day 4: Review the long and short vowel sounds made by the following words. What is the name of the vowel sound in each word that I say? **Words**: 1. crib (short i) 2. sail (long a) 3. sheep (long e) 4. knife (long i) 5. crab (short a) 6. steps (short e) 7. rice (long i) 8. belt (short e) 9. night (long i) 10. lips (short i)

Activity Worksheet: Page 112 The students are to complete each sentence with the correct word. Answer Key: 1. game 2. bell 3. lid 4. pen 5. bit 6. bike 7. bee 8. bag

Day 5: Auditory and Visual Discrimination Tests: Use the following instructions to test your students' ability to recognize the long vowels 'a, e, i' and the short vowels 'a, e, i.'

A. Auditory Test: Listen to each word that I say. Circle the vowel sound that you hear in each word.
Words: 1. chick 2. van 3. pea 4. way 5. web 6. nine 7. egg 8. pine 9. leaf 10. pile
Answer Key: 1. short i 2. short a 3. long e 4. long a 5. short e 6. long i 7. short e 8. long i 9. long e 10. long i

B. Auditory and Visual Discrimination Test: Circle the vowel sound that you hear in each picture.
Picture Key: Row 1: fire, mat, pen Row 2: milk, ear, dish Row 3: jeep, game, mice
Answer Key: Row 1: long i; short a, short e Row 2: short i, long e, short i Row 3: long e, long a, long i

Name: ______________________________ Day 1 | Week 18

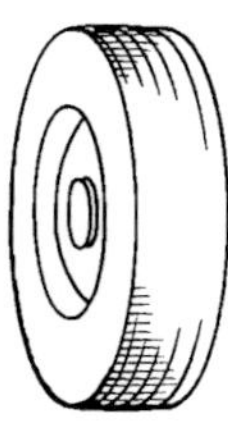

tire

fish

The letter **'i'** can make **two** sounds. It has a **long 'i'** sound in the word **tire** and the **short 'i'** sound in **fish**.

Circle all the pictures that have the **short i** sound and **colour** all the pictures with the **long i** sound.

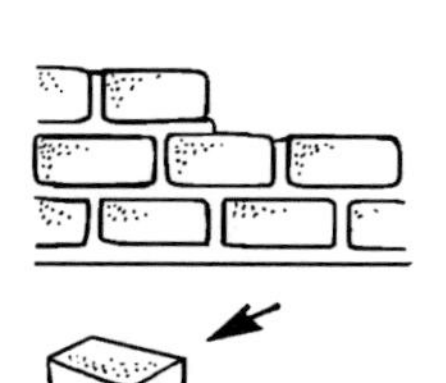

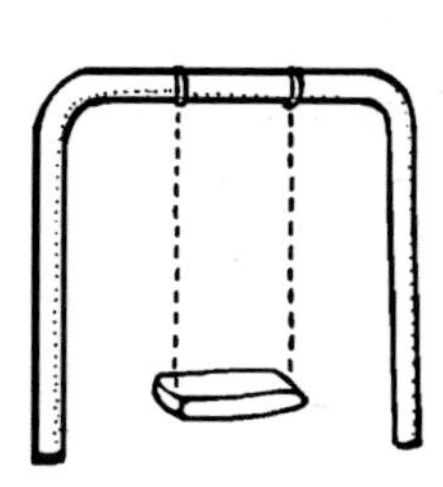

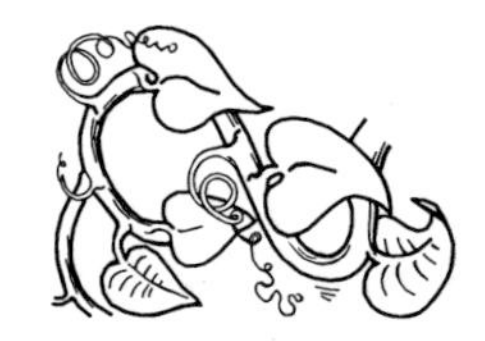

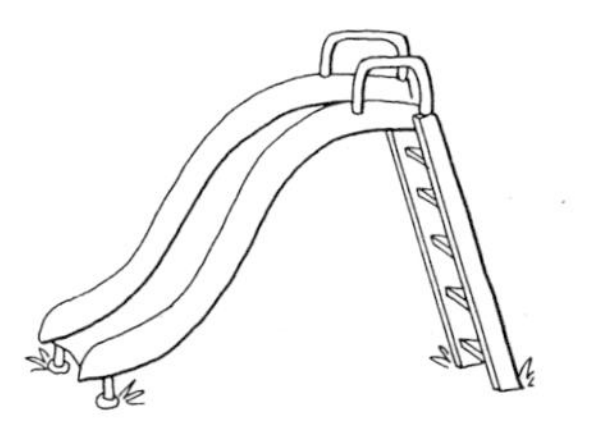

Name: ______________________________

Day 2	Week 18

Name each picture. **Print** the vowel sound heard in each picture to complete each picture's name.

Examples:

slide

pig

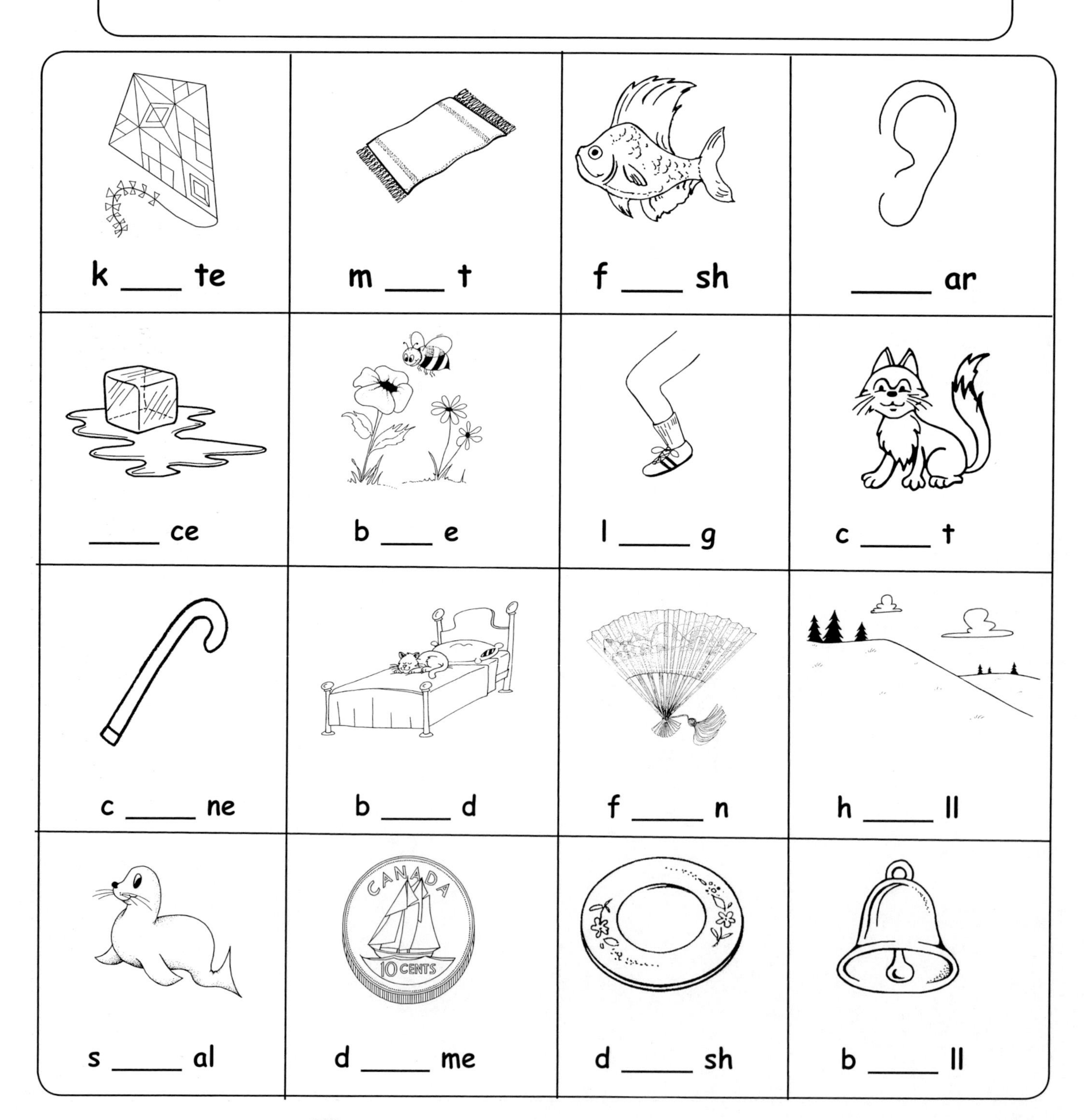

SSR1140 ISBN: 9781771586863

Name: ______________________________ | Day 3 | Week 18 |

Long vowels say their own names.

Short vowels make different sounds

Examples:

Long i  **ice**

Short i  **pin**

Match the words to their pictures. **Draw** a line from each word to its picture in each box

fire wing mice	fish tire tin	vine kick bike
hill fist lips	five kite lid	wind wig dime

 ISBN: 9781771586863

Name: ______________________________

Day 4 | Week 18

The long and short vowels '**a**, **e**, and **i**' are found in many words.

Examples:

long a **short a** **long i** **short i** **long e** **short e**

Print the correct word in each sentence.

1. We can play a ______________. (gate, game, hay)

2. Did you ring the _____________. (ball, bell, bill)

3. Put the ______________ on the pot. (lad, led, lid)

4. The pig is in the _____________. (pan, pin, pen)

5. The dog ____________ the little boy. (bat, bet, bit)

6. The boy can ride on a ____________. (bike, bake, bite)

7. The ____________ flew into the hive. (bin, bee, bite)

8. Put the toys in a ________________ (big, bag, beg)

Name: ______________________________

Day 5	Week 18

A. **Auditory Test** on the long vowels '**a,e,i** and the short vowels '**a,e,i,o,u**

1. ĭ ī ĕ	2. ā ē ă	3. ā ī ē	4. ā ă ĭ	5. ĕ ē ā
6. ē ī ĕ	7. ī ē ā	8. ĭ ĕ ă	9. ī ā ē	10. ī ă ĭ

B. **Auditory and Visual Discrimination Tes**

 ā ī ē	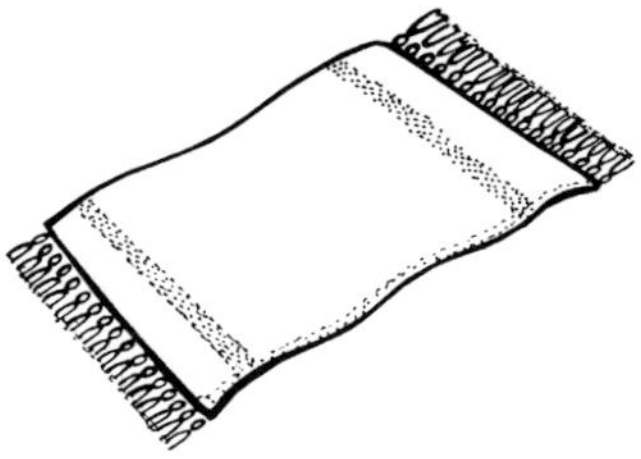 ă ĕ ĭ	 ă ĕ ĭ
 ī ĕ ĭ	 ā ī ē	 ă ĕ ĭ
 ē ī ā	 ā ă ĭ	 ā ī ē

Week 19: Long 'Oo' Vowel Sound

Objective: To teach the recognition of the long vowel 'Oo' in words.

Teacher Information: The long vowel **'Oo'** has the same sound as its name in the alphabet.It is made when the mouth is partially open and comes from the back of the throat. Introduce the symbol '¯' that some times appears over the letter 'Oo' to indicate that it has a long vowel sound.

Day 1: Have your students listen for words that have the long vowel **'Oo'** sound in the following story. **Story**: In an old cold house that sat up high on a hill lived a lonely ghost name Joe. He would float around all over the house going from room to room. He was always looking for something to eat. He especially liked to eat cold oatmeal, toast and yoghurt. Which words in the story have the long o vowel? List the words on a chart and discuss them. The students could mark the letter '**o**' with the ¯ symbol.

Picture Key: Row 1: coat, pot, box, toad Row 2: log, bone, rope, clock Row 3: soap, top, boat, block Row 4: cone, sock, dog, comb

Activity Worksheet: Page 115 The students are to circle the pictures with the long 'o' sound and to underline the pictures with the short 'o' sound.. **Answers:** Pictures to be circled: coat, toad, bone, rope, soap, boat, cone, comb. Pictures to be underlined: pot, box, log, clock, top, block, sock, dog

---

Day 2: Review long and short vowels '**a, e, i,** and **o**. Use the following listening activity. Listen to each word that I say. What vowel sound do you hear in each one. 1. otter (short vowel 'o') 2. dice (long vowel 'i') 3. phone (long vowel 'o') 4. grin (short vowel 'i') 5. wax (short vowel 'a') 6. win (short vowel 'i') 7.beat (long vowel 'e') 8. map (short vowel 'a') 9. yo yo (long vowel 'o') 10. bottle (short vowel 'o')

Picture Key: Row 1: fox, ant, bow, hair Row 2: belt, tie, nose, desk Row 3: ear, pop, six, tent Row 4: van, sink, hose, well

Activity Worksheet: Page 116 The students are to complete each word with its missing vowel sound. They are to indicate the type of vowel sound heard by using the long ¯ and short ˘ symbols above the vowel.

Answer Key: Row 1: ŏ, ă, ō, ā Row 2: ē, ī, ŏ, ĕ Row 3: ē, ŏ, ĭ, ĕ Row 4: ă, ĭ, ō, ĕ

Day 3: On a chart print the following words that have missing vowels. The students are to indicate the vowel that can be used in each word. Words: 1. d __ t 2. c __ b 3. c __ ne 4. f __ re 5. w __ b 6. b__ne 7. l __ d 8. h __ g 9. d __ n 10. __ at **Possible Answers:** dot, cab, cane, fire, web, bone, lid, led, hog, den, eat

Picture Key: Row 1: kite, map, fish, bone Row 2. doll, web, ear, lake Row 3: bag, cape, nose, pond

Activity Worksheet: Page 117 The students are to print the name of each picture on the line under it.

Day 4: Play the game called 'Name That Sound.' Say a word and have the students tell which vowel sound is heard. Words: 1. soap (ō) 2. aim (ā) 3. phone (□) 4. pill (□) 6. yak (□) 7. bean (□) 8. fog (□)

Picture Key: Row 1: kite, map, fish, bone Row 2: doll, web, ear, lake Row 3: bag, cape, nose, pond

Activity Worksheet: Page 117 The students are to complete each sentence with the correct word.

Answer Key: 1. pen 2. set 3. big 4. top 5. bed 6. hair 7. well 8. ball 9. hive 10. pole

---

Day 5: Use the following instructions to test your students ability to recognize the long vowels 'a,e,i,o' and the short vowels 'a,e,i,o'.

A. Auditory Instructions: Listen to each word that I say. Circle the vowel sound that you hear in each word.
Words: 1. flock 2. rail 3. peck 4. grin 5. toast 6. wax 7. tree 8. five 9. shop 10. store **Answer Key:** 1. □ 2. □ 3. □ 4. □ 5. □ 6. □ 7. □ 8. □ 9. □ 10. □

B. Auditory Discrimination Test: Circle the vowel sound that you hear in each picture. **Picture Key:** Row 1: frog, grapes, chick Row 2: jet, slide, teeth Row 3: ax, deer, nose
Answer Key: Row 1: □, □, □ , Row 2: □, □, □, Row 3: □, □, □

Name: ______________________________

Day 1	Week 19

rose

frog

The letter 'o' can make two sounds.

It has a ō sound in rōse and a ŏ sound in frŏg.

Circle all the pictures that have the ō sound and colour all the pictures with the ŏ sound.

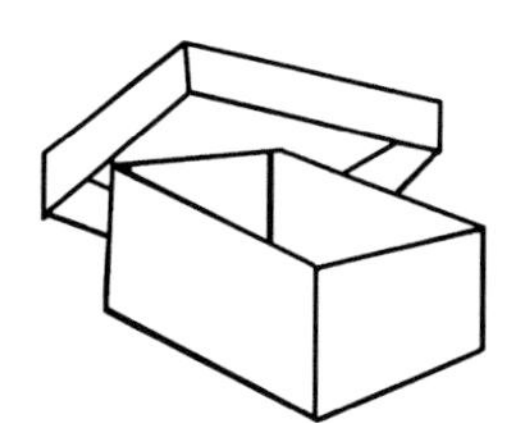

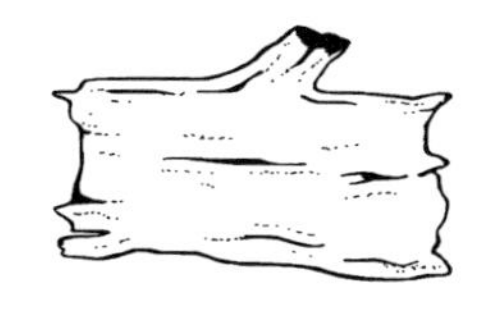
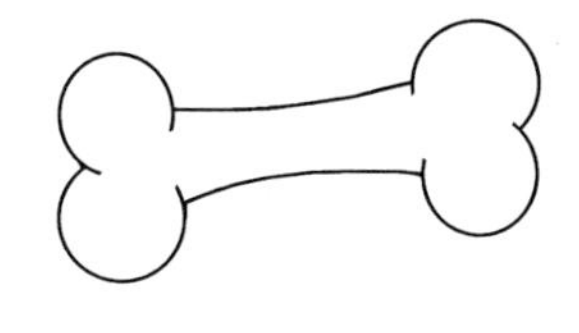

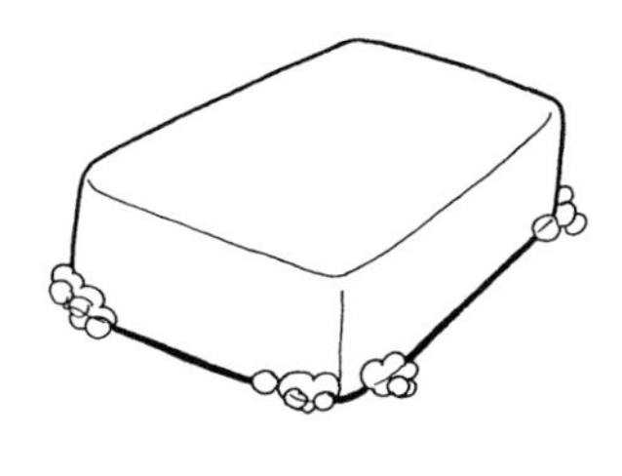

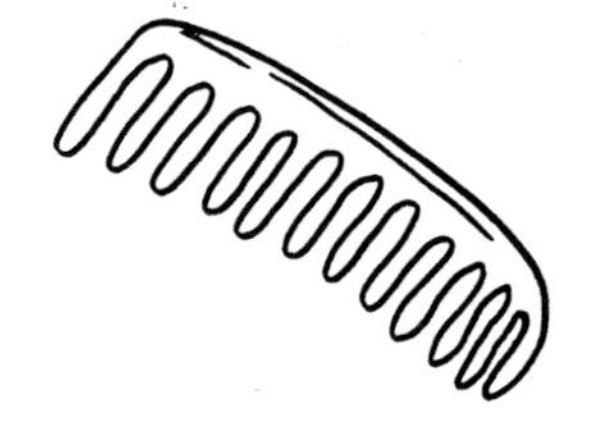

Name: ______________________________

Day 2 | Week 19

Name each picture. **Print** the vowel sound heard to complete each picture's name.

Examples:

tōe

tŏp

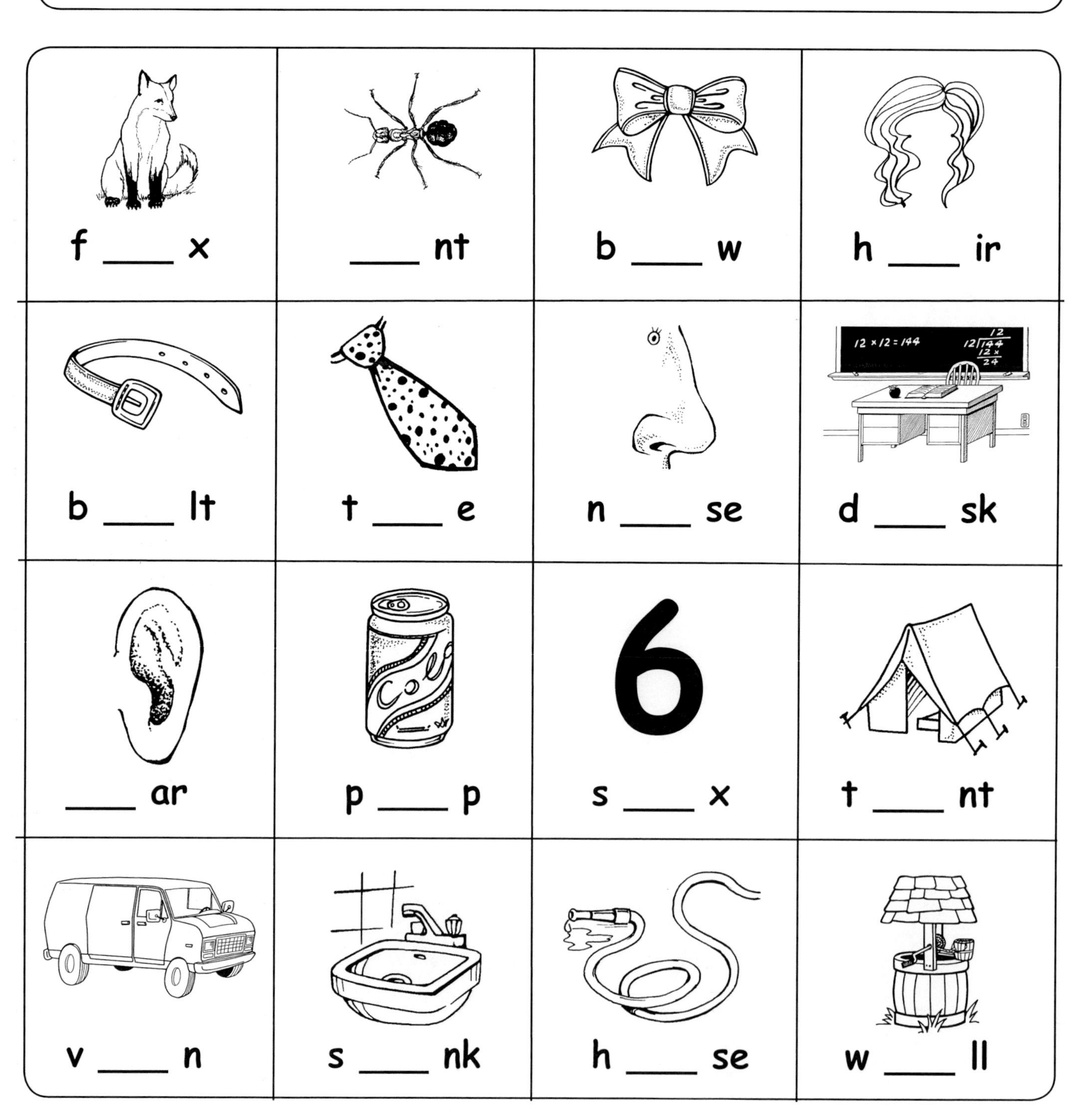

Name: ______________________________ | Day 3 | Week 19 |

Use the following words to name the pictures in the boxes.
Print the picture's name on the line under it.

Names of Pictures:

lake	kite	bone	web	bag
doll	ear	fish	map	cape

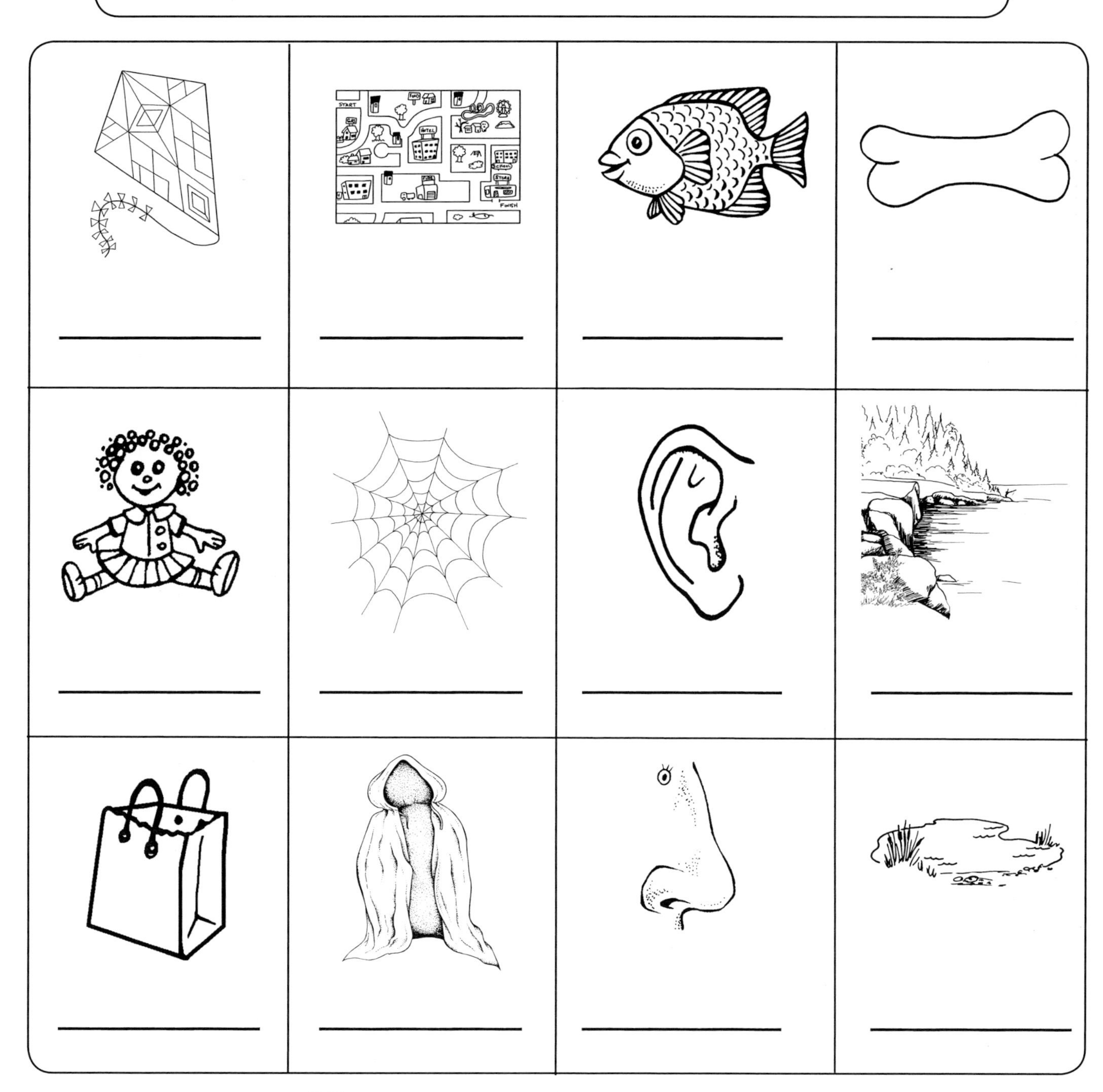

Name: ______________________________

Day 4	Week 19

The **long** and **short** vowels **'a, e, i,** and **o** are found in many words.
Examples:

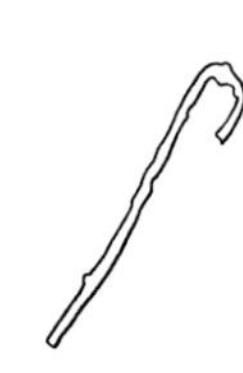
cane

cat

mice

hill

rose

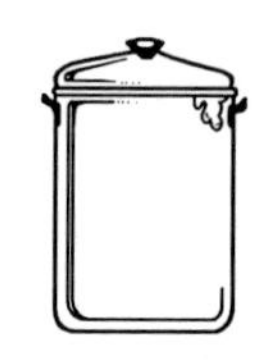
pot

Print the **correct** word from the box that fits each sentence on the line.

1. Look at the __________ pig in the pen. — fit, fat, fin
2. __________ the dish on the table. — sit, sat, set
3. I go to school on a __________ yellow bus. — bag, big, bag
4. The boy likes to play with a __________. — tip, top, tap
5. The bad boy was sent to __________. — bid, bad, bed
6. The girl has brown __________. — hum, him, hair
7. Jane got water from the __________. — will, well, wall
8. We played with a bat and a __________. — bill, bell, ball
9. A __________ is a house for bees. — have, hike, hive
10. A cat can climb up a __________. — pale, pile, pole

Name: ______________________________ | Day 5 | Week 19 |

A. Auditory Test on the long vowels 'a, e, i, o' and the short vowels 'a, e, i, o.'

1.	2.	3.	4.	5.
ō ŏ ā	ē ī ā	ĕ ĭ ă	ĕ ĭ ō	ā ō ē
6.	7.	8.	9.	10.
ă ĭ ŏ	ō ē ī	ĭ ī ŏ	ă ĭ ŏ	ā ē ō

B. Auditory and Visual Discrimination Test:

 ă ĭ ŏ ĕ	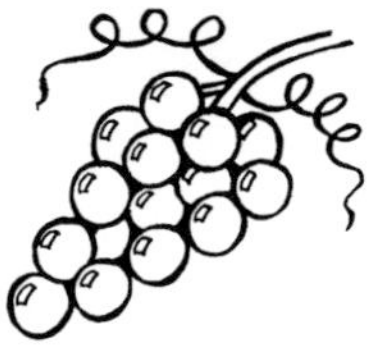 ā ē ī ō	 ă ĕ ĭ ŏ
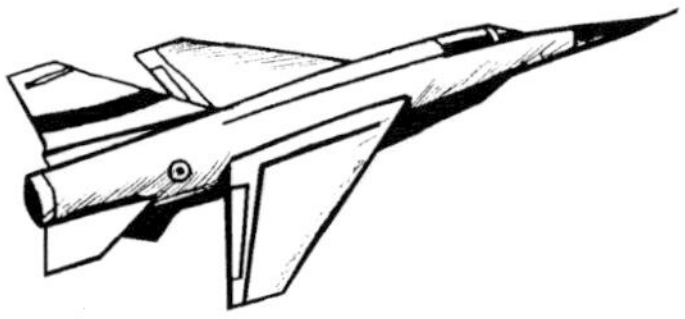 ĕ ŏ ă ĭ	 ī ē ā ō	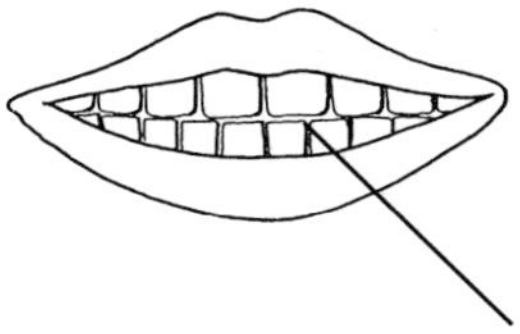 ā ē ī ō
 ā ă ī ĭ	 ā ē ī ō	 ā ō ŏ ĕ

Week 20: Long Vowel 'Uu' Sound

Objective: To teach the recognition of the long vowel **'u'** in words.

Teacher Information: The long vowel '**Uu**' has the same sound as its name in the alphabet. It is made when the mouth is partially open thrusting out the sound with the tongue.

Day 1: Have your students listen for words that have the long vowel '**u**' sound in the following story.
Story: Once upon a time a unique little mule lived on a dude ranch in the United States. He was called Hugo by his owners and had shaggy brown hair on his body. Hugo felt it was his duty to sing hee-haw tunes for visitors. They enjoyed hearing his cute hee-haw songs. Hugo was also used to carry people or supplies on riding trails. List the words with the long **'u'** sound on a chart and discuss them.

Picture Key: Row 1: sun, bus, unicorn, gun 2. nut, ruler, music, flute Row 3: gum, duck, skunk, tub Row 4: hump, rug, mule, trumpet

Activity Worksheet: Page 121 The students are to circle the pictures with the long **'u'** sound and to underline the pictures with a short **'u'** sound. **Answers:** Pictures to be circled: Row 1: unicorn Row 2: ruler, music, flute Row 4: mule, Pictures to be underlined: Row 1: sun, bus, gun Row 2: nut Row 3: gum, duck, skunk, tub Row 4: hump, rug, trumpet

Day 2: Review the long and short vowels 'a,e,i,o,u' with the following exercise. On chart paper record the following words and have the students mark the vowel sound that they can hear in each word **long 'ū'** or short 'ŭ.
Words: căb, jŭg, pŏnd, pāil, nĕt, pīpe, trēe, rūle, pōle, dĭsh

Picture Key: Row 1: mŭd, tŏp, dĭsh. cōat Row 2: ănt, jēep, jŭg, tāil Row 3: lĕg, brŭsh, cūbe, pĭck Row 4: fŏx, dīce, cōne, hŭmp

Activity Worksheet: Page 121 The students are to complete each word with its missing vowel sound. They are to indicate the vowel's sound using the symbols ¯ and ˘ above each one in each word. See the Picture Key for the correct answers.

Day 3: Play the following listening activity with your students. Listen to each group of words that I say. Tell me which vowel sound is heard in the word. Words: 1. snow, hole, cone (long o) 2. bite, pile, nice (long i) 3. back, wax, dad (short a) 4. deer, teeth, beet (long e) 5. hug, bush, pup (short u) 6. rob, dot, doll (short o) 7. kiss, king, pit (short i) 8. face, cane, safe (long a) 9. neck, head, leg (short e) 10. cute, cube, tube (long u)

Picture Key: Row 1: tub, log, nine, fan Row 2: hole, gate, nut, well Row 3: cube, hill, bus, jeep

Activity Worksheet: Page 122 Students are to record the missing word on the line under each picture.

Day 4: Review the vowel sounds made in the long and short form in words. On a chart print the following groups of words with missing vowels. Tell the students they are going to make new words by changing the vowel sound.
Words: 1. l___mp, l___mp, l___mp (lamp, limp, lump) 2. s___ ck, s___ck, s___ck, (sack, sick, suck, sock) 3. r___d, r___d, r___d (rid, red, rod) 4. f___ll, f___ll, f___ll, f___ll (fall, fill, full, fill) 5. b___g, b___g, b___g, b___g) (big, bag, bug, bog)

Activity Worksheet: Page 123 Students will print the correct word in the sentence to complete it.
Answer Key: 1. beg 2. ham 3. fell 4. cub 5. puck 6. dock 7. net 8. limp

Day 5: Use the following instructions to test your students ability to recognize the long and short vowels 'a, e,i, o, u.

A. Auditory Instructions: Listen to each word that I say. Circle the vowel sound that you hear in each word.
Words: 1. plum 2. ship 3. hope 4. pure 5. prize 6. grass 7. teeth 8. coal 9. nod 10. check Answer Key: Row 1: ŭ, 2. ĭ 3. ā 4.ū 5. ī 6. ă 7. ē 8. ō 9. ŏ 10. ĕ

B. Auditory and Visual Discrimination Test:
Circle the vowel sound heard in each picture. **Picture Key:** Row 1: vest, rain, mice, cube Row 2: ghost, grass, seeds, frog Row 3: drum, toe, hill, truck
Answer Key: Row 1: ĕ, ā, ī, ū, Row 2: ō, ă, ē, ŏ Row 3: ŭ, ō, ĭ, ŭ

Name: ______________________________ | Day 1 | Week 20 |

The letter **'u'** can make two sounds.

It has a **ū** sound in cube and a **ŭ** sound in cup.

Circle all the pictures with the **long 'u'** sound and **underline** the pictures with the **short 'u'** sound.

Name: ______________________________ | Day 2 | Week 20

Name each picture. **Print** the vowel sound heard to complete each picture's name.

Examples:

cŭbs

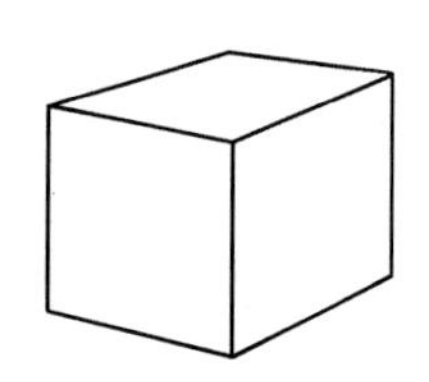

cūbe

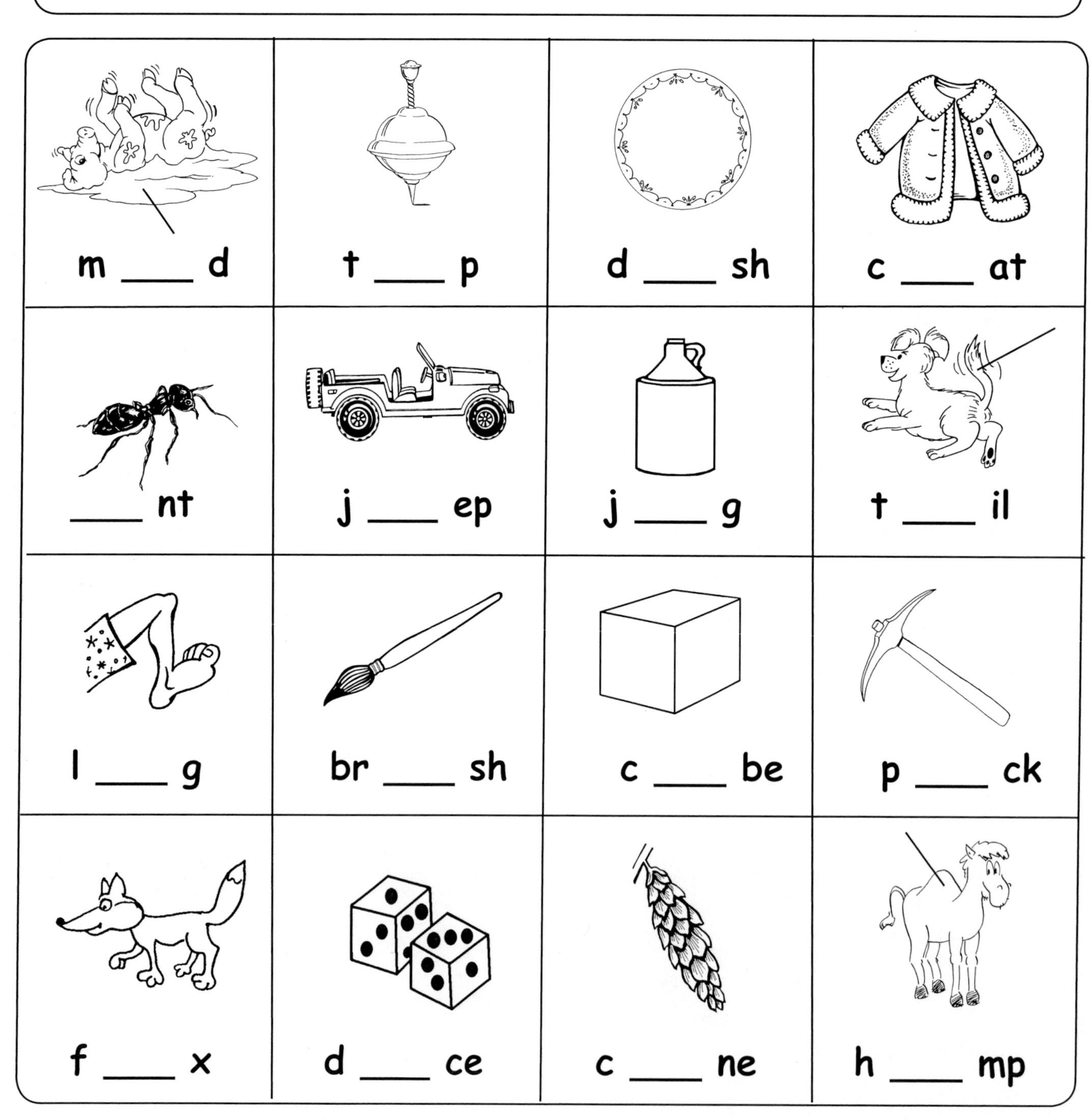

SSR1140 ISBN: 9781771586863

Name: ______________________________ | Day 3 | Week 20 |

Use the following words to name the pictures in the boxes.
Print the name of the picture on the line under it.

Names of Pictures:

jeep	hill	gate	well	nine	tub
fan	hole	nut	cube	bus	log

 ____________	 ____________	9 ____________	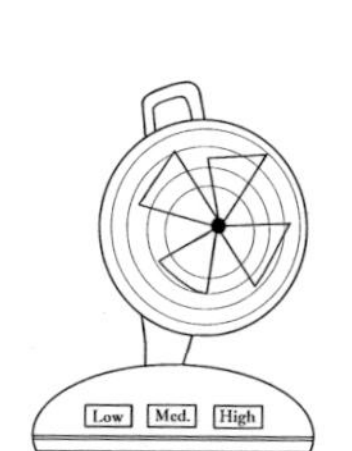 ____________
 ____________	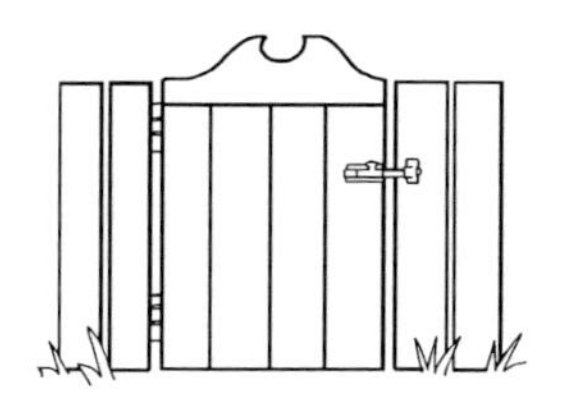 ____________	 ____________	 ____________
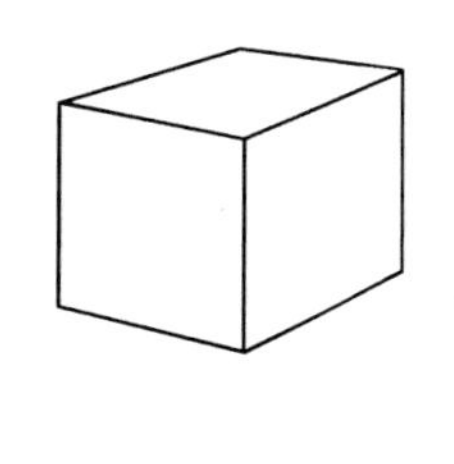 ____________	 ____________	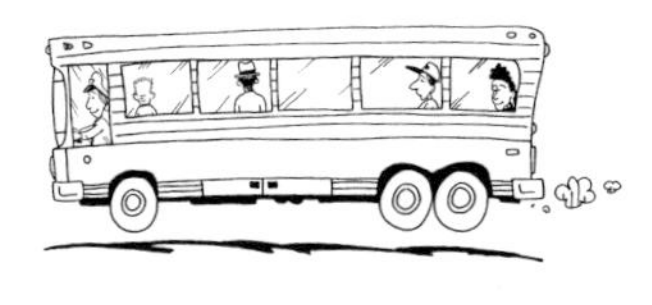 ____________	 ____________

Name: ______________________________ | Day 4 | Week 20 |

The long and short vowels '**a**,**e**,**i**,**o**, and **u**' are found in many words.
Examples:

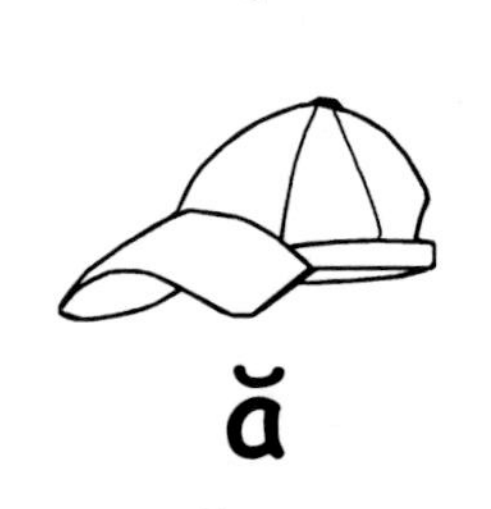    

ă **ĕ** **ĭ** **ŏ** **ŭ**

  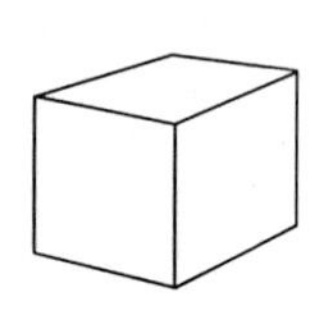

ā **ē** **ī** **ō** **ŏ**

Print the correct word from the box on the line in each sentence

1. The little dog likes to ___________. | bag, big, beg
2. I like to eat ___________ and eggs. | him, hem, ham
3. The boy ___________ down the hill. | full, fell, fill
4. A baby bear is called a ___________ . | cab, cub, cod
5. We play hockey with a ___________. | puck, pick, pack
6. A big boat came to the ___________. | deck, dock, duck
7. You can catch a fish with a ___________. | not, net, nut
8. The man walks with a ___________. | limp, lamp, lump

Name: ______________________________

Day 5	Week 20

A. **Auditory Test** on the long and short vowels '**a, e, i, o, and u**'

1.	2.	3.	4.	5.
ū ŭ ă	ĭ ĕ ā	ā ō ū	ŭ ō ū	ē ū ī
6.	**7.**	**8.**	**9.**	**10.**
ŭ ŏ ă	ū ī ē	ŏ ō ĭ	ă ŏ ĕ	ă ĭ ĕ

B. **Auditory and Visual Discrimination Test:**

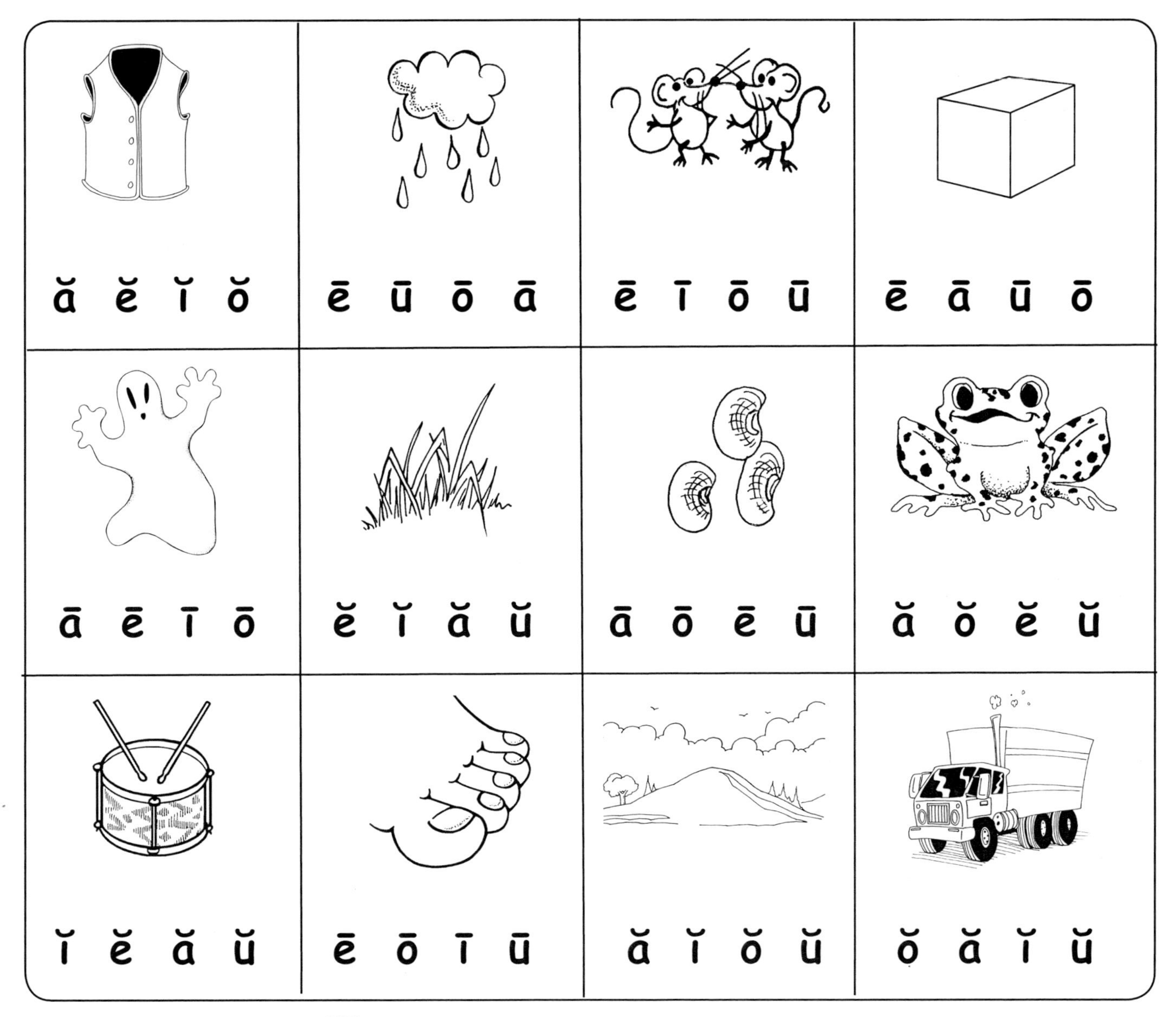

 ISBN: 9781771586863

Week 21: Teach 's' Blends: st, sk, sm, sn, sl, sw, sp, sc

Teacher Information: A **blend** is a combination of two and sometimes three consonants. 'S' blends contain the letter '**s**' in the initial position and another consonant. They may be heard at the beginning or at the ending of a word.

Day 1: Print the letter '**s**' on a chart. Have the students say the sound that it makes. Add the letter '**l**' and combine both sounds to make the blend '**sl**'. Have the students sound and say the blend. Repeat this process for the blends '**sk**' and '**sm**'. Record the following words that begin with the blends and have the students sound them out. **Words:** sled, smell, skin, slap, small, skip, slip, smile, skull

Picture Key: Row 1: smile, slippers, skate, sled Row 2: smell, skull, slide, smoke Row 3: skeleton, sleeve, skirt, skunk

Activity Worksheet: Page 127 Students are to record the correct '**s**' blend heard in each picture on the line provided. **Answer Key: Row 1:** sm, sl, sk, sl **Row 2:** sm, sk, sl, sm **Row 3:** sk, sl, sk, sk

Day 2: Teach the blends **st**, **sn**, and **sp** using the same process as Day 1. Print the letter '**s**' on a chart and add the letter '**t**' to form a different '**s**' blend. Have the students sound out and say the blend. Repeat this process for '**sn**' and '**sp**'. Record the following words on the chart and have the students sound them out. **Words:** stop, snug, spot, snap, star, spin, snow, stuck, spell

Picture Key: Row 1: snail, spinning wheel, star, sleep, Row 2: smile, skunk, spider, snowman Row 3: stairs, stamp, skip, spin

Activity Worksheet: Page 128 Students are to record the correct '**s**' blend heard in each picture on the line. **Answer Key:** Row 1: sm, sl, sk, sl Row 2: sm, sk, sl, sm Row 3: sk, sl, sk, sk

Day 3: Teach the blends '**sw**' and '**sc**' using the same format used for Day 1 and Day 2. Have the students sound out the following words that begin with the blends 'sw' and 'sc'. **Words:** swim, scale, sweep, swing, scare, scat, sweet, scarf

Picture Key: Row 1. scarecrow, sweater, skunk, stairs Row 2: sleigh, smoke, spider, snake Row 3: spool, swim, skeleton, stamp

Activity Worksheet: Page 129 Students are to record the correct '**s**' blend heard in each picture on the line. **Answer Key:** Row 1: st, sw, sk, st Row 2: sl, sn, sk, sw Row 3: sc, sp, sm, sc

Day 4: Review the '**s**' blends with the following riddles. Record the '**s**' blends on a chart. The students are to point to the '**s**' blend that begins the answer to each riddle. **Riddles:** 1. I am a part of a tree left in the ground when I am cut down. (stump) 2. I am the bone in your head. (skull) 3. You do this to a floor with a broom. (sweep) 4. You wrap me around your mouth and neck when it is very cold. (scarf) 5. I am the part of a plant that holds up the flower. (stem) 6. You may do this when you walk on ice. (slip) 7. You may do this when you sleep. (snore) 8. When you are happy this may be on your face. (smile)

Activity Worksheet: Page 130 The students are to record the correct word from the word box that will complete each sentence. **Answer Key:** 1. sleep 2. spin 3. smile 4. scare 5. swing 6. snack 7. sky 8. stuck 9. skate 10. snail

Day 5: Use the following instructions to test your students' ability to recognize the '**s**' blends sl, st, sk, sm, sn, sw, sp, sc.
A. Auditory Test Instructions: Listen to each word that I say. Circle the '**s**' blend that you hear at the beginning of the word. **Words:** 1. snap 2. speak 3. smash 4. slash 5. steam 6. skinny 7. swoop 8. scare 9. swish 10. space **Answer Key:** 1. sn 2. sp 3. sm 4. sl 5. st 6. sk 7. sw 8. sc 9. sw 10. sp

B. Auditory and Visual Discrimination Test: Print the correct '**s**' blend on the line under each picture.
Picture Key: Row 1: sled, smoke, spoon, snowflake Row 2: stem, scarf, swim, skull Row 3: swan, skates, scarecrow, steam Row 4: spider, snail, smell, sleigh
Answer Key: Row 1: sl, sm, sp, sn Row 2: st, sc, sw, sk Row 3: sw, sk, sc, st Row 4: sp, sn, sm, sl

Name: ______________________________ | Day 1 | Week 21 |

Some words begin with two sounds that make a blend.
Examples:

sl **sl**ide   **sk** **sk**irt   **sm** **sm**art

Print the **blend** that each picture begins with on the line

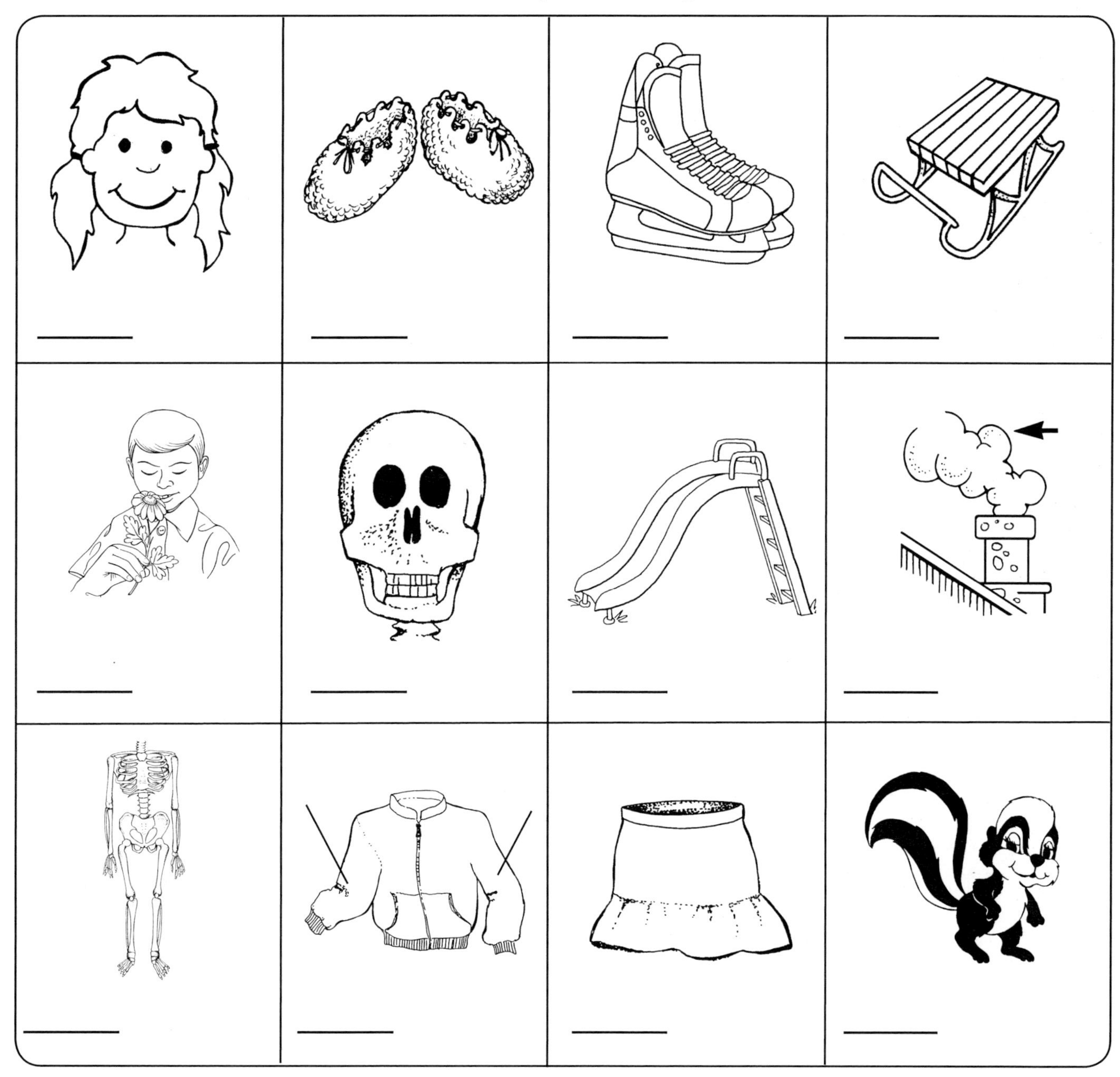

Name: ______________________________

Day 2	Week 21

Some words begin with **two** sounds that make a **blend**.

Examples:

sn **sn**owball

sp spoon

st stool

Print the 's' blend that each picture begins with on the line in each box

Name: ______________________________ | Day 3 | Week 21 |

Some words begin with **two sounds** that make a **blend**

Examples:

sw swing

sc scared

Print the **blend** that each picture begins with on the line in each box.

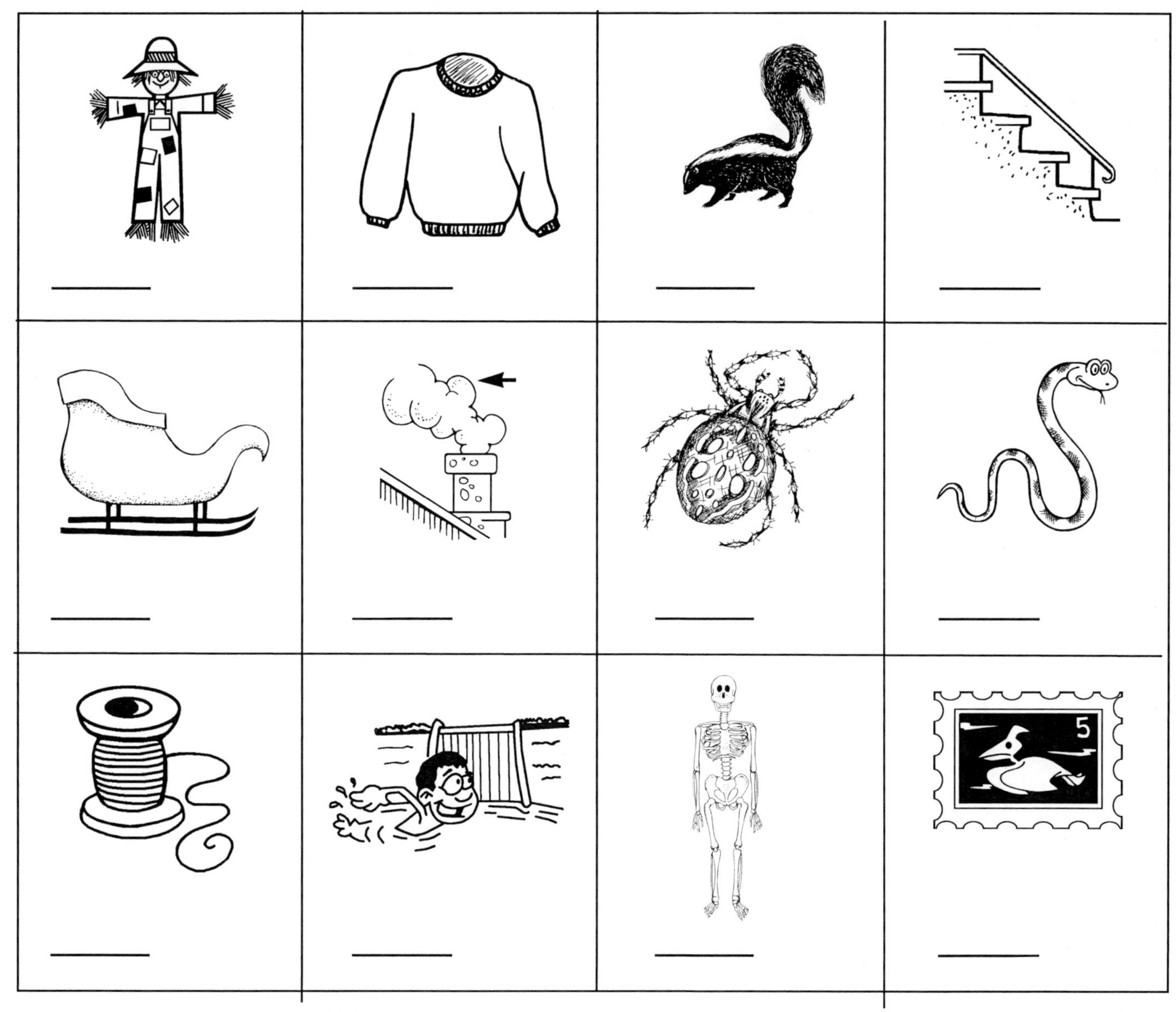

Name: ______________________________ | Day 4 | Week 21 |

Many words that we use begin with an '**s**' blend.

They are '**sl**, **sm**, **sn**, **sp**, **sc**, **st**, **sk**, and **sw**.'

Use the words in the box to complete the sentences below.

snail	skate	stuck	sky	snack
swing	scare	smile	spin	sleep

1. I like to ____________ in my new bed.

2. The boy can make his top ____________ fast.

3. We ____________ when we feel happy.

4. The big bear likes to ____________ the bees.

5. The little girl likes to play on her ____________.

6. I like to eat an apple for a ____________.

7. Rain fell from the ____________ and made the grass wet.

8. The car got ____________ in the snow.

9. Children like to ____________ on a pond in the winter.

10. A ____________ moves very slowly on the ground.

Name: ______________________________

Day 5	Week 21

A. **Auditory Test** on 's' blends **sl**, **sp**, **sm**, **sn**, **sk**, **sc**, **st**, **sw**

1. sm sn sp	2. sl sp st	3. sn sm sl	4. st sn sl	5. sp sk st
6. sl sk sm	7. sw sp sn	8. sl sc st	9. sp, sw, sn	10. sm sn sp

B. **Auditory and Visual Discrimination Test:**

______	______	______	______
______	______	______	______
______	______	______	______
______	______	______	______

Week 22 Recognition of 'L' Blends: bl, cl, fl, gl, pl, sl

Objective: To teach the recognition of the 'l' blends **bl, cl, fl, gl, pl, sl**

Teacher Information: In some words the letter **'l'** follows another consonant to form a **blended** sound. In order to say words that begin with a consonant and the letter 'l' , the two sounds must be blended together to make one sound at the beginning or ending of a word.

Day 1: Introduce the **'l'** blends **'bl, cl,** and **fl'** using the following groups of words recorded on a chart. **Words:** Row 1: blue, black, blow Row 2: class, clap, clam Row 3: flag, fly, flap Direct the students' attention to the words on the chart. Draw their attention to the beginning of each group of words. What letter do you notice is the same at the beginning of each word? (l) Explain that the letter 'l' and another consonant will become partners in a word and they will make a sound together. This sound is called a **'blend.'** Have them listen to the following words. What blend do you hear at the beginning of the words that I am going to say. **Words:** 1. block (bl) 2. clock (cl) 3. flock (fl) 4. bleed (bl) 5. close (cl) 6. flat (fl) 7. blew (bl) 8. flute (fl)

Picture Key: Row 1: flower, blouse, cloud, flag Row 2: clap, clam, blade, blow Row 3: club, flame, flute, clown

Activity Worksheet Page:133 The students are to record the missing blend to make the word that describes each picture. **Answer Key:** Row 1: fl, bl, cl, fl Row 2: cl, cl, bl, bl Row 3: cl, fl, fl, cl

Day 2: Introduce the **'l'** blends **'gl, pl,** and **sl.'** Review the concept of an 'l' blend. Explain that there are other sounds that use 'l' in a blend. Have them listen to this group of words, glass, glow, glue. What blend do you hear at the beginning of each word. (gl) Listen to this group of words, plate, plum, play. What blend do you hear at the beginning of each word? (pl) Listen to this group of words, slip, slap, slow. What blend do you hear at the beginning of these words. (sl) On a chart record 'bl, sl, fl, gl, pl, and cl. Have the students listen to the word that you say and then have one of them locate the blend on the chart. **Words:** plate, bleed, clown, floating, glass, plow, slip, blind, flat, glide

Picture Key: Row 1: gloves, sleigh, plate, slippers Row 2: plane, pliers, glass, slide, Row 3: planet, globe, plum, clothes

Activity Worksheet: Page 134 The students are to record the blend on the line to complete each word below the picture. **Answer Key:** Row 1: gl, sl, pl, sl Row 2: pl, pl, gl, sl Row 3: pl, gl, pl, cl

Day 3: Review all the **'l'** blends with your students. Have them tell the name of the 'l' blend that they hear at the beginning of each of the following words. Words: plenty (pl); slump (sl); glow (gl); flick (fl); blew (bl); clean (cl); blister (bl); plastic (pl); flood (fl); glad (gl)

Picture Key: Row 1: slide, plane, gloves, floor Row 2: flower, block, clown, flag, Row 3: cloud, fly, globe, class

Activity Worksheet: Page: 135 The students are to complete each word with the correct **'l'** blend.
Answer Key: Row 1: sl, pl, gl, fl Row 2: fl, bl, cl, fl Row 3: cl, fl, gl, cl

Day 4: Review the 'l' blends with your students. Have them suggest **'l'** blends that could be placed at the beginning of the following endings. The endings could be written on a chart or a chalkboard and the students use the **'l'** blends to make new words. **Endings:** ___ ock; ___ ake; ___ at; ___ ide; ___ed; ___ ub; ___ ay; ___ ad; ___ ip; ___ ick

Picture Key: Row 1: flag, clap, slide Row 2: plane, flute, globe Row 3: plate, clown, block Row 4: fly, plant, sled

Activity Worksheet: Page 136 The students are to circle the word that describes the picture in each box.

Answer Key: Row 1: flag, clap, slide Row 2: plane, flute, globe Row 3: plate, clown, blocks Row 4: fly, plant, sled

Day 5: Use the following instructions to test your students ability to recognize the 'l' blends bl, cl, fl, gl, pl, sl

A. Auditory Test Instructions: Listen to each word that I say. Circle the 'l' blend that you hear at the beginning of the word. **Words:** 1. glass 2. please 3. flicker 4. blind 5. clean 6. slice 7. plenty 8. sleeve 9. fling 10. glitter **Answer Key:** 1. gl 2. pl 3. fl 4. bl 5. cl 6. sl 7. pl 8. sl 9. fl 10. gl

B. Auditory and Visual Discrimination Test: Print the correct 'l' blend heard on the line under each picture. **Picture Key:** Row 1: flame, glass, plane, sleigh Row 2: blade, clam, flashlight, gloves Row 3: sleeve, plate, globe, flag Row 4: cloud, club, flower, plum **Answer Key:** Row 1: fl, gl, pl, sl Row 2: bl, cl, fl, gl Row 3: sl, pl, gl, fl Row 4: cl, cl, fl, pll

Name: ______________________________

Day 1 | Week 22

In some words the letter 'l' follows another consonant to make a sound called a **blend**.
The two sounds mix together to make **one** sound.
Examples:

block

clock

fly

Use an **'l' blend** to make a word to match each picture in the box.

_____ ower	_____ ouse	_____ oud	_____ ag
_____ ap	_____ am	_____ ade	_____ ow
_____ ub	_____ ame	_____ ute	_____ own

Name: ______________________________ | Day 2 | Week 22 |

In some words the letter 'l' follows different consonants to make a **blend**.

The **two** sounds blend together to make one sound.

Examples:

glue

plant

sled

Use an **'l' blend** to make a word to match each picture.

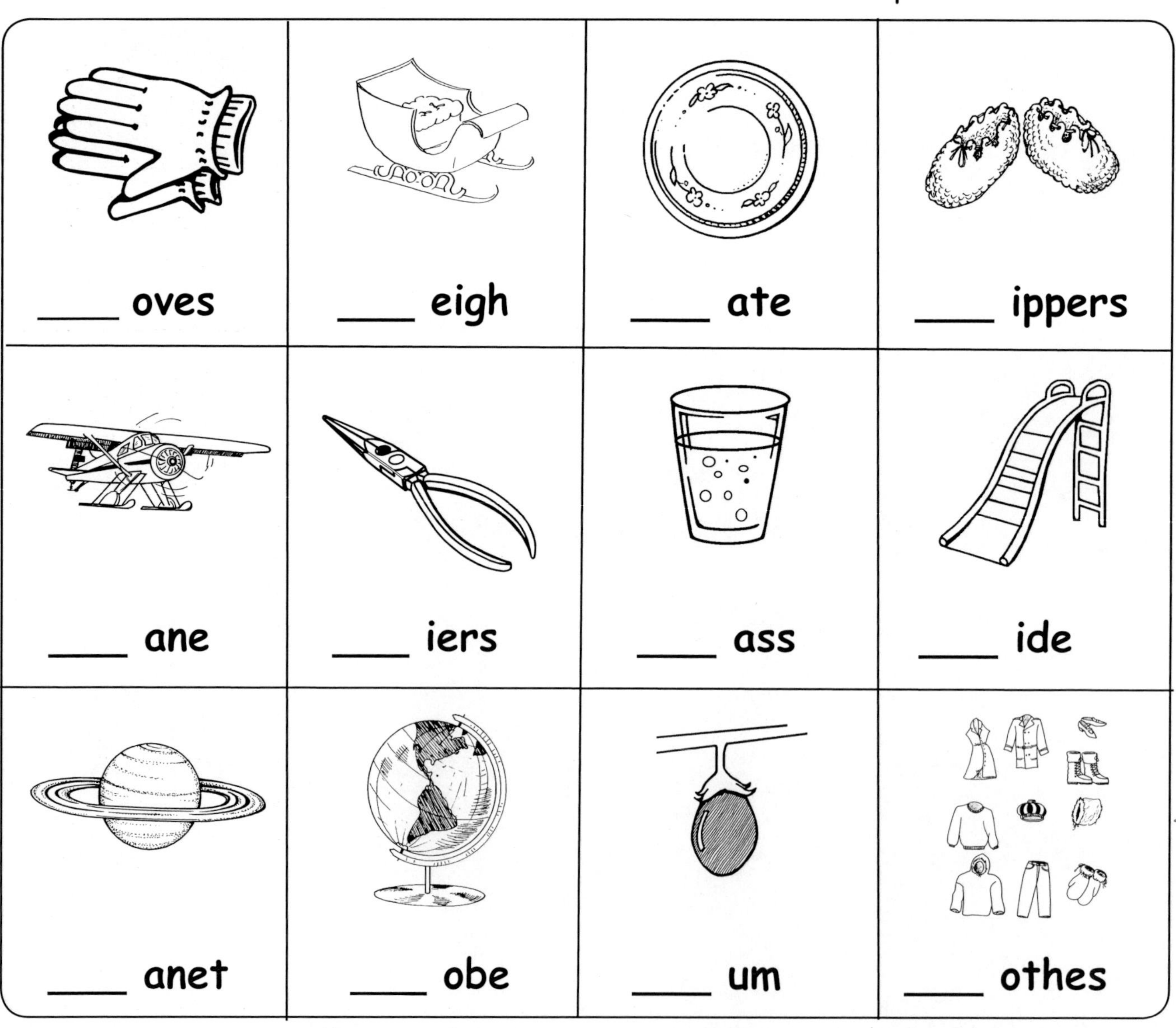

Name: ______________________________

Day 3 | Week 22

Many words begin with 'l' blends.

They may begin with **'cl, bl, fl, gl, pl** and **sl.'**

Examples:

black **cl**ip **fl**at **gl**ad **pl**um **sl**eep

Use an 'l' blend to complete each word under the picture.

bl cl fl gl pl sl

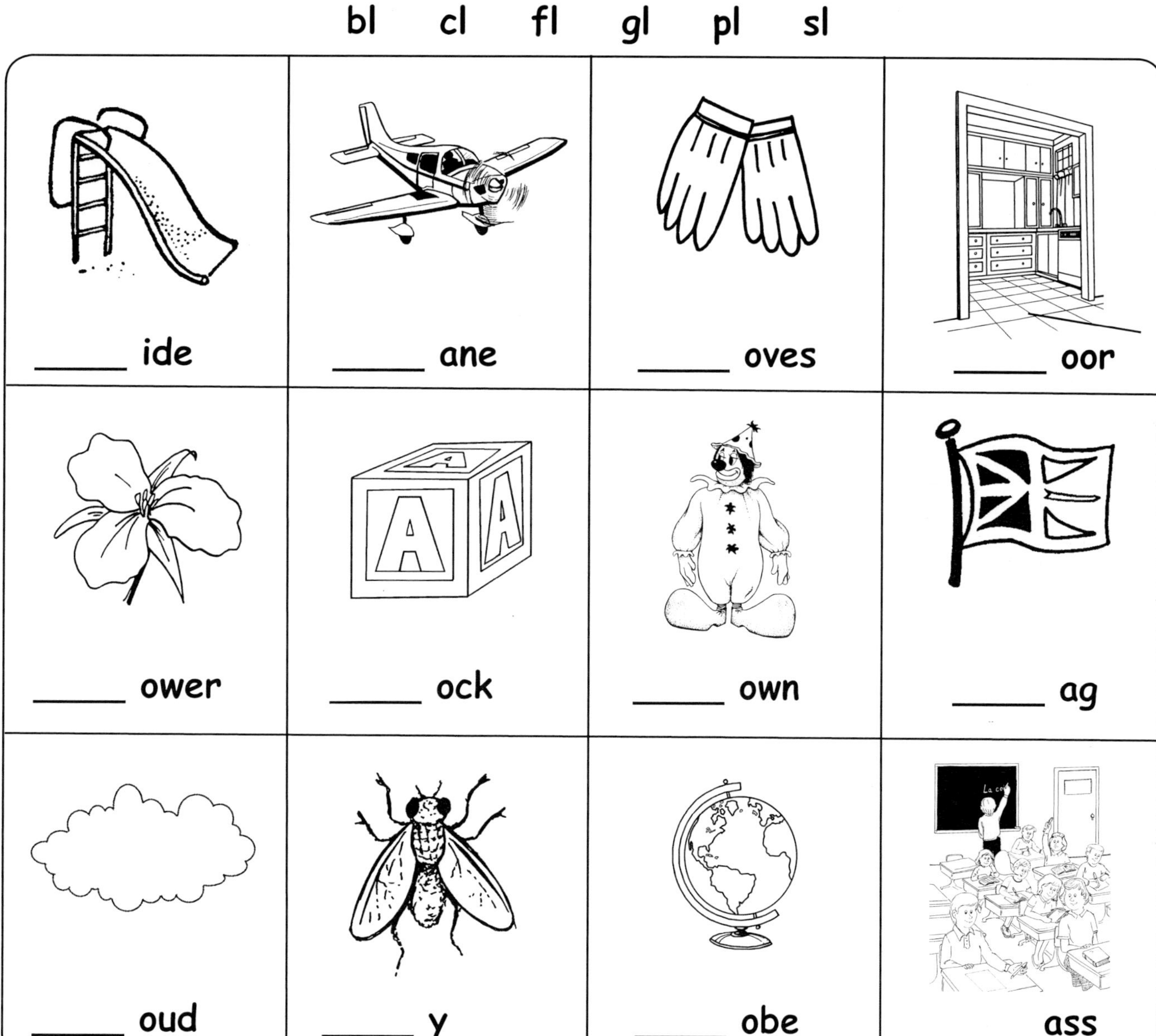

Name: ______________________________

Day 4 | Week 22

Read the group of words beside each picture.
Circle the word that names each picture

flip glad flag clip	play clap flap glad	clam slide glass play
globe plane slate flake	plate blade flute club	flake play club globe
blew clock plate flick	flat clown plum glue	plate sled click blocks
glad fly plan sled	glide flat blew plant	fled blue sled clam

Name: ______________________________

Day 5	Week 22

A. Auditory Test on the 'l' blends bl, cl, fl, gl, pl, sl

1. bl cl gl	2. bl pl cl	3. gl fl pl	4. pl bl cl	5. sl bl cl
6. pl gl sl	7. bl cl pl	8. sl pl gl	9. pl fl bl	10. pl bl cl

B. Auditory and Visual Discrimination Test:

____	____	____	____
____	____	____	____
____	____	____	____
____	____	____	____

Week 23 Recognition of 'R' Blends 'br, cr, fr, gr, pr, tr

Objective: To teach the recognition of the '**r**' blends

Teacher Information: In some words the initial consonant '**r**' follows another consonant to make a blended sound. In order to say words that begin with a consonant and the letter '**r**', the two sounds must be blended together to make one sound at the beginning of words.

Day 1: Introduce the '**r**' blends '**br**, **cr**, and **fr**'. Record the following sentences on a chart: 1. Frank's friend has freckles all over his face. 2. Brenda likes to brush her long brown hair. 3. The crowd of people watched the crocodile crawl out of the creek and cross the road. Underline the words as indicated. Read each sentence to your students and discuss the underlined words. What do you notice about the underlined words in sentence # 1? They all begin with the same two letters. What are the letters called? (**f** and **r**) What sound do they make? How are the underlined words in sentence two the same? (They all begin with the same two letters) What are the letters called? (**b** and **r**) How are the underlined words in sentence three the same. (They all begin with the same two letters) What are the letters called? (**f** and **r**) How are the underlined words in sentence three the same? (They all begin with the same two letters. Record '**br**, **cr**, and **fr** on the chart. Explain to your students that these letters are called '**r**' blends. Each one has the letter '**r**' in it.

Picture Key: Row 1: frog, crayon, brush Row 2: branch, crown, braids Row 3: fruit, crab, bridge

Activity Worksheet: Page 139 The students will record the 'r' blend that each picture begins with on the line. **Answer Key:** Row 1: fr, cr, br Row 2: br, cr, br Row 3: fr, cr, br

Day 2: Introduce the '**r**' blends '**dr**, **gr**, **tr**, and **pr**.' Tell your students there are other '**r**' blends. On a chart print the blends '**dr**, **gr**, **tr**, and **pr**' at the top of four columns. Discuss the sound each '**r**' blend makes. Have the students listen to each word that you say and have them classify the words to make a chart of '**r**' blend words. **Words:** prince, dragon, truck, ground, present, tricycle, grass, drain, tricks, grab, train, draw, proud Add other words if the students can think of them.

Picture Key: Row 1: dress, tree, grass, princess Row 2: truck, grin, prize, drum Row 3: frame, dragon, grasshopper, proud

Activity Worksheet: Page 140 The students are to identify the 'r' blends used at the beginning of each picture and print it on the line under it. **Answer Key:** Row 1: dr, tr, gr, pr Row 2: tr, gr, pr, dr Row 3: fr, dr, gr, pr

Day 3: Review all the 'r' blends with the following riddles. Say, listen to each riddle and tell us the answer and the ' r' blend that it begins with. **Riddles:** 1. I am used for drawing and colouring. I am a crayon. (cr) 2. I am a kind of horn used for playing music. I am a trumpet. (tr) 3. It is a kind of fruit that grows in bunches.They are called grapes. (gr) 4. I am a lady all dressed in white. I am a bride. (br) 5. I am the son of a king and queen. I am called a prince. (pr) 6. It lives in a pond and hops about on land. It is a frog. (fr) 7. I am a large animal that breathes fire. I am a dragon. (dr)

Picture Key: Row 1: crab, bread, triangle, crying Row 2: drum, frog, present, broom Row 3: tree, cradle, truck, grass

Activity Worksheet: Page 141 The students are to complete each word with the correct 'r' blend. Answer Key: Row 1. cr, br, tr, gr Row 2: dr, fr, pr, br Row 3: tr, cr, tr, gr

Day 4: Print the following word endings on a chart: (cr)y, (tr)ay, (gr)ade, (tr)eat, (tr)ee, (gr)in. (br)at, (pr)int, (dr)ill, (tr)uck, (fr)ee Which ending would you use to make the word cry, drill, free, brick, tray, treat, grin, print, brick, grade, drill

Activity Worksheet: Page 142 The students will circle the correct word in the brackets and print it in the sentence to complete it. Answer Key: 1. tray 2. grin 3. fry, 4. drive 5. tree 6. drill 7. brook. 8. crown

Day 5: Use the following instructions to test your students' ability to recognize the 'r' blends br, cr, dr, fr, gr, pr, tr

A. Auditory Test Instructions: Listen to each word that I say. Circle the 'r' blend that you hear at the beginning of the word. **Words**: 1. prince 2. brother 3. friend 4. creature 5. trailer 6. drain 7. grind 8. tractor 9. groan 10. crack **Answer Key:** 1. pr 2. br 3. fr 4. cr 5. tr 6. dr 7. gr 8. tr 9. gr 10. cr

B. Auditory and |Visual Discrimination Test: Print the correct '**r**' blend that you hear at the beginning of each picture on the line under each picture. **Picture Key:** Row 1: truck, crown, grapes, present Row 2: brick, grass, bracelet, frog Row 3: drink, train, dragon, fruit Row 4: tricycle, cradle, bride, treasure **Answer Key:** Row 1: tr, cr, gr, pr Row 2: br, gr, br, fr Row 3: dr, tr, dr, fr Row 4: tr, cr, br, tr

Name: ______________________ | Day 1 | Week 23

Some words begin with an '**r**' blend.
The first consonant blends with the letter '**r**' to make a sound at the beginning of a word.

Examples:

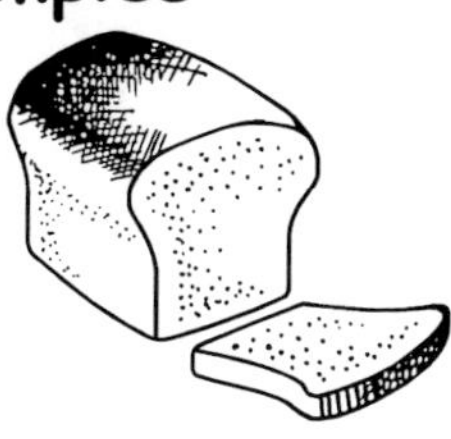

bread **cr**ane **fr**iends

Print the **blend** that each picture begins with on the line in each box.

Is it the blend **br**, **cr**, or **fr**?

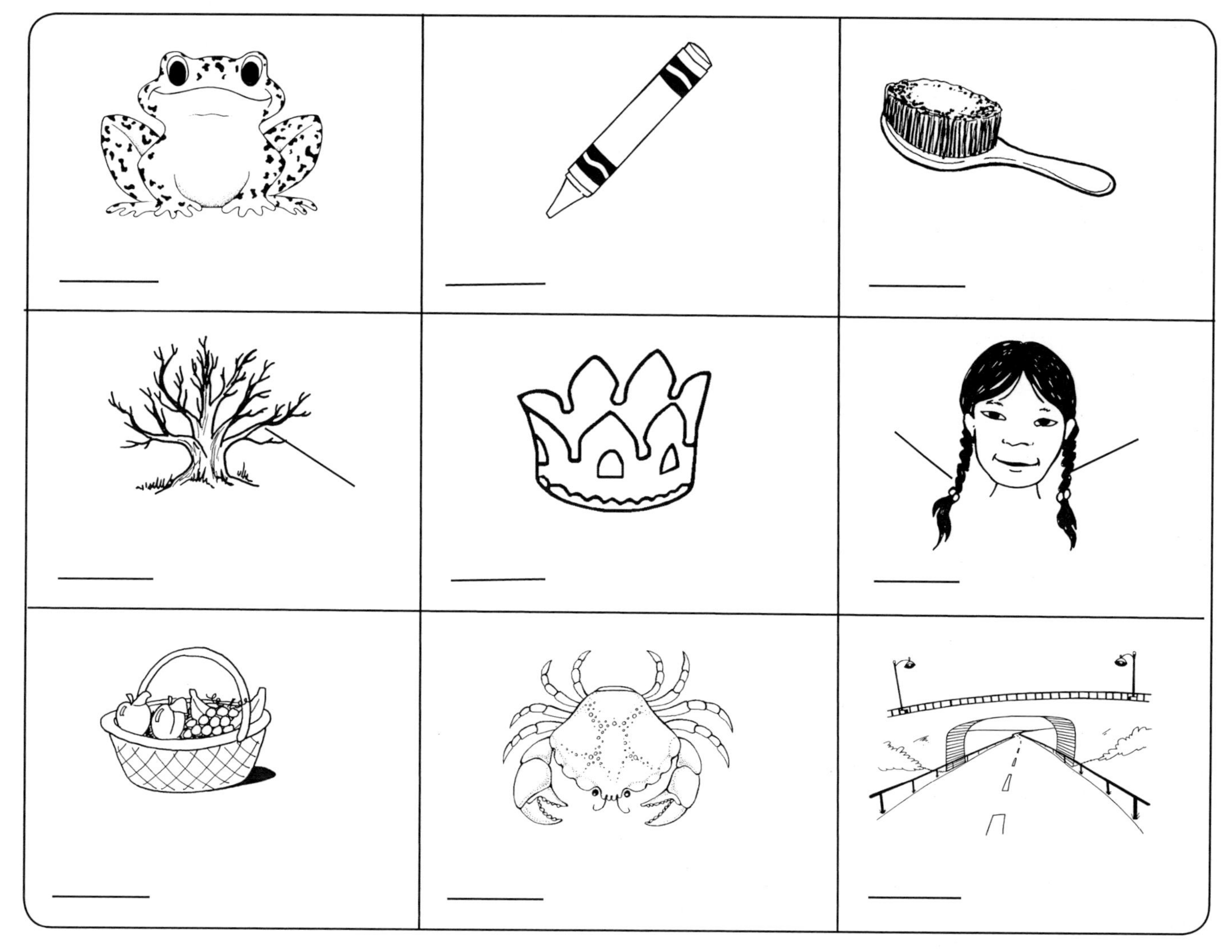

Name: ______________________________

Day 2	Week 23

Other words also begin with an **'r' blend.**

They are:

drink 	**gr**apes	**tr**ain	**pr**esent

Print the correct 'r' blend on the line under each picture.

Does the picture begin with '**dr**, **gr**, **tr** or **pr**' ?

_____	_____	_____	_____
_____	_____	_____	_____
_____	_____	_____	_____

Name: ______________________________

Day 3	Week 23

Many words begin with **'r'** blends.

They may begin with '**br**, **cr**, **dr**, **fr**, **gr**, **pr**, and **tr**.'

Use and **'r' blend** to complete each word that tells the name of the picture in each box

 ____ab	 ____ ead	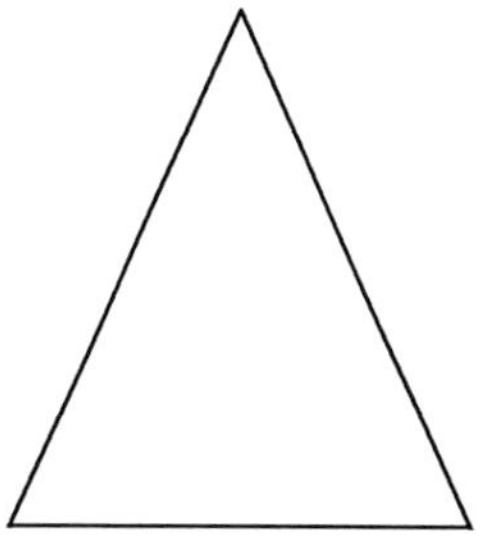 ____iangle	 ____ying
 ____um	 ____og	 ____esent	 ____oom
 ____ee	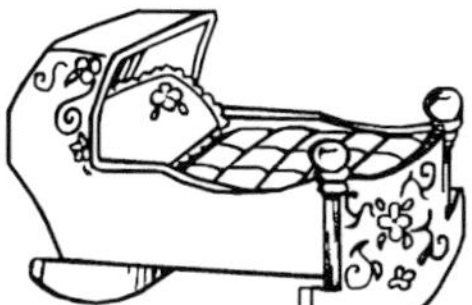 ____adle	 ____uck	 ____ass

Name: ______________________________

Day 4 | Week 23

Read each sentence and the words beside it.

Choose **one** of the words to complete the sentence.

Print the word on the line in the sentence.

1. Put the dish on the ____________. (bray, stay, tray)

2. The boy had a big ____________ on his face. (frill, tree, grin)

3. I will ____________ the eggs in a big pan. (try, fry, dry)

4. Will you ____________ me to school. (drum, drive, drop)

5. The wind blew the ____________ down. (free, green, tree)

6. The man made a hole with his ____________ (frill, grill, drill)

7. Fish like to swim in a ____________. (crook, brook, drum)

8. The king will wear a ____________ today. (crown, drown frown)

Name: ______________________________

Day 5	Week 23

A. **Auditory Test** on the **'r'** blends **br, cr, dr, fr, gr, pr, tr**

1.	2.	3.	4.	5.
br dr pr	fr br tr	br gr fr	br gr cr	fr gr tr
6.	7.	8.	9.	10.
dr br gr	gr pr dr	dr tr pr	gr pr fr	pr cr tr

B. Auditory and Visual Discrimination Test:

____	____	____	____
____	____	____	____
____	____	____	____
____	____	____	____

Week 24 Recognition of Final Consonant Blends: st, lt, nk, lf, nt, mp, sk

Objective: To teach the recognition of blends that are found at the end of words.

Teacher Information: Some words end with a consonant blend. Some sounds are blended together at the end of words to make one sound.

Day 1: Introduce the final consonant blends '**st**, **lt**, **nk**, and **sk**.' Explain to your students that consonant blends are often located at the end of words. On a chart record the words **nest**, **best**, **rest**. Ask your students to tell how these words are similar. (They all end with the same two sounds 's and t.') Where else have you seen the blend '**st**' in words. (at the beginning of words) Explain that some blends begin or end a word. Record the words **belt**, **felt**, **melt** on the chart. Ask the students how these words are the same. (They all end with the blend '**lt**.') Record the words **bank, sank**, **tank,** and **yank** on the chart. How are these words similar? (They all end with '**nk**.') Record the words **mask**, **task**, **ask** on the chart. How are these words the same? (They all end with '**sk**.') Print the following words on the chart and have the students use their word attack skills to sound them out. **Words:** desk, post, belt, tank, most, halt, ask, gift, ramp, bent,

Picture Key: Row 1: ghost, desk, quilt, sink Row 2: tank, nest, tusk, melt Row 3: chest, wrist, skunk, post

Activity Worksheet: Page 145 The students are to circle the final consonant blend heard in each picture.

Answer Key: Row 1: st, sk, lt, nk Row 2: nk, st, sk, lt Row 3: st, st, nk, st

Day 2: Introduce the final consonant blends '**lf**, **nt**, **mp**.' Remind your students that final consonant blends are found at the end of words. On a chart record the following groups of words: elf, wolf, shelf; ant, tent, went; pump, jump, lamp. Discuss each group of words having the students note their endings are the same in each group. On a chart print the endings 'lf, mp, and nt.' Have the students listen to the following riddles and classify the word to one of the endings. **Riddles:** 1. I am a place where you live outside in a tent. (camp) 2. I am a baby cow. (calf) 3. I am a very small insect. (ant) 4. I like to do this with a brush. (paint) 5. It lives in the woods and hunts for things to eat. (wolf) 6. I am a place to sleep in outside. (tent)7. It is a place where things can be placed. (shelf) 8. It grows in the ground. (plant)

Picture Key: Row 1: cent, calf, lamp, jump Row 2: wolf, ant, tent, stamp Row 3: plant, pump, chest, stump

Activity Worksheet: Page 146 The student will circle the final blend heard in each picture.

Answer Key: Row 1: nt, lf, mp, lf Row 2: lf, nt, nt, mp Row 3: nt, mp, st, mp

Day 3: Review the following final consonants '**st**, **lt**, **nk**, **lf**, **nt**, **mp**, **sk**.' Have the students listen to the following words and tell the final blend heard in each one. **Words:** crest; pelt; mink; clump; gulf; went; dusk; spent; shelf; dump; think; melt; cast

Picture Key: Row 1: tusk, belt, lamp Row 2: stump, mask, tank Row 3: pump, desk, post 4: hump, bank, colt

Activity Worksheet: Page 147 The students are to circle the word that describes each picture.
Answer Key: Row 1: tusk, belt, lamp Row 2: stump, mask, tank 3. pump, desk, post 4. camel's hump, piggy bank, colt

Day 4: Review the final blends '**st**, **lt**, **nk**, **lf**, **nt**, **mp**, and **sk**. Record them at the top of a chart. Under the final blends record the following endings. Have the students apply the proper ending to each word and then say the word. **Exercise:** 1. ne___ 2. be___ 3. si___ 4. bu___ 5. wo___ 6. se___ 7. hu__ 8. po___ 9. ba___ 10. ju___ Possible Answers: 1. nest 2. belt 3. sink 4. bunk 5. wolf 6. self 7. hump 8. post 9. bank 10. jump

Activity Worksheet: Page 148 The students are to choose the correct word from the box and record it in the sentence. **Answer Key:** 1. pest 2. cost 3. bunk 4. best 5. limp 6. calf 7. hump 8. belt

Day 5: Use the following instructions to test your students' ability to recognize the final consonant blends '**st**, **lt**, **nk**, **lf**, **nt**, **mp**, **sk**

A. Auditory Test Instructions: Listen to each word that I say. Circle the consonant blend that you hear at the end of each word. **Words**: 1. tramp 2. task 3. bent 4. shelf 5. drank 6. melt 7. past 8. clamp 9. smelt 10. skunk
Answer Key: 1. mp 2. sk 3. nt 4. fl 5. nk 6. lt 7. st 8. mp 9. lf 10. nk

Auditory and Visual Discrimination Test: Circle the correct final consonant blend that you hear at the end of each picture. **Picture Key:** Row 1: nest, quilt, sink, stamp Row 2: calf, paint, pump, tank Row 3: gift, wrist, dump, think
Answer Key: Row 1: st, lt, nk, mp Row 2: lf, nt, mp, nk Row 3: ft, st, mp, nk

Name: ______________________________

Day 1	Week 24

Sometimes **two** letters will join together to make one sound at the **end** of a word. They make a sound called a '**blend**.'

Examples:

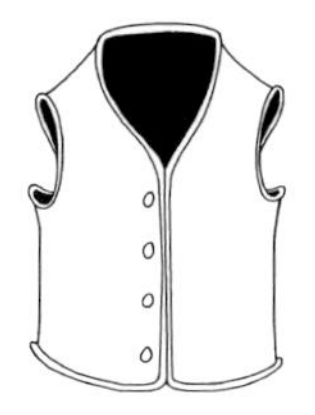
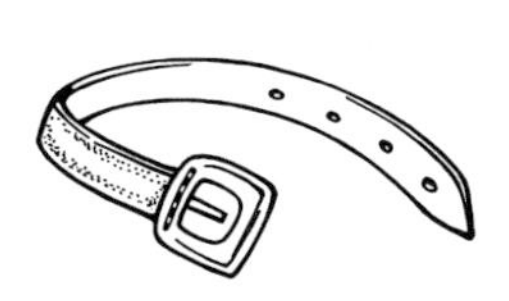

ve**st** be**lt** ba**nk** ma**sk**

Circle the **blend** that you hear at the **end** of each picture.

lt sk st	st nk sk	lf st sk	nk sk st
sk nk lt	lt st sk	lt st sk	lt nk sk
sk lt st	lt nk st	st sk nk	lt st sk

Name: ______________________________ | Day 2 | Week 24 |

There are other letters that join together to make a **blend**.

They are:

 elf  pai**nt**  pu**mp**

Circle the blend that you hear at the **end** of each picture.

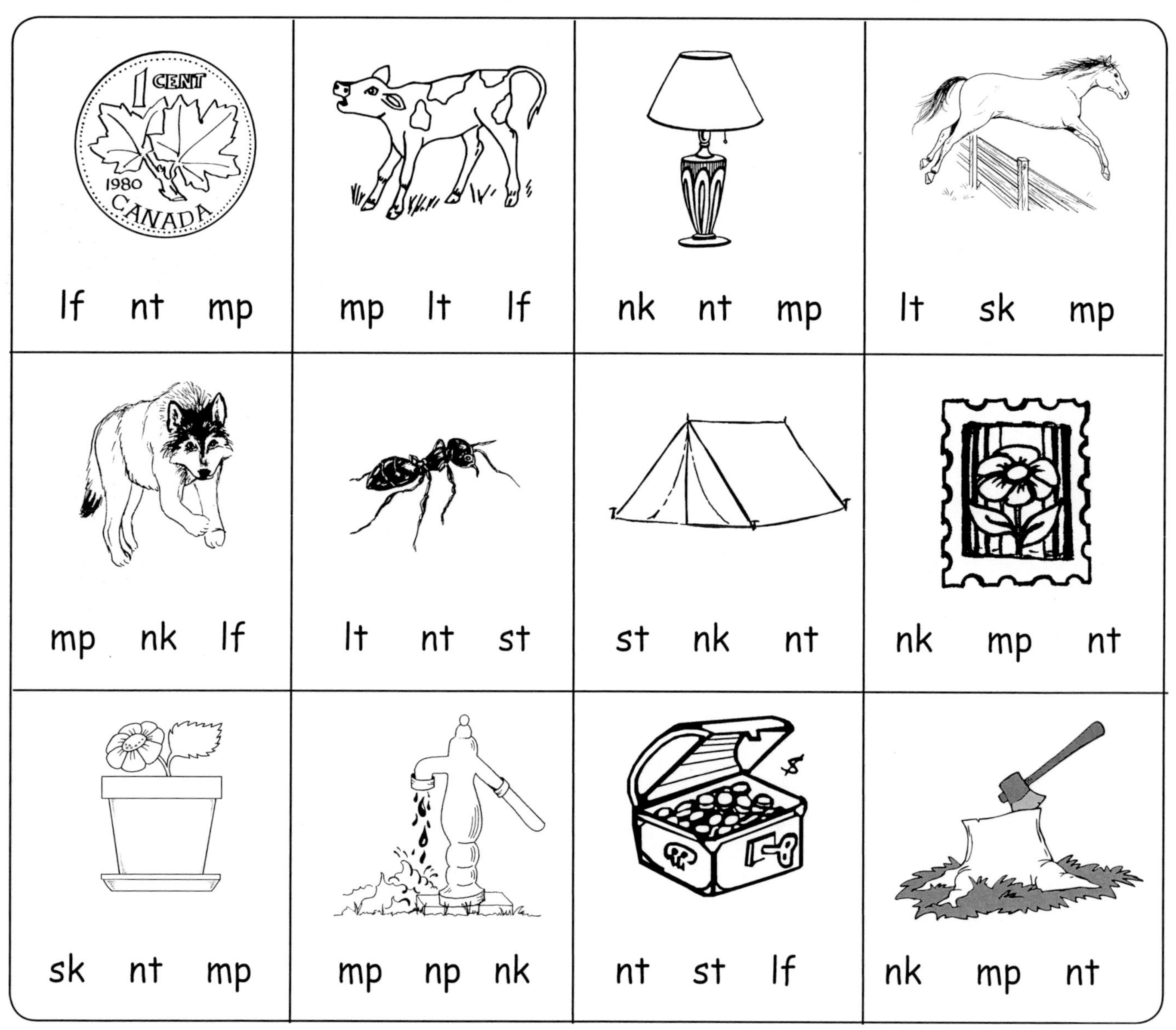

Name: ______________________________

Day 3	Week 24

Read the words and **look** at each picture carefully.
Circle the word that **matches** each pictures.

tusk best cast	elf belt best	bump sent lamp
self sink stump	mink mask mast	thank blink tank
pest pump paint	damp dent desk	post lost most
lamp hump limp	bunk bank bonk	cast camp colt

Name: ______________________________ | Day 4 | Week 24 |

Many words end with final blends.
Some of the final blends are listed below.

st lt nk nt mp sk

Complete each sentence below with the correct word.
Print it on the line in the sentence

1. My little brother can be a big ______________. (pelt pest pent)

2. How much did your bike ______________? (colt conk cost)

3. I sleep in the top ______________ at camp. (bust bump bunk)

4. I always try to do my ____________ work. (belt bent best)

5. The old man walks with a ______________. (limp list link)

6. A baby cow is called a ____________. (cast calf camp)

7. A camel has a big ____________ on its back. (hunt hunk hump)

8. A _____________ will hold up your pants. (bent best belt)

Name: ______________________________

Day 5	Week 24

A. Auditory Test on the final consonants **st**, **lt**, **nk**, **lf**, **nt**, **mp**, **sk**

1. nt mp nk	2. lt sk lf	3. nt mp nk	4. nt lt lf	5. sk nt nk
6. lf lt sk	7. sk lt st	8. mp nt nk	9. lf lt nt	10. nk nt sk

B. Auditory and Visual Discrimination Test:

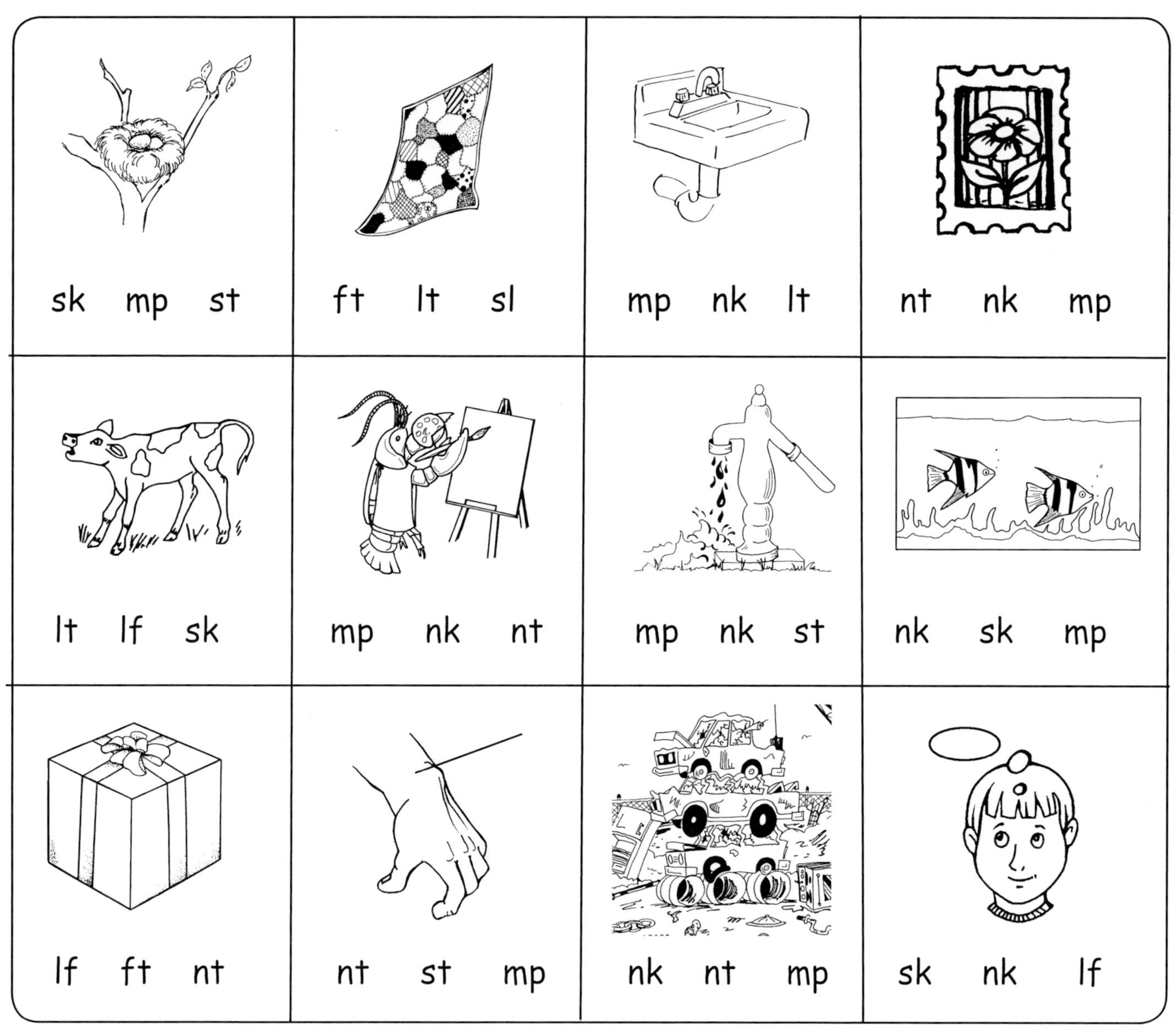

Week 25: Initial Consonant Digraphs 'sh, ch, wh, th'

Objective: To teach the recognition of the initial consonant digraphs and the sound each one makes.

Teacher Information: A digraph is a single sound made by two letters. It may be found at the beginning or ending of a word. A digraph has two letters but makes only one sound.

Day 1: Introduce the digraph '**sh**' with the following story. **Story:** Sharon the Sheep On a large farm lived a little sheep called Sharon. She shared a large shady field with many other sheep who were cared for by a shepherd called Shane. Shane was always watching out for shapes and shadows of wolves and foxes who were sneaking around the herd of sheep waiting for a chance to catch a shaggy one to kill and eat. Sharon would shiver and shake if she thought an enemy was nearby. Shane was a very good shepherd and if he saw an enemy sneaking about, he would shoot at it with his shotgun to scare it away. Record the digraph '**sh**' at the top of a chart. Tell your students the letters '**s**' and '**h**' together make one sound. This sound is one we use when we want everyone to be quiet and to listen. Have them make the sound. Have them listen to the story again for words that begin with the '**sh**' sound and then list them on the chart.

Picture Key: Row 1: shovel, slide, ship, chair, shoe Row 2: star, shirt, smoke, shark, shapes Row 3: shed, skirt, shingle, snake shower

Activity Worksheet: Page 151 The students are to circle and colour only the pictures that begin with the digraph 'sh.' **Answer Key:** shovel, ship, shoe, shirt, shark, shape, shed, shingle, shower

Day 2: Record the following sentences on a chart. Sentences: 1. Charlie Chipmunk chased the cheeky squirrel down the tree. 2. The mice cheered when they stole the cheese from the trap. 3.The chilly air made the children's cheeks rosy. 4. Everyone cheered when Chuck won playing checkers. Read each sentence to your students and have them locate words that begin the same way as the word '**chocolate**.' Explain that the letters '**c**' and '**h**' make one sound when they are together in a word. The '**ch**' sound makes the same sound as a train starting up on the tracks. Review '**sh**' and '**ch**' with this game. Say one of the following words and have the students tell which digraph it begins with. Words: 1. cherry 2. shatter 3. chimney 4. chuckle 5. shallow 6. shingle 7. choke 8. shiny

Picture Key: Row 1: church, shell, chesterfield, shamrock Row 2: shark, cheese, shed, cherries Row 3: chain, shirt, children, shoe

Activity Worksheet: Page 152 The students will circle the digraph each picture begins with. **Answer Key**: Row 1: ch, sh, ch, sh Row 2: sh, ch, sh, ch Row 3: ch, sh, ch, sh

Day 3: Print the following words on a chart: *that, this, they, than.* Have the students circle the letters that are the same in each word. The students should say them out loud. Have them notice what their tongue does at the beginning of each word. The digraph '**th**' makes you stick out your tongue. Play this listening game with your students. What sound do you hear at the beginning of these words: 1. thorn 2. ship 3. choose 4. shame 5. chuckle 6. thunder 7. thumb 8. shave 9. chest 10. thump

Picture Key: Row 1: thimble , chair, shovel, thief Row 2. shadow, thermometer, chipmunk, shed 3. chimney, shingle. thumb, church

Activity Worksheet: Page: 153 The students are to record the correct digraph that the picture begins with on the line in each box. **Answer Key:** Row 1: th, ch, sh, th Row 2: sh, th, ch, sh Row 3: ch, sh, th, ch

Day 4: Introduce the '**wh**' digraph with the following story: "One day a whopper of a fish was swimming through the swirling whirling waters of Whisper Bay. It kept swimming closer towards the wharf filled with people who were standing on it. They watched the whopper of a fish wham and whack its tail in the whirling waters. Suddenly someone knew who the whopper was as it whizzed by the wharf. One man shouted out loudly, 'Why that's Willie the Whale!' Ask the following questions about the story. 1. What size was the fish seen swimming in the bay? (whopper) 2. Where was the fish swimming? (Whisper Bay) 3. What was the water in the bay doing? (whirling) 4. What did the big fish do with its tail on the water? (whammed, whacked) 5. Who was the whopper of a fish? (Willie the Whale) Record the words whopper, whale, wham on a chart. Discuss the letters that each one begins with and the sound that it makes. Have the students place their hand in front of their mouths and say the words. They will discover that 'wh' is a windy sound. Review sh, ch, th, and wh with the following listening activity. Which word does not beloing in each group of words that I am going to say. **Word Groups:** 1. who, why, these, whiskers 2. thick, thin, them, shop 3. chin, chain, thaw, chess 4. shut, cheese, shore, shoot 5. cheer, they, them, the

Picture Key: Row 1: whiskers, thumb, chest, whistle Row 2: shower, whale, chimney, thermometer Row 3: wheelbarrow, shovel, cheek, wheelchair

Activity Worksheet: Page 154 The students are to record the correct digraph on the line in each box. **Answer Key:** Row1: wh, th, ch, wh Row 2: sh, wh, ch, th Row 3: th, sh, ck, sh

Day 5: Use the following instructions to test your students' ability to recognize the sounds made by the initial digraphs 'sh, ch, th, wh

A. Auditory Test Instructions: Listen to each word that I say. Circle the digraph that you hear at the beginning of each word. **Words:** 1. shame 2. chocolate 3. thankful 4. whimper 5. whirl 6. thought 7. chunk 8. shutters 9. chapter 10. thirsty **Answer Key:** 1. sh 2. ch 3. th 4. wh 5. wh 6. th 7. ch 8. sh 9. ch 10. th

B. Auditory and Visual Discrimination Test: Circle the correct digraph that you hear at the beginning of each picture. **Picture Key:** Row 1: shirt, whiskers, cheek, thimble Row 2: shell, thumb, children, shark Row 3: wheel, thief, chick-a-dee, wheelbarrow **Answer Key:** Row 1: sh, wh, ch, th Row 2: sh, th, ch, sh Row 3: wh, th, ch, wh

Name: ______________________________

Day 1	Week 25

The two letters in the sound '**sh**' make only **one** sound together at the beginning of a word. It is a sound that we make when we want everyone to be quiet.

Examples:

sheep

shells

Circle and **colour** all the pictures that begin with '**sh.**'

Name: ______________________________

Day 2	Week 25

The two letters in the sound '**ch**' make one sound at the beginning of a word. The sound it makes is like a train starting down the tracks.

Examples:

chair

chicken

Circle the sound that begins the name of each picture.

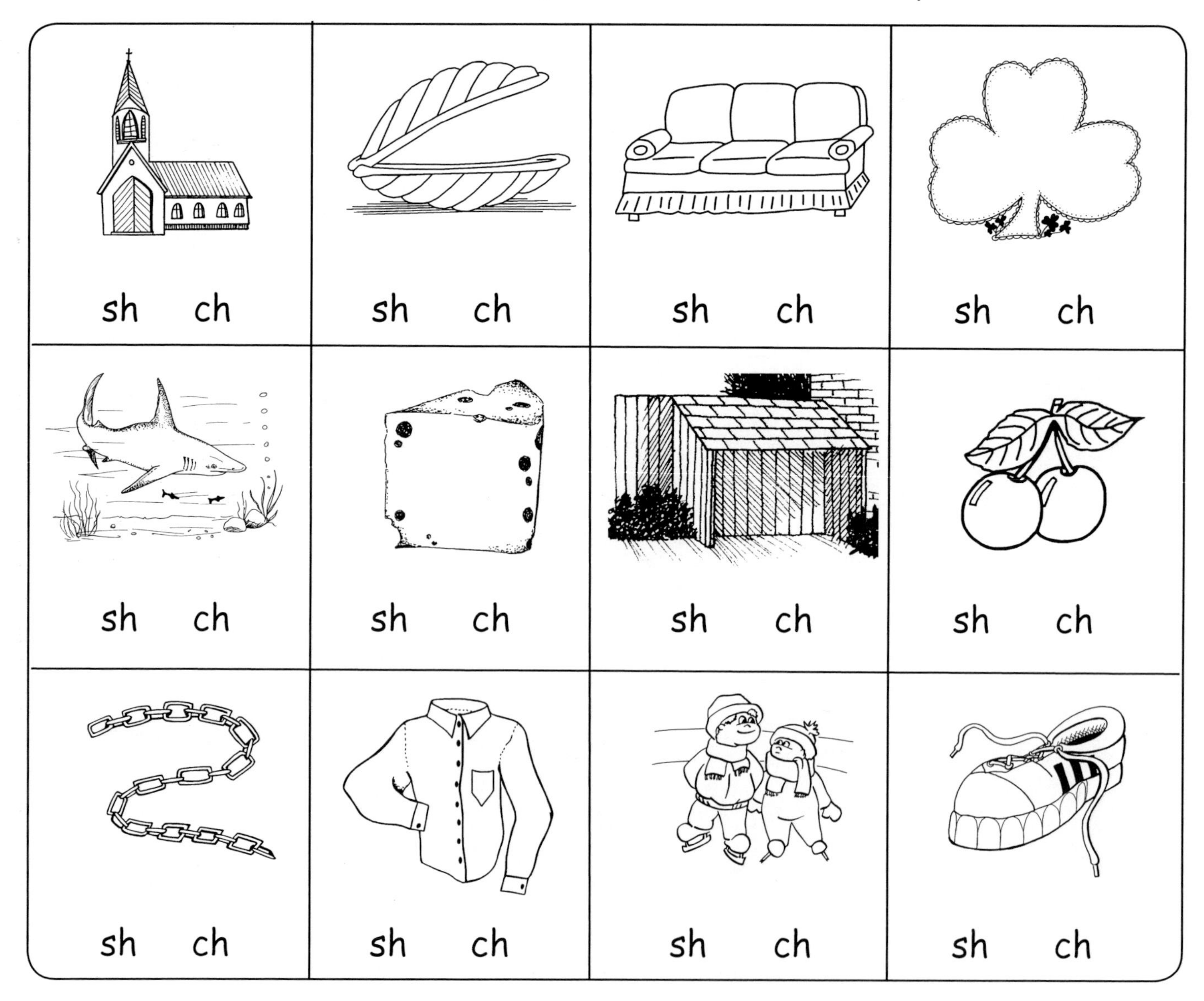

Name: ______________________________

Day 3	Week 25

The two letters in the sound **'th'** make only one sound together at the beginning of a word. This sound is when you stick out your tongue. It is a windy sound.

Examples:

thimble

13

thirteen

Print the sound that you hear at the beginning of each picture.

Is it **ch**, **sh**, or **th**?

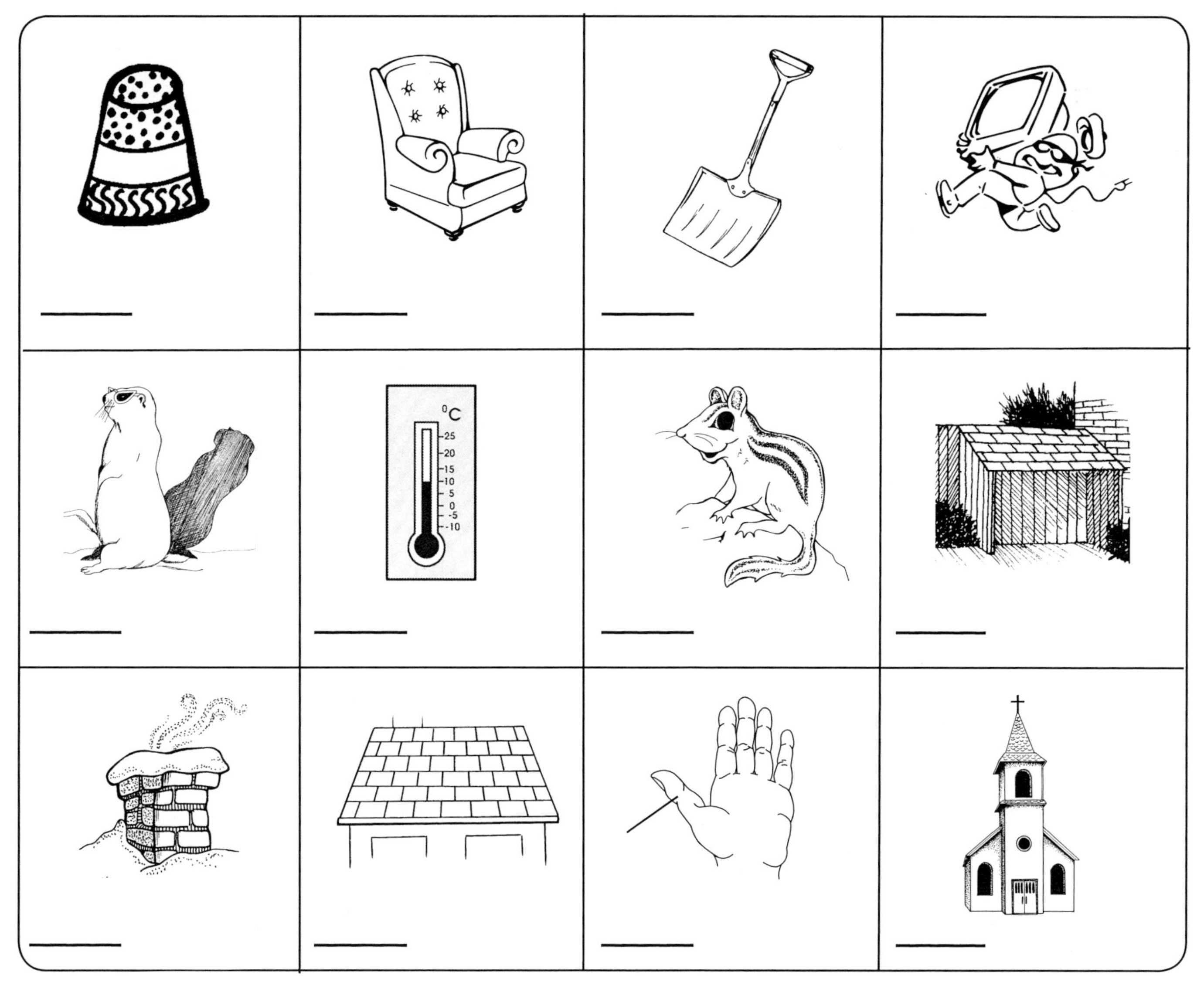

Name: ______________________________

Day 4	Week 25

The two letters in the sound '**wh**' make only **one** sound together at the beginning of a word. It is also a windy sound as air comes out when it is said.

Examples:

wheat 

whip 

Print the sound that you hear at the beginning of each picture.
Is it **sh**, **ch**, **th**, or **wh**?

 ISBN: 9781771586863

Name: ______________________________

Day 5	Week 25

A. Auditory Test on the digraphs **'sh, ch, th, wh'** in the **initial** position

1. th ch sh	2. wh sh ch	3. th wh sh	4. th wh sh	5. sh wh ch
6. ch wh th	7. sh ch th	8. wh ch sh	9. ch sh th	10. sh wh th

B. Auditory and Visual Discrimination Test

Week 26: Final Digraphs sh, ch, th

Objective: To teach the recognition of the final consonant digraphs sh, ch, and th and the sound each one makes.

Teacher Information: A digraph is a single sound made by two consonants. It may be found at the beginning or ending of a word. Final digraphs make the same sound as initial digraphs

Day 1: Introduce the '**sh**' digraph in the initial and final position in words. On a chart list the following words in two columns. **Word List 1:** fish, wish, dish, bush, push **Word List 2:** shell, ship, shoe, she, shake Have the students read the words silently. Then ask them what they have noticed about the two groups of words. (Both groups have the letters '**sh.**' Is there any difference in where '**sh**' is placed in both groups? In list one the words begin with 'sh.' In group 2 the words end with 'sh.' What does this tell you about the digraph 'sh?' It may be at the end of a word or at the beginning of a word. Listen to these words. Does 'sh' start or stop each word? **Words:** 1. shutters (Start) 2. smash (stop) 3. shovel (start) 4. shear (start) 5. trash (stop) 6. shear (start) 7. shore (start) 8. flash (stop) 9. crush (stop) 10. show (start)

Picture Key: Row 1: shells, trash, fish, shorts Row 2: shamrock, shape, cash, shark Row 3: leash, shirt, ship, shore Row 4: wash, dish, shadow, brush

Activity Worksheet: Page 157 The students are to place the digraph '**sh**' on the beginning line or ending line in each box to indicate its position in the word. **Answer Key:** Row 1: B, E, E , B Row 2: B, B, E, B Row 3: E, B, B, E Row 4: E, E, B, E

Day 2: Introduce the '**ch**' digraph in the final position in words. Listen to this group of words: cash, dash, mash, What sound do they all end with? (sh) Listen to this group of words: birch, march, search. What sound do they end with? (the digraph 'ch') Record the digraphs 'sh' and 'ch' on a chart. Have the students listen and tell which digraph they heard and its position in the word. Words could be recorded on the chart. **Words:** 1. wrench 2. crush 3. hash 4. plush 5. speech 6. bench 7. dash 8. couch 9. smash 10. crouch

Picture Key: Row 1: children, brush, peach, torch Row 2: trash, church, shirt, couch Row 3: churn, bench, porch, chain

Activity Worksheet: Page 158 The students are to record the digraph in its initial or fina position in each picture. **Answer Key:** Row 1: ch, n; br, sh; p, ch; t, ch, Row 2: tr, sh; ch, ch; sh, t; c, ch; Row 3: ch, n; b,ch . p, ch; ch, n

Day 3: Introduce the digraph '**th**' in the final position. Use the following story and have your students listen for words that end with the digraph '**th.**' Story: Seth is an aimal called a sloth. He lives in a jungle in South America. During the day Seth may travel north or south in the jungle swinging from tree to tree using both of his feet and both of his hands that have very long claws. Seth also likes to hang upside down using the strength in his strong legs. He seldom travels on paths that wander through the jungle beneath him. Seth enjoys eating leaves with his long tongue and chews them with his small teeth. Hiding in Seth's fur may be some insects such as a moth, a beetle or a cockroach. On a chart list the words that end with the digraph 'th.' You may have to read the story to your students again.

Picture Key: Row 1: wreath, moth, thumb, church Row 2: porch, teeth, beach, trash Row 3: match, tooth, brush, hatch

Activity Worksheet: Page 159 The students will record the initial and final sound heard in each picture on the lines in the box. **Answer Key:** Row 1: wr, th; m, th;cl, th; ch, ch Row 2: p, ch; t, th; b, ch; tr, sh Row 3: m, ch; t, th; br, sh; p, th

Day 4: Day 4: Review the initial and final consonant digraphs sh, ch, wh, and th in the initial and final position in words. Have the students listen for and tell the position of sh, ch, wh and th in each word. Say: Listen to each word that I am going to say. Tell how it begins and ends. Words: 1. broth (br, th) 2. pouch (p, ch) 3. flush (fl, sh) 4. trash (tr, sh) 5. speech (sp, ch) 6. beneath (b, th) 7. smooth (sm, th) 8. crunch (cr, ch) 9. smash (sm, sh) 10. clench (cl, ch)

Picture Key: Row 1: moth, lunch, chest, match Row 2: wreath, watch, brush, thief Row 3: chipmunk, mouth, bunch, beach Row 4: witch, tooth, trash, wheel

Activity Worksheet: Page 160 The student is to record the beginning and final sound to complete the word that refers to the picture. Answer Key: Row 1: Row 1: m, th; l, ch; ch, t; m, ch Row 2: wr, th; w, ch; br, sh; th, f Row 3: ch, k; m,th; b,ch; b, ch Row 4: w, ch; t, th; tr, sh; wh, l

Day 5: Use the following instructions to test your students ability to recognize the correct digraph heard at the beginning and ending of each picture. The digraphs are sh, ch, th, wh

A. Auditory Test Instructions: Page 161 Listen to each word that I say. Circle the correct digraph heard at the end of each picture.
Words: 1. fifth 2. march 3. squash 4. pouch 5. both 6. rash 7. slouch 8. birth 9. bench 10. booth Answer Key: 1. th 2. ch 3. sh 4. ch 5. th 6. sh 7. ch 8. th 9. ch 10. th

B. Auditory and Visual Test Instructions: Print the correct final digraph on the line to complete each word.
Picture Key: Row 1: wreath, hatch, fish, porch Row 2: speech, brush, couch, mouth Row 3: branch, dash, lunch, tooth
Answer Key: Row 1: th, ch, sh, ch Row 2: ch, sh, ch, th Row 3: ch, sh, ch, th

Name: ______________________________ | Day 1 | Week 26 |

The sound '**sh**' may be heard and seen at the **beginning** of a word.
Examples:

 **sh**eep  **sh**oe

The sound '**sh**' may also be seen and heard at the **end** of a word.
Examples:

 da**sh**  wi**sh**

How does each word **begin** or **end**? Print the '**sh**' sound on the beginning line or the ending line in each box.

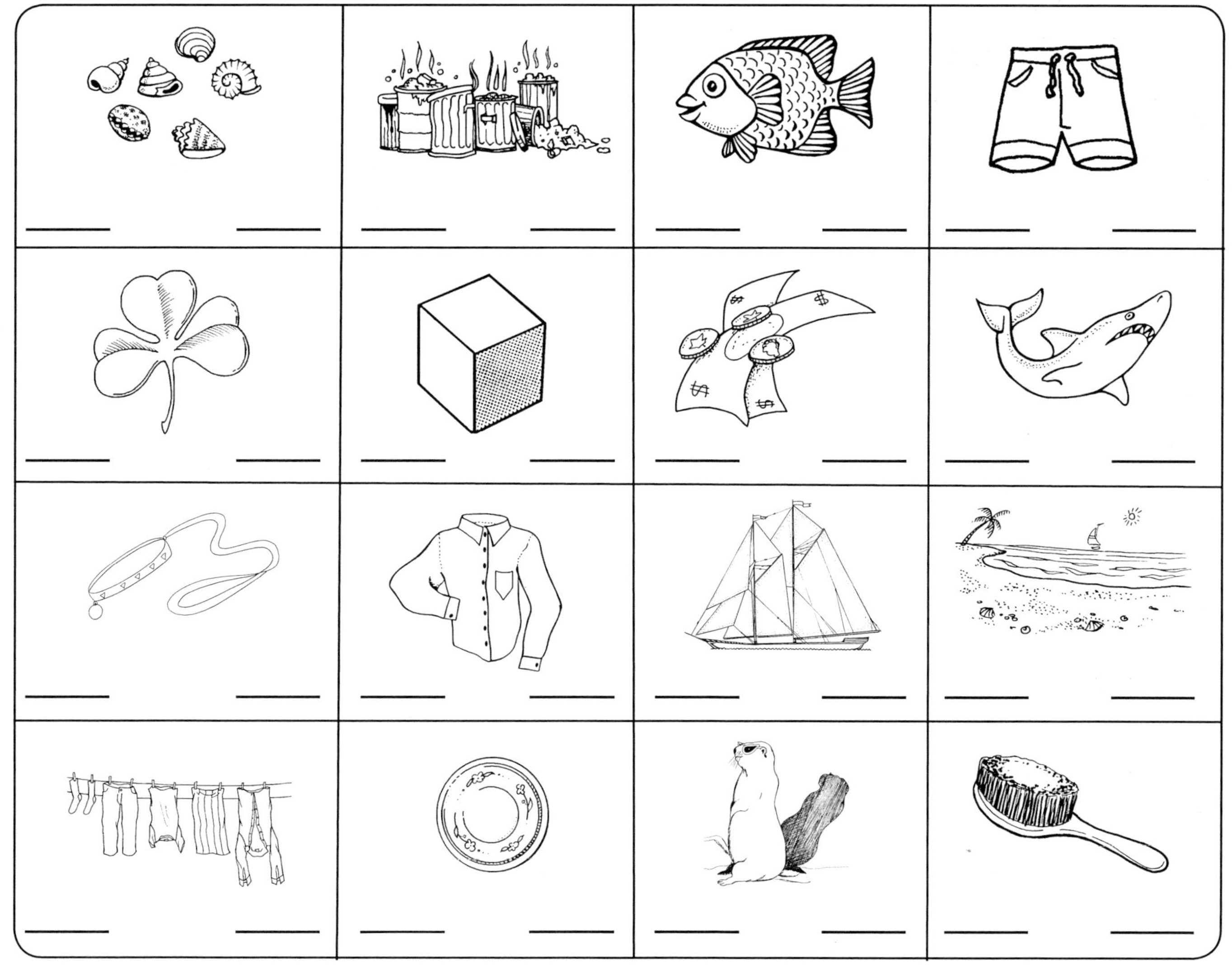

Name: ______________________________

Day 2	Week 26

The sound that '**ch**' maakes may be heard and seen at the **beginning** and **ending** of some words of some word.

Examples:

chicken

bun**ch**

Record the correct sound heard at the beginning and ending of each picture.

Name: ______________________________ | Day 3 | Week 26 |

The sound '**th**' may be heard and seen at the **beginning** or **ending** of a word.

Examples:

thumbtack

pa**th**

Record the correct sound heard at the **beginning** and **ending** of each word.

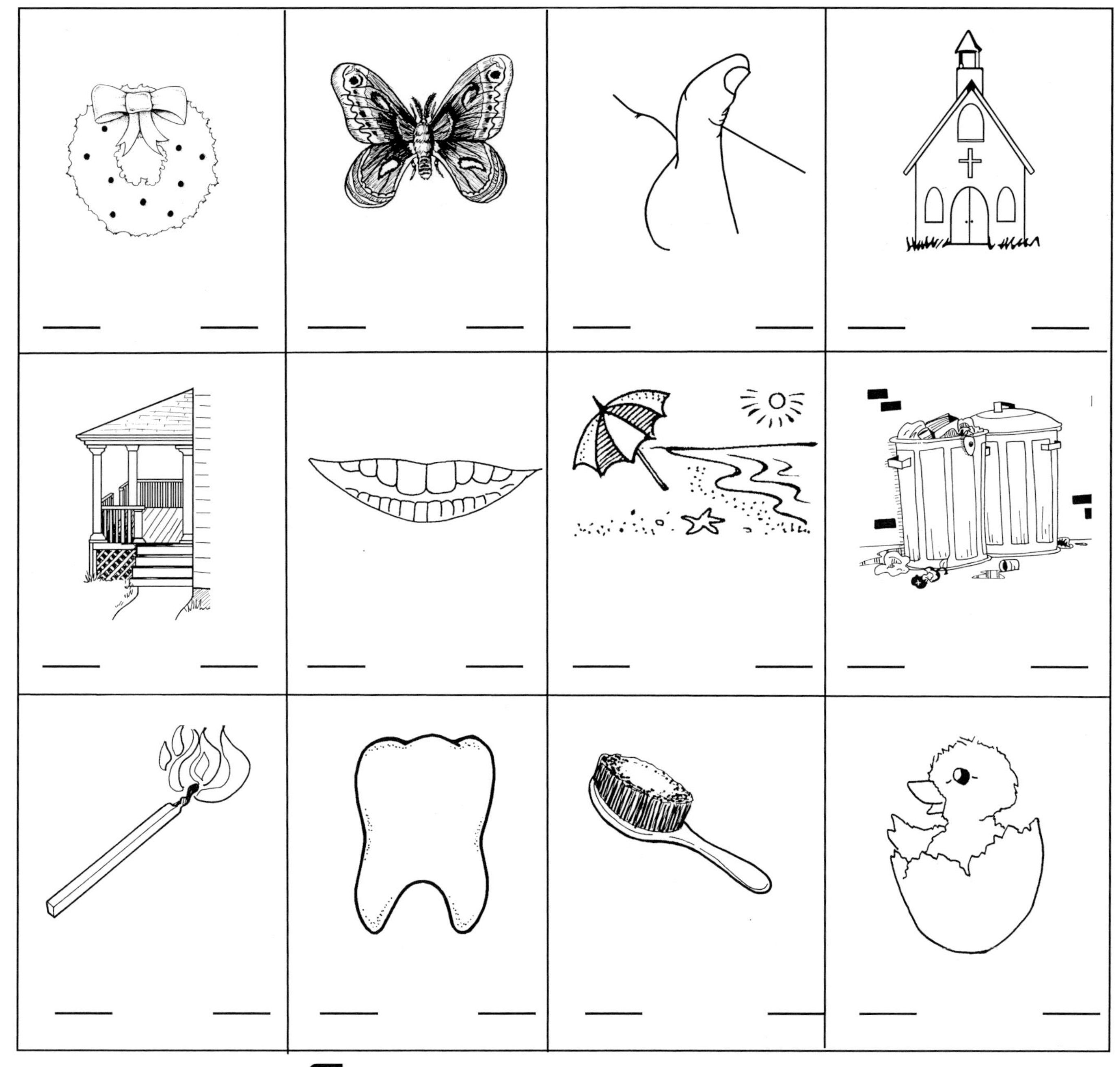

Name: ______________________________

Day 4	Week 26

The sounds '**sh**, **ch**, **wh**, and **th**' may be heard at the beginning and ending of a word.
Examples:

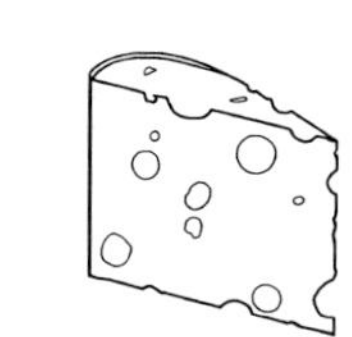
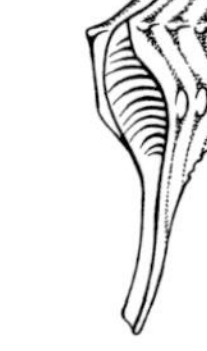

whale **th**umb **ch**eese **sh**ell bru**sh** pea**ch** mou**th**

Print the **first** and **last** sound that you hear in each word on the lines in each box.

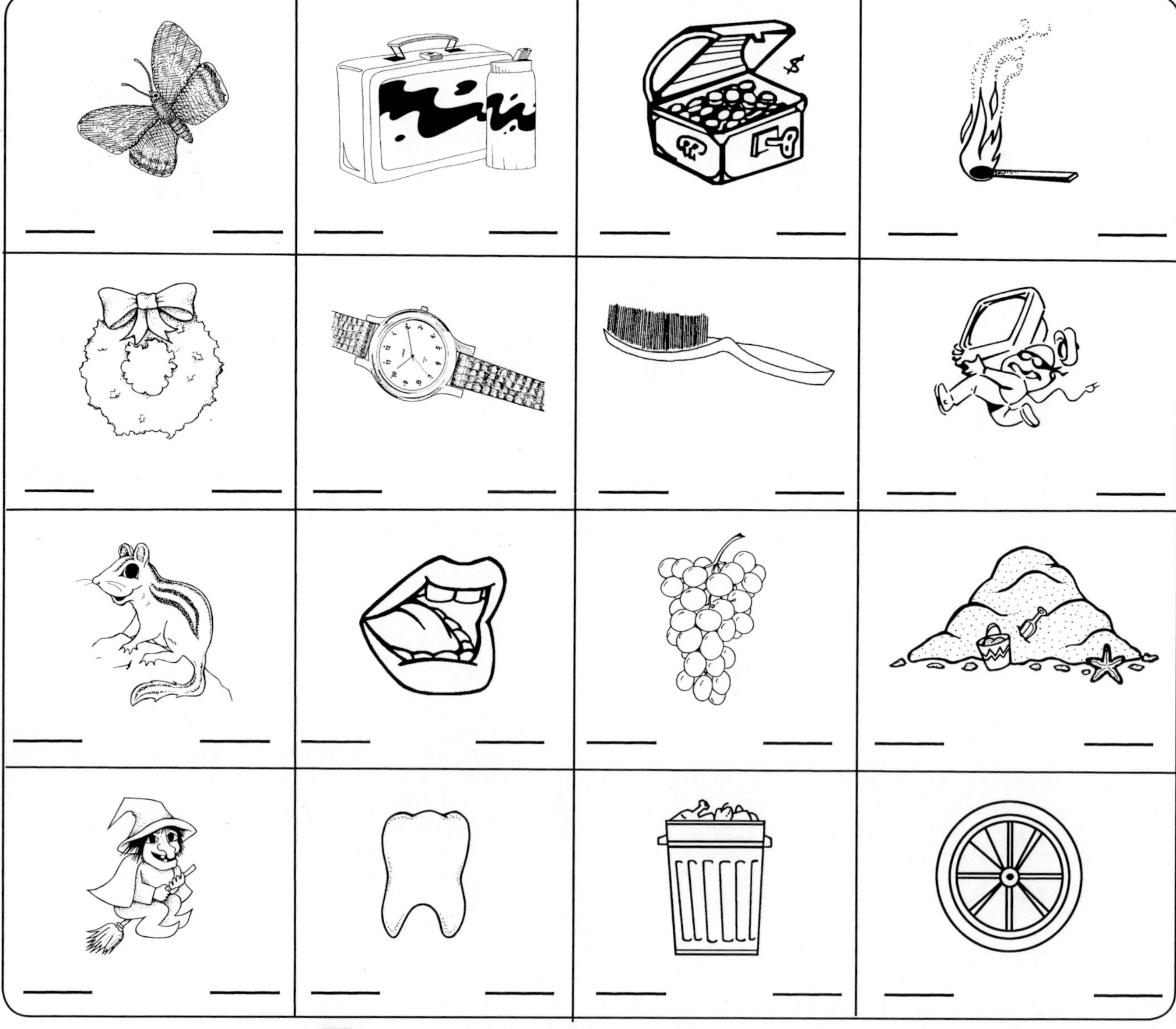

Name: ______________________________

Day 5	Week 26

A. Auditory Test on the final digraphs 'sh,ch,th'

1. sh ch th	2. sh ch th	3. sh ch th	4. sh ch th	5. sh ch th
6. sh ch th	7. sh ch th	8. sh ch th	9. sh ch th	10. sh ch th

B. Auditory and Visual Discrimination Test:

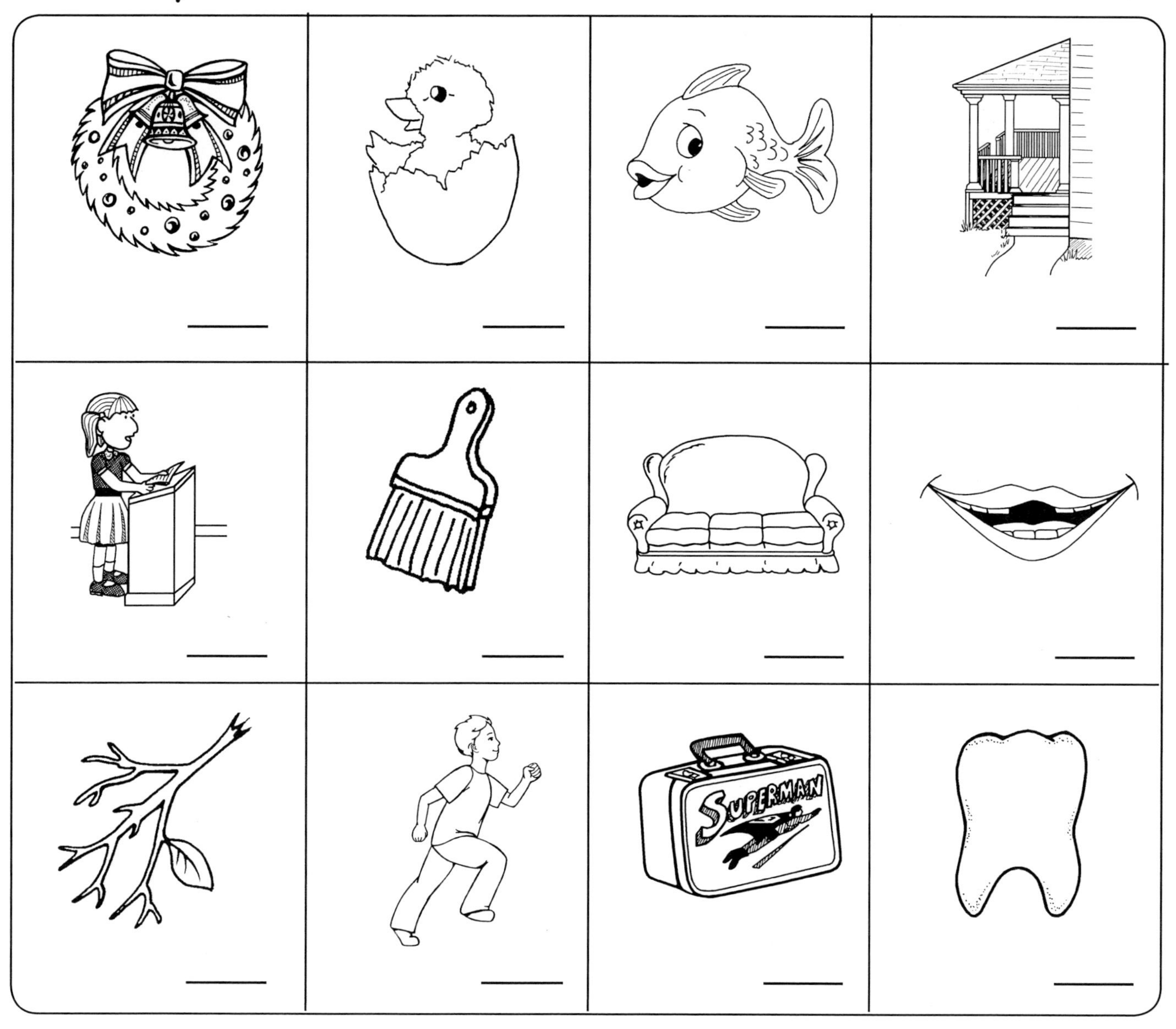

Week 27: Recognition of vowel Pairs 'ai, ay, ee, ea'

Objective: Teach the recognition of vowel pairs 'ai, ay, ee, ea, their sounds, and their placement in words.

Teacher Information: Most vowel combinations are found inside words. Most of the time the first vowel is heard in a vowel combination. For young students tell them this saying to help them to remember which vowel is heard in a vowel combination. 'When two vowels go walking in a word, the first one does the talking because the second vowel pinches the first vowel and makes it shout out its own name.'

Day 1: Introduce the vowel pairs '**ai**' and '**ay**.' Record the vowel pairs at the top of a chart. Say the following riddles to your students and record their answers on the chart in the correct column. **Riddles:** 1. I am a very small girl with a magic wand. (fairy) 2. I am used to colour a picture. (crayon) 3. It can be filled with water and carried. (pail) 4. Children like to do this outside at recess. (play) 5. This machine can pull many cars on a track. (train) 6. Horses like to eat this in their stall. (hay) 7. We get wet if this falls from the sky. (rain) 8. I carry dishes and food to people. (tray) Discuss the two lists and draw to your pupils' attention the vowel combinations in them, which vowel is being heard, which one is silent, and their position in the words.

Picture Key: Row 1: train, tray, tail, jay Row 2: spray, nail, paint, hay Row 3: rain, play, pail, pray

Activity Worksheet: Page 163 The student will complete each word with the correct vowel combination.
Answer Key: Row 1: ai, ay, ai, ay Row 2: ay, ai, ai, ay Row 3: ai, ay, ai, ay

Day 2: Introduce the vowel pairs '**ea**' and '**ee**.' Record the vowel combinations on a chart. Introduce the sounds that each combination makes. Remind your students of the saying about when two vowels go walking in a word. Have the students answer the following clues. 1. You have two that are used for walking. (feet) 2. It grows on a tree. (leaf) 3. You do this in your bed. (sleep) 4. You have this at breakfast, noon and suppertime. (meal) 5. It is a tall plant that gives us shade. (tree) 6. It is a part of your leg that bends. (knee) 7. It is a large body of water. (sea) 8. A car has four of them. (wheels) 9. It is a loud frightening cry. (scream) 10. It is the opposite to dirty. (clean) Draw to your students attention that '**ee**' and '**ea**' may begin a word or are found inside a word. Sometimes they are used to show different meanings. Examples: steal, steel; real, reel

Activity Worksheet: Page 164 The students will complete each sentence with the correct word.
Answer Key: 1. leaf 2. beach 3. team 4. creep 5. meet 6. seals 7. meat 8. peel

Day 3: Review the '**ai**, **ay**, **ee**, and **ea**' vowel pairs. Record the following words on a chart and have the students locate the word that answers each of the following clues. Words: brain, braids 2. tail, trail 3. train, tray 4. jeep, jeans 5. meat, meet 6. sail, snail 7. leap, leaf 8. tea, tray Clues: 1. They are made with long hair. (braids) 2. It is a part of an animal's body. (tail) 3. It makes a loud sound when it travels. (train) 4. They are a name for pants. (jeans) 5. It is a type of food. (meat) 6. It is a slow-moving creature. (snail) 7. It is a big jump. (leap) 8. It is a hot drink. (tea)

Picture Key: Row 1: mail, clam, paint, bee Row 2: meat, leaf, feet, pail Row 3: jeep, seal, snail, heel

Activity Worksheet: Page 165 The students will circle the correct word for each picture. **Answer Key:** Row1: mail, clam, paint, bee Row 2: meat, leaf, feet, pail Row 3: jeep, seal, pail, heel

Day 4: Review the vowel pairs ' ai, ay, ee, and ea' with the following exercise. At the top of a chart print the vowel pairs. Under the pairs print the following words with the vowels missing. 1. t __ __ l 2. gr __ __ 3. p __ __ n 4. thr __ __ 5. qu __ __ n 6. l __ __ p 7. s __ __ t 8. b __ __ f Have the students give the correct vowel pair for each word. **Possible Answers:** tail, gray, pain, three, queen, leap, seat, beef,

Picture Key: Row 1: chain, hay, nail Row 2: feet, train, rain Row 3: pea, tray, beak Row 4: dream, meat, sea
Activity Worksheet: Page 166 The students will circle the word that describes the picture.
Answer Key: Row 1: chain, hay, nail Row 2: feet, train, rain Row 3: pea, tray, beak Row 4: dream, meat, sea

Day 5: Use the following instructions to test your students' ability to recognize the correct vowel pair heard inside each word. The vowel pairs are ai, ay, ee, and ea.
A. Auditory Test Instructions: Listen to each word. Circle the vowel pair that you hear in each word.
Words: 1. bee 2. paid 3. bait 4. say 5. creek 6. faint 7. steep 8. play 9. read 10. dream **Answer Key:** 1. ee 2. ai 3. ai 4. ay 5. ee 6. ai 7. ee 8. ay 9. ea 10. ea
B. Auditory and Visual Discrimination Test Instructions: Print the correct vowel pair heard in each picture on the line provided. **Picture Key:** Row 1: tray, leaf, chain, wheel Row 2: snail, sheep, hay, read Row 3: peach, jail, jeep, teach **Answer Key:** Row 1: ay, ea, ai, ee Row 2: ai, ee, ay, ea Row 3: ea, ai, ee, ea

Name: ______________________________ Day 1 | Week 27

Inside many words two vowels walk together but only the first one does the talking.

Examples:

braids

ray

Complete each word with the correct **vowel pair**.
Is it '**ai**' or '**ay**' that is heard.

tr ___ n	tr ___	t ___ l	bluej ___
spr ___	n ___ l	p ___ nt	h ___
r ___ n	pl ___	p ___ l	pr ___

Name ______________________________

Day 2	Week 27

When **two** vowels go walking together in a word, the **first** one does the talking.

Examples:

bee

beach

Complete each sentence with the correct word.

1. The wind blew the ______________ off the tree.

   (leap, leak, leaf)

2. We like to play in the sand at the ______________ .

   (beep, bee, beach)

3. Jill wants to play on the baseball ______________.

   (teeth, team, tree)

4. The baby can ______________ fast across the floor.

   (cheese, creek, creep)

5. We will ______________ you at the park by the lake.

   (meet, meat, mean)

6. There were six ______________ doing tricks in the big pool.

   (sheep, seals, bees)

7. My dinner did not have any ______________ in it.

   (meet, mean, meat)

8. Can you ______________ the skin from an orange.

   (peal, peek, peel)

Name: ______________________________

Day 3 | Week 27

Inside a word there may be **two** vowels together but it is the **first** one that makes all the noise.

Examples:

train

tray

bee

leaf

Circle the word that matches each picture in each box.

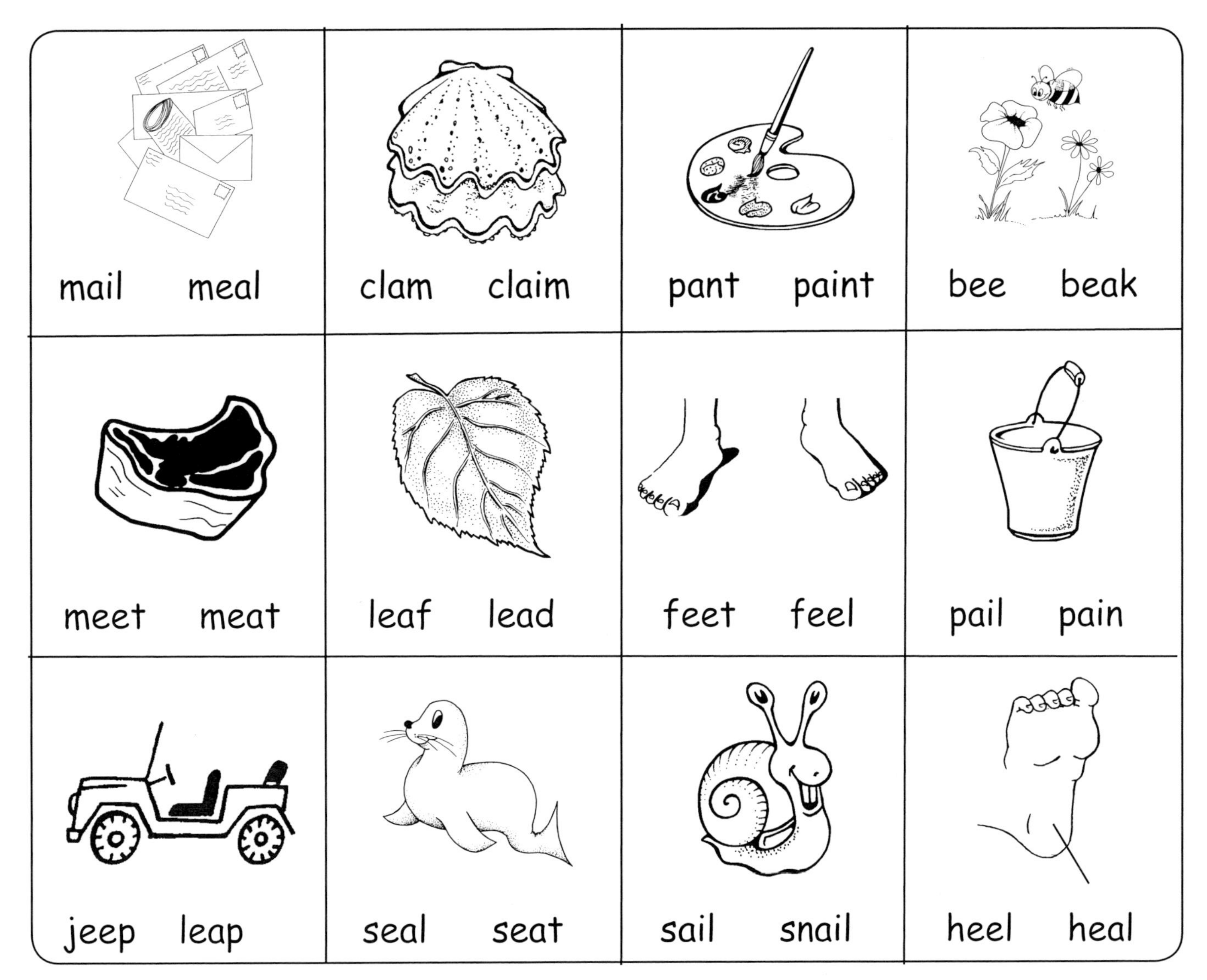

Name: ______________________________

Day 4 | Week 27

Many words have the sounds that '**ai**, **ay**, **ee**, and **ea**' make inside them or at the end of them.

Read the words in the box beside the picture. **Circle** the word that tells about each picture.

 chair cheer chain	 hail hay heat	 need nail neat
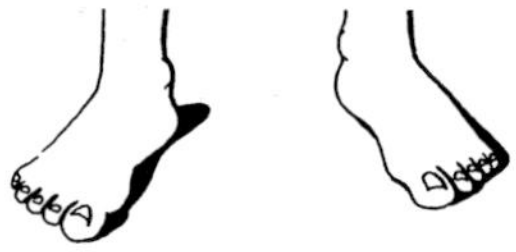 feed feel feet	 trail tail train	 rain rail ray
 pay pain pea	 trap try tray	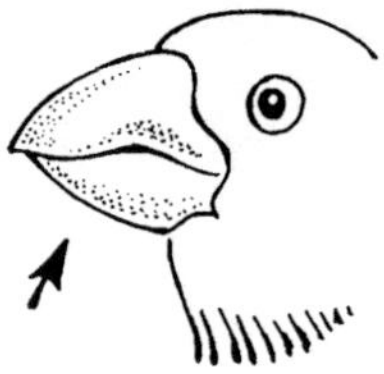 beak bean beam
 deep dream day	 may meat maid	 see say sea

Name: ______________________________

Day 5	Week 27

A. **Auditory Test** on the vowel pairs '**ai**, **ay**, **ee**, and **ea**.'

1. ee ea	2. ai ay	3. ea ai	4. ay ee	5. ee ai
6. ea ai	7. ee ay	8. ay ai	9. ee ai	10. ea ee

B. Auditory and Visual Discrimination Test

Week 28: Recognition of the Vowel Pairs 'oa' and 'ow'

Objective: To teach the recognition of the vowel pairs '**oa**' and '**ow**', their sounds, and their placement in words.

Teacher Information: Most vowel combinations are found inside words while some vowels will form a sound team with a consonant. The vowel combination '**oa**' is found inside a word or it may lead the word as in **oat** and **oar**. The '**ow**' vowel combination is usually found at the end of a word. Examples: **coat, grow** Both combinations usually make the long '**o**' sound.

Day 1: On a chart print the words 'coat' and 'snow.' What sound do you hear in both words? (long o) Which letters in coat make the long 'o 'sound? (oa) Which letters in snow make the long 'o' sound? (ow) Are both letters in the word 'snow' vowels? (No) Which letter is not a vowel? (w) What is the letter 'w?' It is a consonant. Which of the two letters in snow do you hear? (o) Does the 'w' do any talking ? (No) Explain that if the letters 'ow' are found at the end of a word or in a word, the long 'o' sound is usually heard. Have your students listen to the following words and have them tell which group they hear. Listen to each word that I say. Tell me which 'o' sound in each pair is doing the talking in each word. Words: 1. grow (ow) 2. boat (oa) 3. bow (ow) 4. load (oa) 5. slow (ow) 6. float (oa) 7. show (ow) 8. float (oa)

Picture Key: Row 1: goat, bow, toad Row 2: soap, loaf, snow Row 3: road, blow, coat

Activity Worksheet: Page 169 The students are to circle the word that names each picture. Answer Key: Row 1: goat, bow, toad Row 2: soap, loaf, snow 3. road, blow, coat

Day 2: Review the vowel combinations 'oa' and 'ow.' On a chart print the following incomplete words: 1. r___ 2. b___t 3. sh___ 4. sl___ 5. l___f 6. b___ 7. t___m 8. r___d 9. cr___ 10. c___l The students are to supply the missing sounds to make words that have the long 'o' sound. **Answer Key:** 1. now 2. bow 3. show 4. slow 5. leaf 6. bow 7. team 8. road 9. crow 10. coal

Activity Worksheet: Page 170 The students are to complete each sentence with the correct word.

Answer Key: 1. row 2. oats 3. crow 4. toad 5. bow 6. snow 7. load 8. grow 9. soap 10. shadow

Day 3: Review the vowel combinations 'oa' and 'ow.' Listen to each word that I say carefully. Tell me where you hear the '**oa**' and '**ow**' sounds. Is it inside the word or at the end of each word that I say? **Words:** 1. know (end) 2. coach (inside) 3. flow (end) 4. foam (inside) 5. know (end) 6. arrow (end) 7. toast (inside) 8. slow (end) 9. burrow (end) 10. roast (inside)

Picture Key: Row 1: bow, soap, bowl Row 2: toad, float, boat Row 3: crow, coal, loaf Row 4: goat, rain, cow

Activity Worksheet: Page 171 The students will circle the correct word to match each picture.

Answer Key: Row 1: bow, soap, bowl Row 2: toad, row, float Row 3: goat, goal, coach Row 4: roar, roast, loaf

Day 4: On a chart print the vowel combinations '**ai, ay, ee, ea, oa,** and **ow** at the top. Record the beginning, middle, and endings. Example: 1. s___t 2. pl___ 3. gr___ 4. bl___ 5. t___d 6. ___ow 7. p___s 8. tr___ 9. gr___n 10. t___l. Have the students suggest the vowel combinations for each word and record each one on the chart. Have the students read the words aloud

Activity Worksheet: Page 172 The students are to record the correct word in each sentence.
Answer Key: 1. row, boat 2, hay, oats 3. snow 4. grow, year 5. coat, hole 6. toad 7. fairy 8. sleep, chair 9. bee, around 10. play, team

Day 5. Use the following instructions to test your students ability to recognize the following vowel combinations 'ai, ay, ee, ea, oa, and ow'.

Auditory Test Instructions: Listen to each word that I say. Circle the vowel combination that you hear in the word that I say. **Words:** 1. spray 2. cheap 3. snail 4. queen 5. toast 6. bow 7. leap 8. wait 9. free 10. crow **Answer Key:** 1. ay 2. ea 3. ai 4. ee 5. oa 6. ow 7. ea 8. ai 9. ee 10. ow

B. Auditory and Visual Discrimination Test Instructions: Print the correct vowel pair heard in each picture on the line provided. **Picture Key:** Row 1: tray, leaf, chain, wheel Row 2: snail, sheep, hay, eating Row 3: peach, jail, jeep, teach **Answer Key:** Row 1: ay; ea; ai; ee Row 2: ai; ee; ay; ea Row 3: ea; ai; ee; ea

Name: ______________________________

Day 1	Week 28

In the word '**boat**' we hear the **long** '**o**' sound spelled '**oa**.'
In the word '**bow**' we hear the **long** '**o**' sound spelled '**ow**'
Examples:

boat

bowl

Circle the word in each box that tells the **name** of the picture.

glow goat	bow bowl	load toad
soap boat	low loaf	show snow
row rode	blow boat	coat coal

Name: ______________________________ | Day 2 | Week 28 |

Many words have the vowel combinations '**oa**' and '**ow**.'

Use the words in the word box to complete each sentence correctly.

Word Box

shadow	**grow**	**snow**	**toad**	**oats**
row	**crow**	**bow**	**load**	**soap**

1. The boy can ___________ the big boat well.
2. The goat likes to eat ___________ for lunch every day.
3. The ___________ flew to the top of the big maple tree.
4. A little ___________ lived under the pile of leaves.
5. The girl had a red ___________ in her brown hair.
6. The ___________ slowly fell and was all over the ground.
7. We will ___________ our car with things for our big trip.
8. In the spring plants will ___________ in the gardens.
9. Wash your hands well with the ___________.
10. Did the groundhog see its ___________ today?

Name: ______________________________

Day 3 | Week 28

You can hear and see the vowel sounds '**oa**' and '**ow**' in many words.

boat

snow

coat

bow

Put an **'x'** beside the word that **does not name** the picture in each box.

bowl bow	sow soap	bowl boat
tow toad	float row	coat float
grow goat	goal coal	poach coach
roar row	coast roast	low loaf

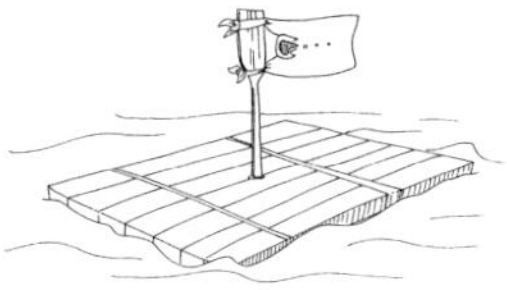

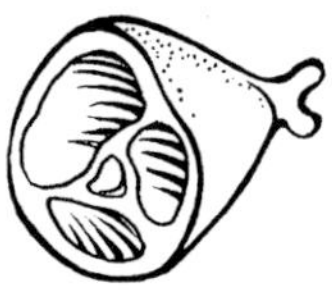

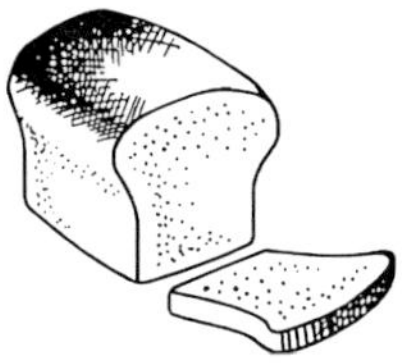

 ISBN: 9781771586863

Name: ______________________________

Day 4 | Week 28

Read each sentence carefully.

Choose **words** from the **Word Box** that will complete the sentences. **Print** the word on the line to complete each sentence.

Word Box

coat	hole	year	boat	oars	snow	chair	grow	row
hay	toad	fairy	sleep	bee	team	around	play	

1. Can you ____________ your ____________ across the lake.

2. The boy fed the horses some ____________ and ____________ for a snack.

3. The children loved to make things with the ____________.

4. Did the plants ____________ well in your garden this ____________.

5. Bill tore his ____________ on the fence and made a big ____________ in it.

6. The ____________ hopped all over the garden looking for some flies.

7. The tooth ____________ left some money under Lisa's pillow.

8. The cat went to ____________ in the big ____________.

9. The ____________ flew all ____________ the garden.

10. Jim wants to ____________ on the school's baseball ____________.

Name: ______________________________

Day 5	Week 28

A. Auditory Test on the Vowel Combinations: ai, ay, ee, ea, oa, and ow

1. ee ea ay	2. ow ea ay	3. ai ee ay	4. ee ow ay	5. oa ee ai
6. ea ay ow	7. ai ay ea	8. ai ay ee	9. ay ow ee	10. ow ay ea

B. Auditory and Visual Discrimination Test:

____	____	____	____
____	____	____	____
____	____	____	____

Week 29: Double Vowel Combinations of 'oo, oa, and ow'

Objective: To teach the long and short sounds of **'oo'** as in sch**oo**l' and in '**hook**'.

Teacher Information: The double vowel combination '**oo**' has two different sounds. One makes a long sound as in 'm**oo**n' and the other is a short sound as in 'b**oo**k.' The **long 'oo'** sound makes you slightly close your lips and the sound comes from the back of the throat. The **short 'oo'** sound is made inside the mouth and shoots out quickly. Its sound is similar to the short **u** vowel sound. Teach the '**oa**' sound and the '**ow**' sound as well

Day 1: On a chart print the following sentences. 1.The loon swam smoothly across the cool water. 2. A kangaroo lives in a herd called a troop. 3. The moose got loose and zoomed around the forest. Underline the words as indicated. Read or have a student read sentence #1. Discuss the underlined words. What two letters are the same and together in each word? (oo) What sound does the 'oo'make in each word? (an 'oo' sound) Continue the exercise with sentences 2 and 3.

Picture Key: Row 1: moon, hook, goose, book Row 2: crook, broom, foot, moose Row 3: loon, school, wood, cook Row 4: spool, pool, boots, wool

Activity Worksheet: Page 175 The students will colour the pictures that have the 'oo' sound as in 'moon.'

Answer Key: Pictures to be coloured and labelled. Row 1: moon, goose Row 2: broom, moose Row 3: loon, school Row 4: spool, boot

Day 2: On a chart record the words '**good**' and '**goose**' side by side. Ask your students how the two words look the same. (They look the same because they each begin with the initial consonant 'g' and have the two letters 'oo' following it. Say the word '**good**'. Say the word '**goose**.' Do the letters '**oo**' in each word make the same sound? (No) What does the '**oo**' say in 'good?' (uh) What does the '**oo**' say in 'goose?' (ooh) Listen carefully to the words that I say and tell me in which list I should print it. **Words:** 1. shook (good) 2. food (goose) 3. spoon (goose) 4. roof (good) 5. moon (goose) 6. hoop (goose) 7. brook (good) 8. school (goose) 9. tooth (goose) 10. hood (good)

Picture Key: Row 1: spool, broom, book Row 2: moose, boot, hook Row 3: hood, stool, cook Row 4: foot, roof, pool

Activity Worksheet: Page 175 The students will circle the word that describes the picture.

Answer Key: Row 1: spool, broom, book Row 2: moose, boot, hook Row 3: hood, stool, cook Row 4: foot, roof, pool

Day 3: Introduce the vowel consonant combination '**ow**' that makes the same sound as '**oa**' and '**oo**.' Record the following sentences on a chart. Underline the 'ow' words. Have the students read them. **Sentences:** 1. The crow is a big black bird. 2. Plants grow in gardens in the spring. 3. Snow fell all over the ground. What can you tell us about the underlined words in the sentences? (They all have the same sound at the end.) What are the letters in the sound? (ow) What sound does the 'ow' make? (long o) Which letter is the only one heard? (o) Is it the long or short 'o' vowel sound? (long) Look at these words on the chart and say them. **Words:** blow, now, low, cow, row, plow, slow, Which words have the 'ow' sound that makes the long o vowel sound? What sound does the '**ow**' make in the other words. (The sound is the same sound that you make when you hurt yourself.)

Picture Key: Row 1: moon, snow, goat Row 2: crow, broom, book, Row 3: toad, soap, stool Row 4: bow, roof, boat

Activity Worksheet: Page 176 The students is to circle the word that describes the picture. **Answer Key:** Row 1: moon, snow, goat Row 2: crow, broom, book Row 3: toad, soap, stool, Row 4: bow, roof, boat

Day 4: On a chart record the vowel combinations '**oo**' as in **moon**; '**oo**' as in **book**; and '**ow**' as in **flow.** Print the following list of words on the chart with missing sounds. Have the students finish the word with one of the vowel combinations at the top of the chart and say it. **List of Words:** 1. b__t (oo) 2. b__ (ow or oo) 3. gr ___ (ow) 4. b __m (oo) 5. sl __ (ow) 6. r __ t (oo) 7. bl __ (ow) 8. h __ k (oo) 9. w__d (oo) 10. sh __ (ow)

Activity Sheet: Page 177 The students are to print the missing words in its correct sentence.
Answer Key: 1. moose 2. foot 3. boat 4. soap 5. crow 6. broom 7. blow 8. grow 9. toad 10. loaf

Day 5: Use the following instructions to test your students' ability to recognize the correct sound combination heard inside each word. The sound pairs are '**oo**, **oa**, and **ow**.'

A. Auditory Test Instructions: Listen to each word that I say. Circle the vowel pair that you hear in each word.
Words: 1. hook 2. stool 3. flow 4. bow 5. tool 6. boat 7. look 8. slow 9. coat 10. grow
Answer Key: 1. oo 2. oo 3. ow 4. ow 5. ow 5. oa 7. oo 8. ow 9. oa 10. ow

B. Auditory and Visual Discrimination Test Instructions: Print the correct sound pair heard in each picture on the line provided. **Picture Key:** Row 1: stool, brook, crow Row 2. hook, pool, boat 3. boot, coat, roof 4. snowman, soap, broom **Answer Key:** Row 1: oo; oo; ow Row 2: oo; oa; oa Row 3: oo; oa; oo Row 4: ow; oa; oo

Name: ______________________________

Day 1	Week 29

In the word '**moon**' the two letters '**oo**' make **one** sound. This sound can be heard when we don't like to taste, touch or see something nasty.

Examples:

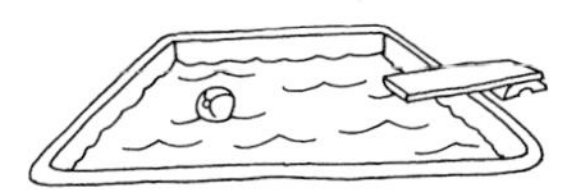

pool

stool

Colour only the pictures with the '**oo**' sound as in **pool** and **stool**. **Print** the sound heard inside on the line.

______	______	______	______
______	______	______	______
______	______	______	______
______	______	______	______

Name: ______________________________

Day 2 | Week 29

The vowels **'oo'** are often seen together in a word. In some words they say '**uh**' as in **brook** while in the word **spoon**, they say '**o-o-o-h**.'
Examples:

br**oo**k

sp**oo**n

Circle the word in each box that is the **name** of the picture.

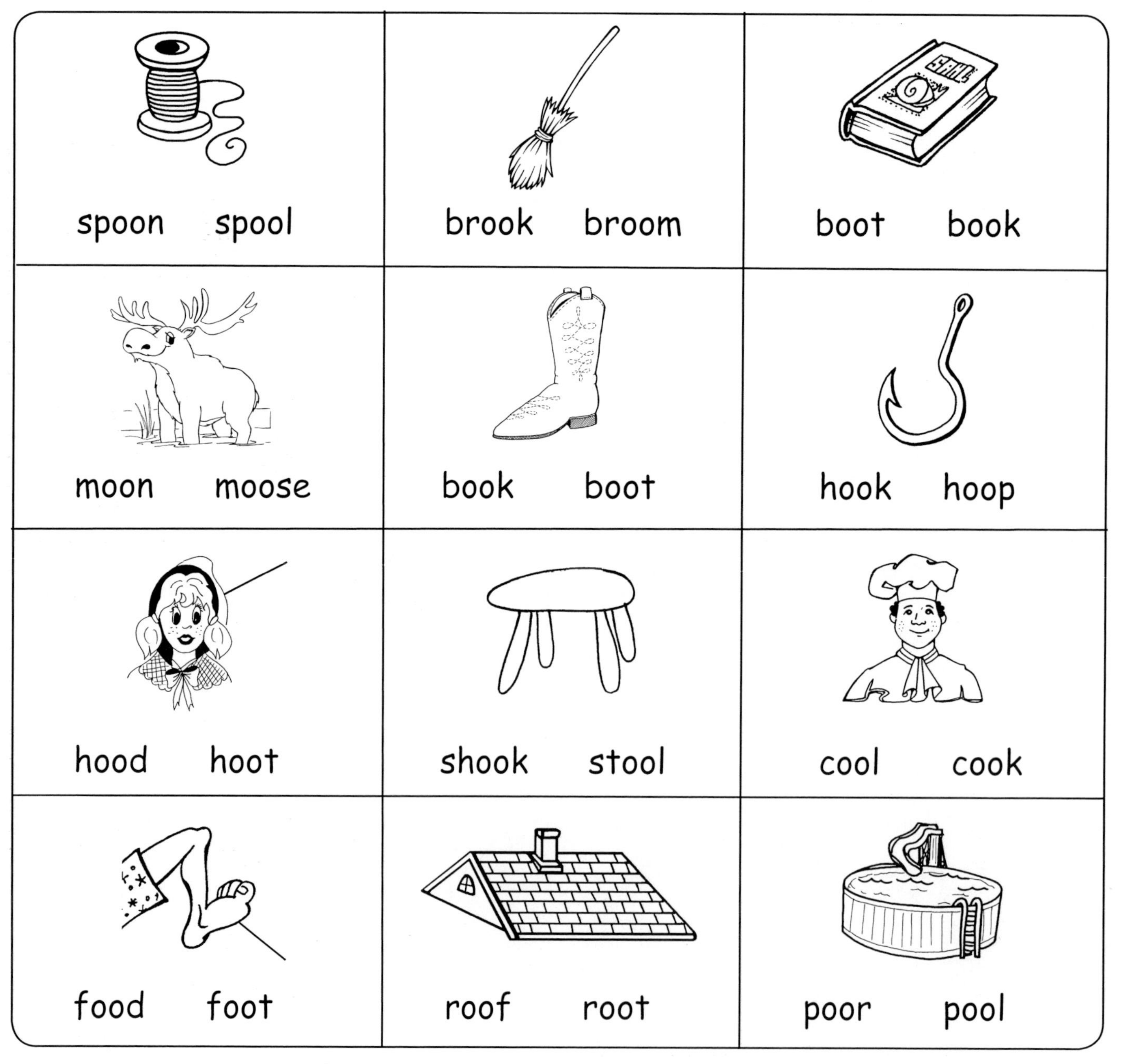

SSR1140 ISBN: 9781771586863

Name: ______________________________ | Day 3 | Week 29 |

The sounds '**oa**' and '**ow**' often make the same sound in words. The sound '**oa**' is often found in '**coat**.' The sound '**ow**' is often found in '**blow**.'

Examples:

coat  **blow** 

Circle the word that names each picture.

moo moon moan	sow snow slow	goal grow goat
cool coal crow	broom book boom	boot book boat
toad took tool	slow spoon soap	snow stool stood
bow blow book	road roof row	boot boat bow

Name: ______________________________ | Day 4 | Week 29

The sound '**oo**' can make **two** sounds.

One is a **long** sound as in moon and the other is a **short** sound as in hook.

The vowel sound '**ow**' can make **two** sounds as well.

It can say '**ow**' as in **how** or '**ow**' as in **snow**.

moon

book

bow

crow

Print the correct word in each sentence.

toad	**broom**	**soap**	**foot**	**loaf**
moose	**boat**	**crow**	**blow**	**grow**

1. A ____________ is a very big animal.
2. The boy cut his ____________ on the glass.
3. The ____________ sailed across the lake.
4. Did you wash your hands with the ____________?
5. A ____________ is a big black bird that caws.
6. Sweep the floor with this new ______________.
7. Can you ____________ out all the candles on your cake?
8. The boy did not ____________ very tall.
9. A ____________ has bumpy skin and big eyes.
10. I went to the store to buy a ____________ of bread.

Name: ______________________________

Day 5	Week 29

A. **Auditory Test** on the vowel sounds **'oo, ow,** and **oa.'**

1. oo ow	2. oo ow	3. oa ow	4. oo ow	5. oa ow
6. oo oa	7. oo ow	8. oo ow	9. oa ow	10. oo ow

B. **Auditory and Visual Discrimination Test**

________	________	________
________	________	________
________	________	________
________	SOAP ________	________

 ISBN: 9781771586863

Week 30: The Two Sounds of 'Yy' as a Vowel and the One Sound as a Consonant

Objective: To introduce the letter 'y' as a vowel and a consonant and its three sounds.

Teacher Information: The letter '**Yy**' can be a consonant at the beginning of a word that says 'yuh.' It can also be a long or short vowel at the end of a word. When it is a long vowel it says '**e**' as in 'city' and as a short vowel it has the long vowel '**i**' sound as in 'by.'

Day 1: Record the following words on a chart. **Words:** happy, city, funny. Ask your students the following questions. How are these words the same? (They all have the letter 'y' at the end.) Let's say the words. How are these words the same when you say them? (They have the long 'e' sound at the end.) When the letter 'y' is a vowel it has a long 'e' sound. This happens at the end of a word. When the letter 'Yy' is a consonant it is heard at the beginning of a word. Listen to these words. Is the letter 'y' a vowel or a consonant? Did you hear it at the beginning or the end of the word? **Words:** 1. fairy (end, vowel) 2. young (beginning, consonant) 3. yard (beginning, consonant) 4. funny (end, vowel) 5. pony (end, vowel) 6. yellow (beginning, consonant) 7. easy (end, vowel) 8. yes (beginning, consonant) 9. funny (vowel, ending) 10. young (beginning, consonant)

Picture Key: Row 1: baby, fly, canary Row 2: hockey, yawn, yarn Row 3: sky, yard, yolk

Activity Worksheet: Page 181 The student is to circle the 'y' as a consonant or as a vowel in each picture. **Answer Key:** Row 1: vowel; consonant, vowel Row 2: vowel, consonant, consonant Row 3: vowel, consonant, consonant

Day 2: On a chart record the following words: funny, baby, fairy, bunny, story. Read them to your students or have them read them independently. What do you notice about the group of words. (They all end with the letter "y.') What sound does the letter 'y' make? (long e sound) Is the 'y' in this group of words a consonant or a vowel? (a vowel) What other vowel sound can the letter 'y' make? (long 'i') Listen to each word that I am going to say. Does it end with the long 'e' sound or the long 'i' sound? **Words:** 1. poppy (long e) 2. spy (long i) 3. puppy (long e) 4. try (long i) 5. happy (long e) 6. shy (long i) 7. easy (long e) 8. poppy (long e)

Picture Key: Row 1: baby, fly, bunny, sky Row 2: family, cry, buy, puppy Row 3: spy, happy, fry, money

Activity Worksheet: Page 182 The students will record the name of the vowel sound heard at the end of each word as long 'i' or long 'e'. **Answer Key:** Row 1: long e, long i, long e, long i Row 2: long e, long i, long i, long e Row 3: long i, long e, long i, long e

Day 3: On a chart record the following words in columns. Column 1: buy, my, sky Column 2: bunny, fairy, funny Column 3: yellow, yard, yell Have the students read column 1's words. Ask: In what ways are these words the same? (They all end with the letter 'y'.) What sound does the letter 'y' make? (Long vowel 'i' sound) Read the words in Column 2. In what way are they the same? (They all end with the letter 'y.') What sound does the letter 'y' make at the end of the words? (long vowel 'e') Read the words in Column 3: How is this group of words different? (They all begin with the letter 'y.') How is this sound different? (It begins each word as a consonant.) What three things did you learn about the letter 'y?' (The letter 'y'is a consonant when it is found at the beginning of a word or a vowel at the end of a word. At the end of a word the letter 'y' makes the long 'e' or long 'i' sound.

Picture Key: Row 1: bunny, sky, yarn Row 2: fly, yard, fairy Row 3: cry, lady, yawn

Activity Worksheet: Page 183 The students will circle the name of the sound made by the letter "Yy' in each box. **Answer Key:** Row 1: long e; long i.; consonant Row 2: long i, consonant, long e Row 3: long i; long e; consonant

Day 4: Play the following game with your students. Listen for the sound that the letter 'Yy' makes in each word. If you hear the long vowel 'e' in the word, clap once. If you hear the long vowel 'i', clap twice and if the 'y' is a consonant, clap three times. **Words:** 1. city (1 clap) 2. spy (2 claps) 3. yank (3 claps) 4. ugly (1 clap) 5. cry (2 claps) 5. yell (3 claps) 6. yacht (3 claps) 7. pry (2 claps) 8. ivy (1 clap) 9. yak (3 claps) 10. party (1 clap)

Activity Worksheet: Page 184 The students will select the correct word to complete each sentence. **Answer Key:** 1. buy 2. sky 3. fry 4. pony 5. yawn 6. puppy 7. baby 8. penny 9. yard 10. shy

Day Five: Use the following instructions to test your students' ability to recognize the correct vowel sounds and the consonant sound made by the letter 'Yy.' **Auditory Test Instructions:** Listen to each word that I say. Circle the sound made by the letter 'Yy' in each box. **Words:** 1.yank 2.money 3. shy 4. yell 5. hurry 6. spy 7. tiny 8. dry 9. yelp 10. heavy **Answer Key:** 1. y 2. e 3. i 4. y 5. e 6. i 7. e 8. i 9. y 10. e

B. Auditory and Visual Discrimination Test Instructions: Circle the sound heard made by the letter 'Yy' in each picture. **Picture Key:** Row 1: bunny, yawn, puppy, cry 2. fly, yoyo, baby, ivy Row 3: sky, family, yolk, pony **Answer Key:** Row 1: long e, consonant y, long e, long i Row 2: long i, consonant y, long e, long e Row 3: long i, long e, consonant y, long e

Name: ______________________________ | Day 1 | Week 30 |

Did you know that the letter 'y' can be a **consonant** and a **vowel**?

When **'y'** is heard at the **beginning** of a word it is a **consonant**.

When the **'y'** is heard at the end of a word sometimes it makes the long 'i' vowel sound.

Examples:

yoyo

cry

If the letter 'y' is a vowel in the picture, **circle** the word **vowel**.
If the letter 'y' is a consonant, **circle** the word **consonant**.

vowel consonant	vowel consonant	vowel consonant
vowel consonant	vowel consonant	vowel consonant
vowel consonant	vowel consonant	vowel consonant

Name: ______________________________

Day 2	Week 30

The letter '**y**' as a **vowel** can make **two** sounds.

If it is a **long vowel** it makes the same sound as the **long** '**e**' vowel.

If the letter '**y**' is a **short vowel**, it makes the same sound as the **long** '**i**' vowel.

Examples:

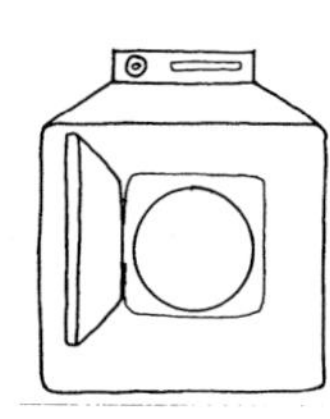

dry

lady

What sound does the letter '**y**' say at the end ofeach picture.
Is it the long '**e**' or the long '**y**' sound?

Name: ______________________________

Day 3	Week 30

The letter **'Yy'** can be consonantand a vowel.
It can make **three** different sounds.
It can be a **consonant** at the beginning of words or **two** different **vowel** sounds at the ends of words.

Examples:

		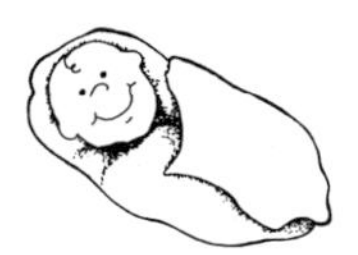
yoyo **consonant**	**fly** **long vowel 'i'**	**baby** **long vowel 'e'**

Circle the sound that the letter **'Yy'** makes in each picture.

long e long i consonant	 long e long i consonant	 long e long i consonant
 long e long i consonant	 long e long i consonant	 long e long i consonant
 long e long i consonant	 long e long i consonant	 long e long i consonant

Name: ______________________________ | Day 4 | Week 30 |

The letter 'y' is a consonant at the **beginning** of a word.
Examples: yes, yellow, you

The letter 'y' can be a **vowel** and can make the **long 'e'** or **long 'i'** sound at the end of words.
Examples: happy (**long e**), cry (**long i**)

Read each sentence. **Choose** a word from the word box to complete it.

1. I went to the store to __________ some candy. (baby buy busy)

2. The blue __________ has fluffy white clouds. (sly shy sky)

3. Dad will __________ the fish in a pan. (funny furry fry)

4. I rode the little brown __________ at the farm. (penny pony party)

5. The sleepy boy made a big __________. (yank yard yawn)

6. Maggie is our new white __________. (puppy penny pretty)

7. The __________ was asleep in its crib. (bunny puppy baby)

8. I found a __________ in my coat pocket. (penny party puppy)

9. The children like to play in their __________. (yarn yard yawn)

10. The __________ little boy hid behind his mom. (sky sly shy)

Name: ______________________________

Day 5 Week 30

A. **Auditory Test** on the sounds made by the letter **'Yy'**

1. i e y	2. i e y	3. i e y	4. i e y	5. i e y
6. i e y	7. i e y	8. i e y	9. i e y	10. i e y

B. Auditory and Visual Discrimination Test

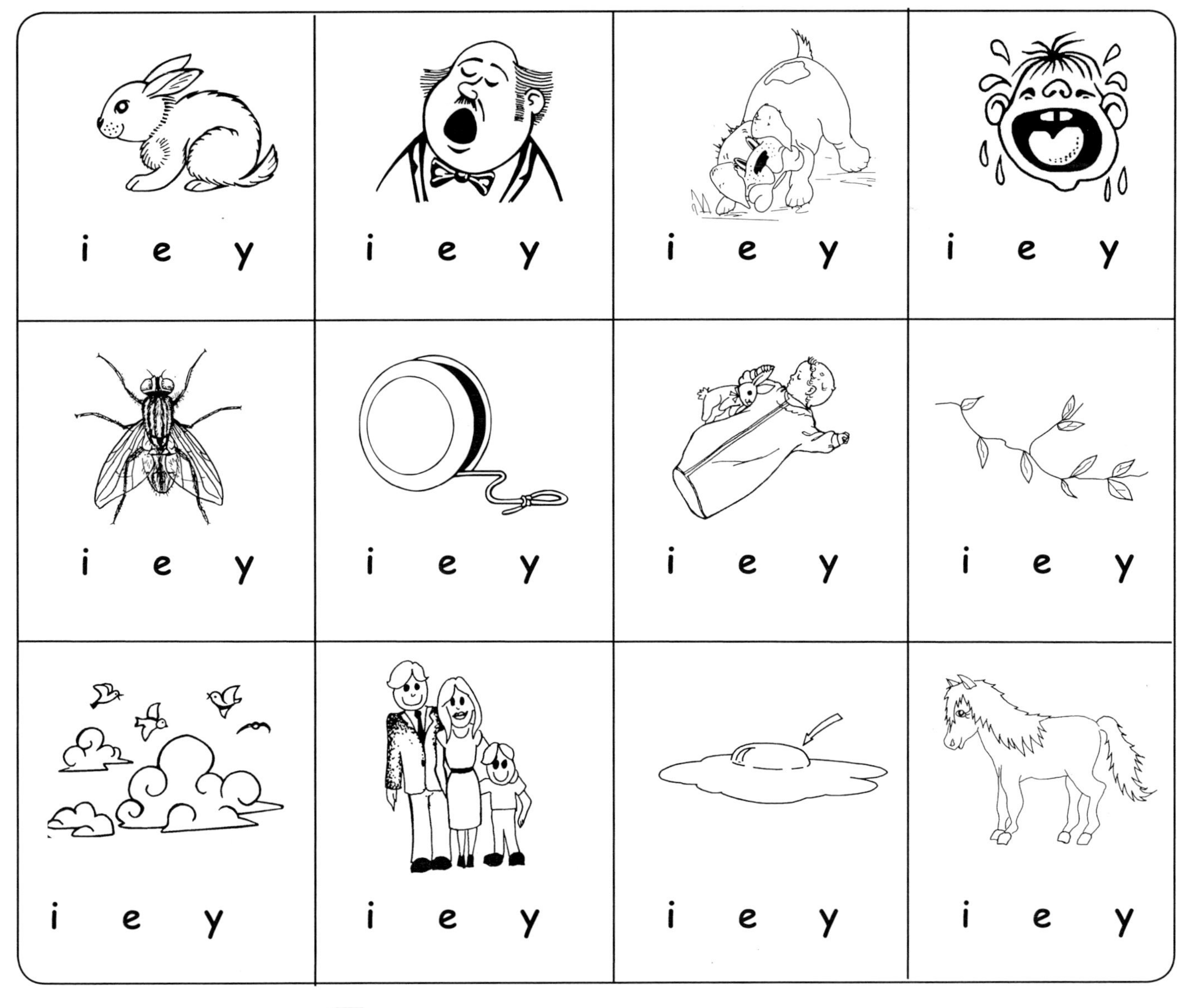

Week 31: Final Consonant Blends 'nt, nd, ng, and nk'

Objective: To introduce the final consonant pairs '**ng**, **nd**, **ng**, and **nk**

Teacher Information: A blend is a combination of two or more consonants grouped together in a word at the beginning or ending of it. The letters blend together while maintaining their own individual sounds.

Day 1: Listen to each word that I say and repeat it. **Words:** paint, front, grant, want What part of each word is the same. (The way that it ends.) What are the names of the letters that you hear at the end of each word? (**nt**) Listen to another group of words. Say each one after me. **Words:** band, find, land, wind Do these words end the same way as paint, front, grant and want? (No) How do they end? They end with the consonants '**nd**.' Let's play a riddle game. Listen to each one. Give the answer and tell how it ends. **Riddles:** 1. I am a black insect that can run fast on the ground. (ant, nt) 2. It is a group of people who play music. (band, nd) 3. It blows leaves all over the place in the autumn. (wind, nd) 4. A dog does this when it is very hot. (pant, nt) 5. This stops light from coming through a window. (blind, nd) 6. It is a place in which people like to sweep outside. (tent, nt)

Picture Key: Row 1: friend, cent, paint, pond Row 2: haunted, hound, tent, round Row 3: stand, wand, front, hunt

Activity Worksheet: Page 187 The student is to circle the final consonant blend to match each picture.
Answer Key: Row 1: nd, nt, nt, nd Row 2: nt, nd, nt, nd Row 3: nd, nd, nt, nt

Day 2: Print the following sentence on a chart. 'Bing, bang, bong rang the big gong.' Read it to your students or have them read it with you. Have them look at each word carefully. Ask them if there is something the same about most of the words. (All of the words but one have the same letters '**ng**' at the end of them) Have the students circle the '**ng**' in each word. Print the following sentence on the chart. 'The chain on the door went clink, clank, clunk in the wind. Read the sentence to or with your students. Are there any words that end with the same letters in this sentence? (Yes) What do the words say? (clink, clank, clunk) What letters are found at the end of the words? (**nk**) Listen to each word that I say. Tell how each word ends. 1. bonk (nk) 2. king (ng) 3. skunk (nk) 4. rang (ng) 5. wing (ng) 6. pink (nk) 7. hang (ng) 8. drank (nk)

Picture Key: Row 1: king, drink, trunk, wing Row 2: junk, sing, sink, ring Row 3: skunk, hang, swing, bank

Activity Worksheet: Page 188 The students are to circle the final consonant blend to match each picture.
Answer Key: Row1: ng, nk, nk, ng Row 2: nk, ng, nk, ng Row 3: nk, ng, ng, nk

Day 3: Review the final blends '**nt**, **nd**, **ng**, and **nk**.' On a chart print the four consonant blends. Have the students make the sounds in each blend. Play a game in which you say a word and a student uses a marker and puts a check mark under its final sonsonant blend. **Words:** bent, round, long, prank, crank, bang, pond, front, stunt, fling, mink, send

Picture Key: Row 1: chipmunk, plant, friends, trunk Row 2: front, rink, drink, hand Row 3: land, think, ant, blind Row 3: king, pond, band, ring

Activity Worksheet: The students are to record the consonant blend heard at the end of the picture.
Answer Key: Row 1: nk, nt, nd, nk Row 2: nt, nk, nk, nd Row 3: nd, nk, nt, nd Row 4: ng, nd, nd, ng

Day 4: Review the final consonants **nt**, **nd**, **nk**, and **ng**. Play this listening game. I am going to say three words. You are to tell me which one doesn't belong and why. **Word Groups:** 1. band, bank, bend (ba**nk**) 2. dent, dint, drank (dra**nk**) 3. bank, bunt drank (bu**nt**) 4. grind, bunk, ground (bu**nk**) 5. band, ring, friend (ri**ng**) 6. hu**nt**, pai**nt**, si**nk** (si**nk**) 7. band, bang, bing (ba**nd**) 8. sank, sunk, sang (sa**ng**)

Activity Worksheet: Page 189 The students will select words from the box to complete the sentences.
Answer Key: blind 2. front 3. drink 4. bank 5. hunt 6. pink 7. pond 8. long

Day 5: Use the following instructions to test your students' ability to recognize the final consonant blends '**nt**, **nd**, **ng**, and **nk**.'

A. Auditory Test Instructions: Listen to each word that I say. Circle the blend that you hear at the end of the word. Words: 1. sent 2. mound 3. bang 4. stink 5. rang 6. bend 7. spent 8. pound 9. sank 10. went
Answer Key: 1. nt 2. nd 3. ng 4. nk 5. ng 6. nd 7. nt 8. nd 9. nk 10. nt

B. Auditory and Visual Discrimination Test Instructions: Circle the consonant blend that you hear at the end of each picture. **Picture Key:** Row 1: paint, band, ring Row 2: skunk, swing, wand Row 3: hang, think paint Row 4: tank, hand, plant **Answer Key:** Row 1: nt, nd, ng Row 2: nk, ng, nd Row 3: ng, nk, nt Row 4: nk, nd, nt

Name: ______________________________

Day 1 | Week 31

Sometimes consonants join together at the end of a word and can be heard . They are called **final consonants**.
Examples:

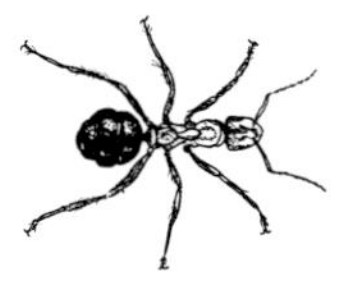 ant

 sand

Circle the sound that you hear at the **end** of each picture.

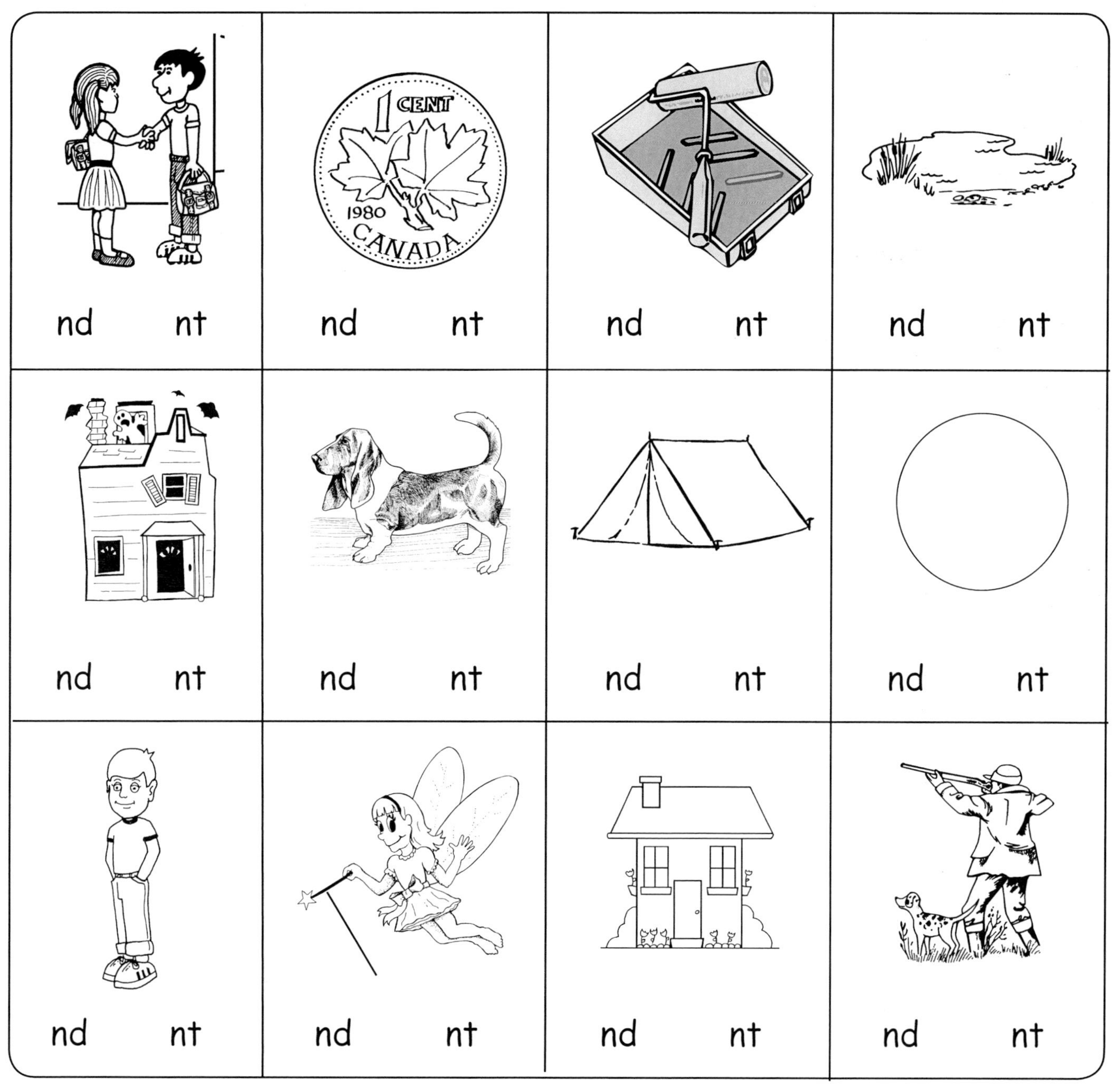

SSR1140 ISBN: 9781771586863

Name: ______________________________ | Day 2 | Week 31 |

Some words end with the final blend of '**ng**.'

Example:

spri**ng**

Some words end with the final blend '**nk**.'

Example:

ba**nk**

Circle the sound that you hear at the **end** of each picture.

ng nk	ng nk	ng nk	ng nk
ng nk	ng nk	ng nk	ng nk
ng nk	ng nk	ng nk	ng nk

Name: ______________________________

Day 3	Week 31

Some words end with the following **consonant blends**.

ce**nt**

bl**ow**

ba**ng**

ba**nk**

Print the **final consonant blend** heard in each word on the line in each box.

Name: ____________________________ **Day 4** | **Week 31**

Many words end with consonant blends such as **'nt, nd, ng,** and **nk.'**
Examples:

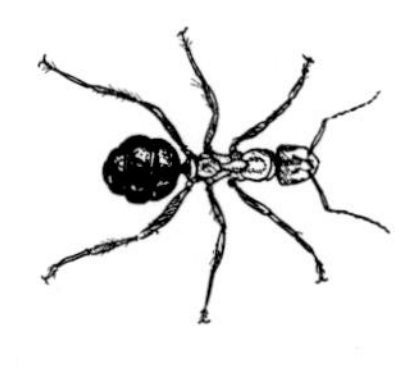

ant **pond** **king** **rink**

Find the word in the **Word Box** that fits each sentence. **Print** it on the line.

Word Box							
pond	long	hunt	drink	front	bank	pink	blind

1. The __________ man needed help to cross the street.
2. At the __________ of our house was a big snowman.
3. The boy likes to __________ lots of milk every day.
4. The girl put the money in her piggy __________.
5. Will you help me __________ for our lost dog?
6. The little girl wore a pretty __________ dress to the party.
7. We saw some ducks swimming on the big __________.
8. The dog had a __________ furry brown tail.

Name: ______________________________

Day 5	Week 31

A. **Auditory Test** on the sounds made by the final consonants **'nt, nd, ng, nk'**

1. nt nd ng nk	2. nt nd ng nk	3. nt nd ng nk	4. nt nd ng nk	5. nt nd ng nk
6. nt nd ng nk	7. nt nd ng nk	8. nt nd ng nk	9. nt nd ng nk	10. nt nd ng nk

B. **Auditory and Visual Discrimination Test**

 ISBN: 9781771586863

Week 32: Singular and Plural Words

Objective: To teach adding 's' and 'es' to make singular words plural.

Teacher Information: Words that end with a consonant are made plural by adding the letter 's'. Words that end with 's, ss, sh, ch and x' have 'es' added to make them plural.

Day 1: Record the following words on a chart: hen hen; hat hat; cat cat . What does the first word say? (hen) How many hens? (1) Add 's' to the second word 'hen.' What does the word say now? (hens) Which word means only one. (hen) Which word means more than one? (hens) Look at the next word. What does it say? (hat) How many hats? (1) What happens if I add an 's' to the end of hat? (It becomes hats.) Do the same process for the word 'cat.' Explain to your students that adding 's' to the end of a word makes it mean more than one or plural.

Picture Key: Row 1: chicks, hat, dog Row 2: hats, ball, coats Row 3: hand, kites, flag

Activity Worksheet: Page 193 The student is to circle the word that matches the picture.
Answer Key: Row 1: chicks, hat, dog Row 2: hats, ball, coats Row 3: hand, kites, flag

Day 2: On a chart print the following words: box, bus, dish, lunch, dress in two rows. Explain that if we want to make some words mean 'more than one' we have to add these letters to certain words. Add the plural form 'es' to the words previously printed on the chart to make the words 'boxes, buses, dishes, lunches, dresses.' What must a word end with in order to have 'es' added to it to make it mean more than one. (The word must end with 's, ss, sh, ch, or x.) Print the following words on the chart and have the students make them plural by adding 's' or 'es.' Words: coat___ lunch___ ball___ dress___ toy___ fox___ bush___ can___ cat ___

Activity Worksheet: Page 194 The students will print the plural form of the singular words.
Answer Key: 1. dishes 2. couches 3. dresses 4. waxes 5. witches 6. kittens 7. pools 8. foxes 9. kisses 10. wishes 11. matches 12. beaches 13. churches 14. bushes

Day 3: Record the following words down a chart. **Words:** party, lily, city, sky Explain to your students that if you want to make these words mean more than one the ending of each word has to be changed. If I want to make the word 'party' mean more than one party, I must change the 'y' to an 'i' and then add 'es.' Tell me how to change city, lily and sky to mean more than one. Tell your students that most words that end with the letter 'y' have their ending changed to an 'i' before adding 'es.'

Picture Key: Row 1: ponies, flies, bunnies Row 2: fairies, puppies, fries, Row 3: pennies, candies, ladies

Activity Worksheet: Page 195 The students are to record the plural word under the correct picture.
Answer Key: Row 1: ponies, flies, bunnies Row 2: fairies, puppies, fries Row 3: pennies, candles, ladies

Day 4: Review the ways words are made plural. Record the following words down one side of a chart. **Words:** boat, dish, lunch, fox, bus, guess, party Have the students read the words. Ask them what they would have to do to make each word mean more than one. Remind them to check the end of each word. Have students tell you how to print the plural form of each word.

Picture Key: Row 1: puppies, dresses, flies, candies, Row 2: foxes, fairies, churches, balls

Activity Worksheet: Page 196 The students will label each set of pictures with the correct word.
Answer Key: Row 1: puppies , dresses, flies, candies Row 2: foxes, fairies, churches, balls

Day 5: Visual Discrimination Test on Plural Words Page 197:
The students will complete each sentence with the correct singular or plural word.
Answer Key: A 1. bunnies 2. matches 3. bus 4. kites 5. bush 6. dish 7. wishes 8. glass B. 1. skies 2. brushes 3. guesses 4. toys 5. ponies 6. lunches 7. wishes 8. eggs 9. classes 10. cars

Name: ______________________________ | Day 1 | Week 32 |

Did you know that words can be changed to mean more than one?

All you have to do to some words is to add the letter **'s'** to the end of it.

Example:

car

cars

Look at the pictures in each box. **Circle** the word that tells what they are.

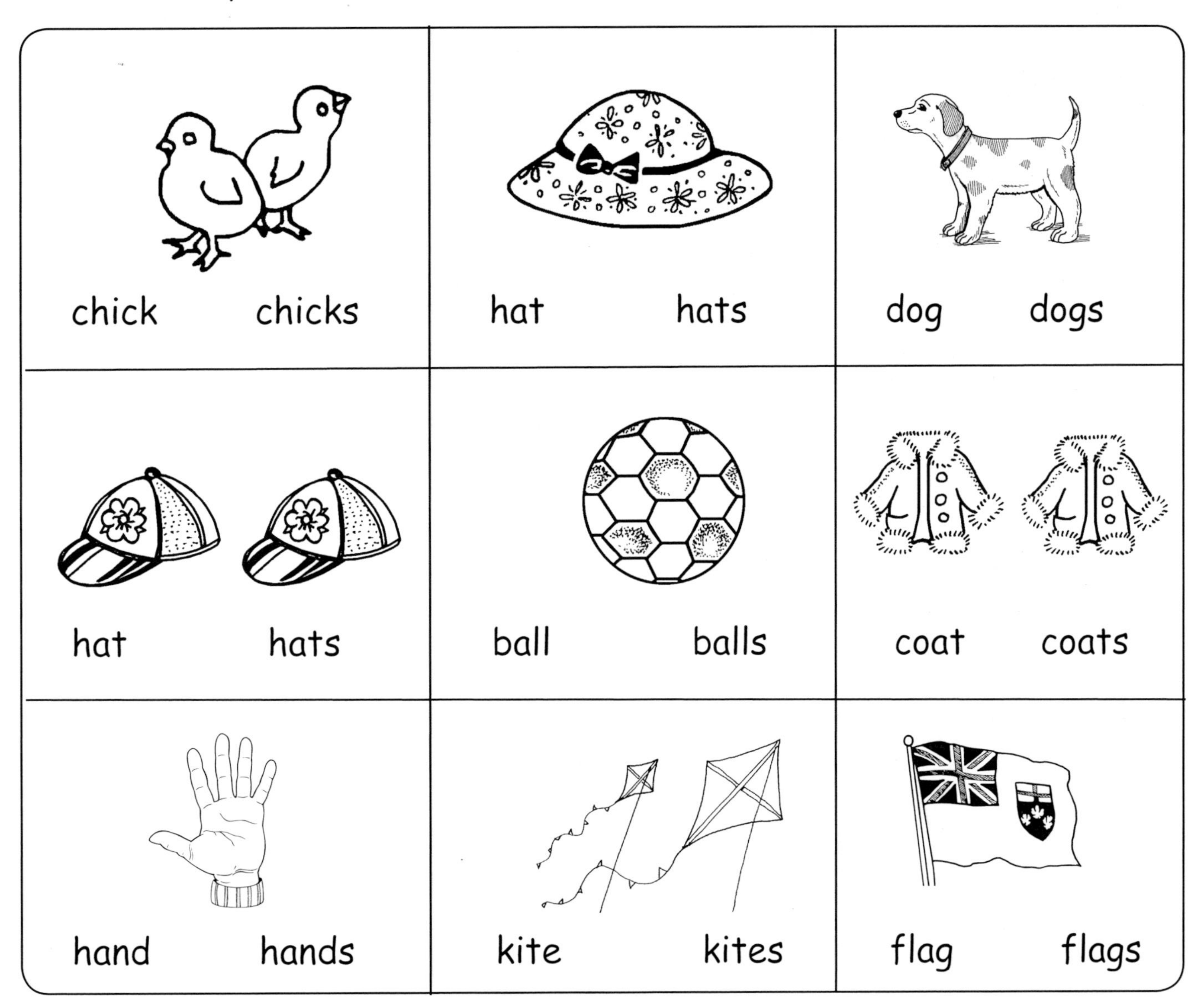

chick chicks	hat hats	dog dogs
hat hats	ball balls	coat coats
hand hands	kite kites	flag flags

 ISBN: 9781771586863

Name: ____________________

Day 2 | Week 32

Some words can become more than one by adding the letter '**s**.'

If a word ends in '**s**, **ss**, **sh**, **ch**, or **x**', the letters '**es**' are added to the **end** of it to make it **mean more than one.**

Examples:

buses

glasses

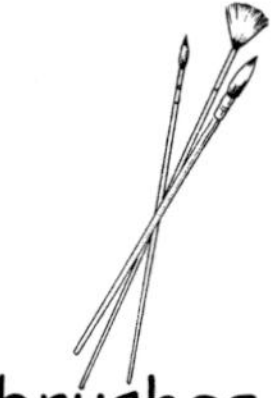

brushes

watches

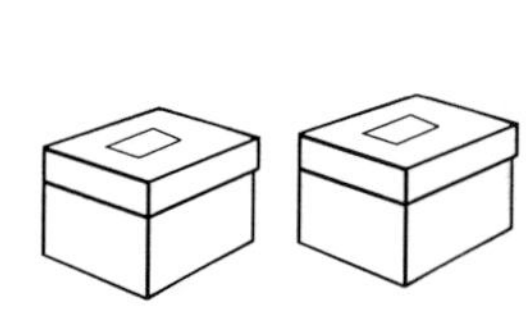

boxes

Add '**s**' or '**es**' to each word to make it mean more than one.

1. dish ____________________
2. couch ____________________
3. dress ____________________
4. wax ____________________
5. witch ____________________
6. kitten ____________________
7. pool ____________________
8. fox ____________________
9. kiss ____________________
10. wish ____________________
11. match ____________________
12. beach ____________________
13. church ____________________
14. bush ____________________

Name: ______________________________

Day 3	Week 32

When a word ends with the letter '**y**', the '**y**' must be changed to the letter '**i**' and then '**es**' is added to the end of it.

Example:

berry

berries

Print the word that means **'more than one'** under each picture.

Words:

flies candies fairies ponies ladies
bunnies pennies puppies fries

______________	______________	______________
______________	______________	______________
______________	______________	______________

 ISBN: 9781771586863

Name: ______________________________ Day 4 Week 32

Plural words mean more than one thing.
If a word ends with a **consonant**, you add only an '**s**' to the end of it.
Examples: bed - beds hat - hats

Words that end with '**s**, **ss**, **ch**, **sh**, or **x**, the letters '**es**' are added to the end.
Examples: axes, buses, dishes, lunches, dresses

When a word ends with the letter '**y**', the '**y**' is changed to the letter '**i**' and '**es**' is added after it.
Examples: party - parties city - cities

Print the word that means **more than one** thing under each picture.

puppies dresses flies churches
foxes fairies candies balls

Name: ______________________________ | Day 5 | Week 32 |

Test on Singular and Plural Words

A. Record the **correct word** in each sentence.

1. ____________ like to hop about in the grass. (Bunnies, Bunny)

2. Boys and girls should not play with ______________. (match, matches)

3. The school ________________ was filled with children. (bus, buses)

4. The _______________ were flying high in the sky. (kite, kites)

5. The baby fox hid under the _______________. (bush, bushes)

6. Put the meat on the big, round _______________. (dish, dishes)

7. The little boy made three _______________. (wish, wishes)

8. Use the _______________ to drink your milk. (glass, glasses)

B. Print the **plural** word for each word that means only one.

1. sky ________________ 6. lunch _______________

2. brush ________________ 7. wish _______________

3. guess ________________ 8. egg _______________

4. toy ________________ 9. class _______________

5. pony ________________ 10. car _______________

Teacher Record:

Development and Progress of Student Phonetic Skills

Name of Student: ______________________________

Phonetic Skills	Teacher Comments
Initial Consonants	
Final Consonants	
Short Vowels	
Long Vowels	
S Blends	
L Blends	
R Blends	
Final Consonant Blends	
Consonant Digraphs	
Vowel Pairs	
Singular/Plural	

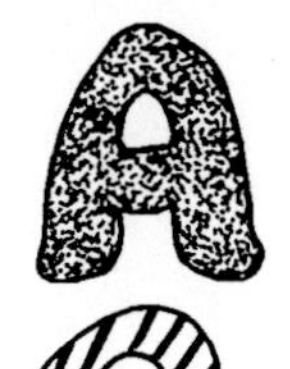

Phonics Award

Congratulations!

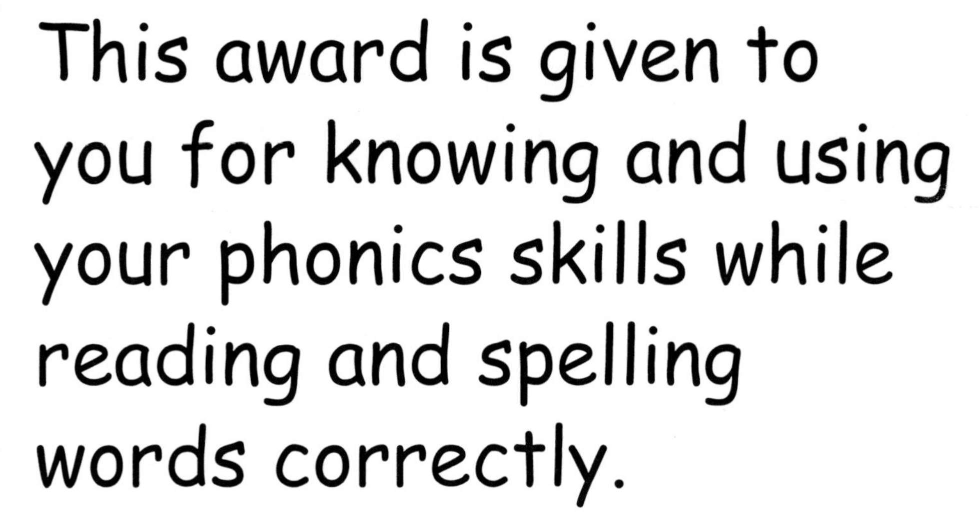

This award is given to you for knowing and using your phonics skills while reading and spelling words correctly.

From

Oliver Owl Phonics Award

This award is presented to ______________________________
for knowing the following phonics skills.

Initial Consonants ________
Final Consonants ________
Long Vowels ________
Short Vowels ________
S Blends ________
L Blends ________
R Blends ________
Digraphs: Sh, Ch, Wh, Th ________
Final Consonant Blends ________

